Flatlining on the Field of Dreams

Flatlining on the Field of Dreams

Cultural Narratives in the Films of President Reagan's America

Alan Nadel

Rutgers University Press

New Brunswick, New Jersey
and London

88096

Library of Congress Cataloging-in-Publication Data

Nadel, Alan, 1947–
    Flatlining on the field of dreams: cultural narratives in the
    films of President Reagan's America / Alan Nadel.
        p.   cm.
    Includes bibliographical references and index.
    ISBN 0-8135-2439-3 (cloth: alk. paper). — ISBN 0-8135-2440-7
(pbk.: alk. paper)
    1. Motion pictures—Social aspects—United States. 2. Motion
pictures—Political aspects—United States.   I. Title.
PN1995.9.S6N33   1997
302.23′43′097309048—dc21   96-49062
                                                      CIP

British Cataloging-in-Publication data for this book is available from the
British Library

Composition by Colophon Typesetting

Manufactured in the United States of America

*To
Alan Sandy Garber,
with whom I saw my first movie,
and
Paul Fussell,
whose tempered indifference to the medium is nearly perfect*

Contents

Preface

I cannot remember being unaware of movies. Long before my parents took me to see my first movie, the Walt Disney version of Robin Hood, I had seen countless movies at home on television. Before we owned a television set, at a neighbor's house I had watched Gabby Hayes (the second greatest toothless film actor in American history) hosting television releases of B westerns, cut into half-hour segments.

When I was four years old, we bought our first television, which reorganized permanently the living space in our very small two-bedroom apartment. We stopped eating in the tiny kitchen, moving instead to the dining table at one end of the living room, situating ourselves so that we could all watch television while we ate, and after dinner moving to the sofa and stuffed chair, also aligned to the best perspectives on the screen. Within that screen's radii my family gathered. Each night over dinner we watched a film—crudely edited to one hour—on *The Early Show*. On weekends, particularly after the Dodgers had left Brooklyn, we usually watched *Picture for a Sunday Afternoon*. At other times we watched *Million Dollar Movie*, a show that, like the local movie houses, played the same film each evening for a week, so that, long before the advent of VCRs, we could see movies we liked several times over.

Watching movies became not only ordinary—in that movies chronically occupied the only real living space our apartment afforded—but also integral to our family life. Hepburn or Bogart, Errol Flynn or Fay Wray were present for our meals, and they spoke to me while I did my homework. This sense of film as commonplace reality was, of course, augmented by the filmed comedy and drama that, by the time I was nine, had replaced most live television in prime time and, aside from soaps and game shows, throughout the day.

I doubt this experience was atypical in its broad parameters. Like most baby boomers, I shared with my parents an exhaustive education in the normality of the cinematic. We accepted not only the pervasiveness of dramatic narrative—a life of virtually uninterrupted comedy, melodrama, adventure, romance—but also the transparent ease with which that narrative assembled itself. Movies demonstrated that it was possible to make a coherent story out of fragmented experience. No wonder movies were so attractive when so little else in my life fulfilled the same promise. Thus movies not only revealed their own narratives, they anchored mine, providing assurance that actions had a shape and a purpose. As I think back on it, our relationship to the television was virtually theological. It is not that we "worshiped" television but rather that it provided voices and images from elsewhere with narratives to orient and center our lives, around which we ritualized our time.

In an educational psychology course I took in college, the instructor showed us a test used to develop psychological profiles, a series of pictures about which people were asked to tell stories. My immediate response, I remember distinctly, was that each picture she held up reminded me of a movie, a shot of Spencer Tracy in *Tortilla Flat*, the moment when Scarlett O'Hara stands on the small bridge watching the convicts who work for her, the final shot in *Sherlock Holmes and the Voice of Terror* when we follow Basil Rathbone's line of sight up through the open rafters, where the RAF will fly by to meet the Nazi challenge. Once again movies provided narratives preferable to the ones I was escaping at the time: that the course was boring and the instructor incompetent, that my reason for taking the course—a reason I shared with two-thirds of the class—was to get a teaching license and thus a draft-differed job. It was 1968 and, like almost all the American men my age, I was in reality a prisoner of war.

To the extent that my saturation in the plots, images, and techniques of film enabled me to escape darker narratives of my life, of my culture, or of my history, I was forging a prophetic kinship with Ronald Reagan. The record now shows beyond question his masterful capacity for substituting movie narratives and cinematic imagination for the lived life or the national history. In that regard he was a man ahead of his time, who managed to live long enough that history caught up to him. In its most concise form, that is the point of this book: Reaganism gained a significant portion of its credibility because it manifested the cinematic notion of reality with which the American public had been indoctrinated since the beginning of the baby boom.

If President Reagan believed, for example, in a universal shield that could defend America from all missiles originating on this planet (or any other), he was merely putting the presidential seal on what we had already learned at the movies. If he really thought that the deficit could be closed by time, he was merely articulating a tacit assumption of film editing. As a population we had already learned supply-side and deregulation narratives through the formal process of watching movies. Ronald Reagan simply told us that our movie lessons applied to such topics as economics and social policy. Having grown up learning movie lessons and continuing to practice them on a regular basis—some people more than forty hours a week—we all may have derived a degree of comfort hearing them repeated as if they were true.

I started making this point just barely after President Reagan had left office, through a series of academic papers and conference sessions. To the audiences at those conferences, particularly those at the International Narrative Conferences in 1991, 1992, 1993, and 1994, I owe much thanks for stimulating questions and suggestions. Similarly, I am indebted to my co-panelists, Dale Bauer, Carol Colatrella, Susan Derwin, Bill Galperin, Gordon Hutner, Ruth Johnston, Pat O'Donnell, Warren Rosenberg, and Lynda Zwinger. I am particularly grateful for sustained intellectual stimulation to Tom Byers, who participated in a number of these panels while completing his own outstanding study of masculinity in the films of this era. Thanks also go to Barbara Foley, for insightful suggestions about Chapter 1, and to Brea Bathel, my superb research assistant during the later stages of this project.

Leslie Mitchner is surely the gem in that most beleaguered and (sometimes justly) underappreciated of professions, editor in chief of a university press. She is a careful reader with a keen intelligence and a clear vision, who gave personal attention to the manuscript as it developed, and selected for it an excellent reader, the benefit of whose detailed commentary can be found throughout this book.

My daughter, Glynnis, made me an extended loan of *The Little Mermaid* video, without which Chapter 3 would have been impossible, and my son, Alexander, continues a dialogue with me about film and culture initiated by his having been an innocent bystander to my "research." My wife, Amy Perkins—companion, lover, intellectual peer—retained our sanity through years when we were represented first in the Senate and then in the executive branch by Dan Quayle. No greater tribute have I.

Flatlining on the Field of Dreams

Introduction

Class, Film, and President Reagan's America

In his penetrating 1984 satire, *Class*, Paul Fussell writes perhaps one of the earliest books to understand incisively the culture of Reaganism. Irvin Ehrenpreis defined satire as a genre that presents readers with one of their cherished prejudices and its extreme example, thus forcing them into the uncomfortable choice between rejecting the prejudice and embracing the example: "The reader is confronted," Ehrenpreis explains, "with the need either to surrender a sound definition or to strip a label from an unsound case."[1] In Jonathan Swift's famous *A Modest Proposal*, for instance, the readers must either acknowledge the efficacy and decency of raising Irish offspring for food, or they must reject their conception of the Irish peasantry as cattle.

Fussell's satire pinpoints the essential contradictions of Reaganism by evoking similar discomfort for his readers, who are denied a mediating context between the extreme authority with which he speaks and the outrageous examples that he presents. Although he identifies nine classes in America, organized in three groups, the book attends primarily to the fence Fussell constructs between "upper-middle" (which is something like "preppy"), in the top group, and "middle," in the second group.[2] That fence, he knows, is built entirely out of his readers' angst. They live teetering on its sharpened pales, like characters in a Spenserian allegory, terrified lest they fall to the lower side, ever hopeful they be perceived as living on the higher. Having

1

built the fence, with true satiric industry, Fussell shakes, kicks, and hacks its foundations, so that not even the most punctilious fence walker can avoid being impaled.

Since the reader of *Class* is supposed to be learning to associate him- or herself with an identifiable group, Fussell constantly taints the desire for association with the aura of guilt by association. Any association with religious fundamentalism thus becomes a negative class indicator, so that Akron, Ohio, "is fatally known as the home of Rex Humbard Ministry," and the way to learn which flowers are vulgar "is to notice the varieties favored on Sunday-morning TV religious programs. . . . There you will see primarily geraniums (red are lower than pink), poinsettias, chrysanthemums, and you will know instantly, without even attending to the quality of the discourse, that you are looking at a high-prole[tarian] setup."[3] Fussell thus forces his readers to acknowledge their bond in taste with Rex Humbard or, without delay, uproot their geraniums and pluck their mums.

And thus it goes for the potential mum pluckers of America, through every aspect of habitation, decor, speech, and manner. If, for example, one likes to wear his shirt collar out, he must do so at the cost of being (or worse, being taken for) middle class or prole. "All you have to know about this practice," he points out, "is that when out riding or otherwise got up in sports costume, the President favors it."[4]

If religious fundamentalists provide sure negative class indicators, then Ronald Reagan becomes Fussell's apotheosis of all that these fundamentalists signify: "[Reagan] of course doesn't need to affect the establishment style, sensing accurately that his low-brow, God-fearing, intellect distrusting constituency regards it as an affront (which, of course, to them it is). Reagan's style can be designated Los Angeles (or even Orange) County Wasp-Chutzpah. It registers the sense that if you stubbornly believe you're as good as educated, civilized people . . . then you are. . . . One hesitates even to speculate about the polyester levels of his outfits."[5]

As these passages make clear, *Class* not only describes the culture of Reaganism, but it also assaults the modes of identification that proliferate it. Although in certain ways just a footnote to this study, Fussell's book provides an instructive entry into the culture of Reaganism, for without ever attending directly to films, Fussell has understood the cinematic conventions at work in those modes of identification, conventions honed to establish character type—history, taste, intellect, wealth—with the terse economy of well-framed, succinctly edited images. Organizing the small details that have been appropriated as class signifiers—the shots and contexts that in films become the cornerstones of class—Fussell creates an iconography of Reaganism so that he may demonstrate in the most discomforting ways imaginable the impossibility of constructing from them a coherent narrative. In contrast to Reagan's unflinching optimism, moreover, Fussell provides a subtle but pervasive fatalism. While often seeming to give self-help advice about how to overcome the trappings of one's class, at crucial points Fussell reminds the reader that everyone is locked into his or her class and thus that there is no effective way to act on that advice. To the adage that it takes three generations to make a gentleman, in other words, Fussell might be inferred to add, yes, but only if he does not retain his own parents.

Reading *Class*, therefore, helped me recognize how much the narratives of contemporary America rely on unspoken reference to the visual community created by the cinematic conventions that television has deployed ubiquitously since the end of World War II. Fussell's class signifiers, therefore, conform to the ideas of neither Karl Marx nor Emily Post. They come instead from cinematic notions, disdain for which motivates Fussell's satiric engine. In this regard, Fussell is Reagan's Other, in that he undermines exactly the assumption Reagan so successfully promoted: that reality is a movie. Because, despite Fussell's brief discussion of pronunciation, his book reveals the hunger of Americans for visual delusion, whether Fussell realizes it or not he describes symptoms of America's acquiescence to the codes of cinematic representation. His iconography of Reaganism describes a culture full of people looking up, just as they do in movie theaters, physically and socially, chronically weighing themselves on a set of invisible scales, taking their own measure, looking for ways to prove to themselves that they have "improved." But tellingly, their mode of proof, like the "proof" they see on a screen, is completely external, based less on logic than on narrative, less on criteria than on display.

For that audience, Ronald Reagan exemplified the power of display as well as a concomitant optimism about the effect of using that power. His presidency prolifically validated his form of display, and his success accrued from embodying narratives that had cultural currency in a given moment of extended optimism, the period that began with the economic recovery of 1983 and ended with the recession that started in the second half of the Bush presidency. Between these two recessions, narratives about credit, deregulation, gender, race, and masculinity define a subtext that might be called "President Reagan's America."

Films are particularly useful in analyzing that subtext in that they are commercial products that represent a large collaborative consensus about ways to commodify a culture's values, to which commercial success lends affirmation. In that context, Susan Jeffords has discussed extensively the pervasive "remasculinization" of American culture during the Reagan presidency, as exemplified by what she calls "Hard Body" films, such as the "Rambo" series and the macho cop films (e.g., *Lethal Weapon, Die Hard*, and *Robocop*).[6] The purpose of my book is to explore other cultural narratives performed by the films of President Reagan's America. I look at the political unconscious not of the former president, therefore, but of the cultural values he signified and the cultural conflicts for which he represented the apparent resolution. These conflicts and resolutions surround the ideas of class that Fussell satirizes, in the process revealing class to be a visual phenomenon.

The ideas and values of President Reagan's America are thus inextricably connected to their mode of representation, which was as the consumables of a hyperconsumptive society situated between two recessions. Identified by John Kenneth Galbraith as the "Culture of Contentment," or more simply by Barbara Ehrenreich as the "Worst Years of Our Lives" (in her "irreverent notes from a decade of greed"), it was marked particularly by what Donald Barlett and James Steele demonstrate, in *America: What Went Wrong,* is the dismantling of the middle class.[7] That dismantling, however, took place in such a way that the middle class, destabilized economically and demographically, maintained its ostensive status through its ability to consume narratives about itself. The popular credit given to those narratives helped provide, I think, the psychological basis for the consumer credit that fueled further consumption and, as well, fueled the production of a more extensive set of narratives made for immediate consumption. When Jean Baudrillard points out that "America has retained power, both political and cultural, but it is now power as a special effect," Baudrillard is using the term "special effect" in very much the cinematic sense.[8] Ronald Reagan, he asserts, "has worked up his euphoric, cinematic, extroverted, advertising vision of the artificial paradises of the West to all-American dimensions."[9]

This does not mean that I think filmmakers, either individually or collectively, have planted hidden narratives within their ostensive stories. A filmmaker's intent or degree of self-consciousness is beyond the range of my knowledge or attention. So are the cultural phenomena surrounding a film's reception. The reception of any mass event, such as a film release, is a topic worthy of study, one potentially rich with insights into the assumptions, motivations, and conditions of perception at any specific historical moment. Certain films—*Fatal Attraction*, for example, or *Batman*—for sundry reasons become cultural events worthy of analysis, in the same way that notable flops can reveal the superannuation of a popular myth, a shift in audience assumptions or expectations or both. The same is true of the vicissitudes of stardom. Much no doubt could be said, for example, about shifts in the popular construction of masculinity in the mid-1990s simply by contrasting the film careers of Travolta and Stallone.

My interests, however, lie elsewhere, in what films *tell* an audience, not what they tell us *about* that audience. I am trying to describe the cultural narratives that groups of films accept as credible referents, so that we may better understand some of the stories we tell ourselves about who we are and what we believe. Fundamentally, I believe that a culture constitutes social reality by accepting specific narratives complacently enough to make them virtually transparent. Popular films as collaborative ventures promote a consensus in order to draw on these narratives, a consensus about the themes and tropes with which the audience can "identify." That consensus also "overlooks" those problems, concerns, and dilemmas the makers fail to see as problematic for themselves or for their audience. Consider, for example, how many films in earlier periods portrayed blacks by drawing, without apparent problems, on racial narratives that would seem today extremely problematic, or consider the thorough absence of blacks (and thus of segregation) in the 1950s southern television town of Mayberry, sheriffed by Andy Griffith, to cite some obvious examples of narratives that have been tacitly accepted or tacitly overlooked in the historically specific construction of cinematic and televisual realities.

In trying to describe the films of "President Reagan's America," therefore, I am referring to a reality constructed out of the tension between privileged narratives and overlooked ones. It is my belief that they affect, beyond intention or reception, almost all of the films produced for a mass audience in

America. This is a function, in part, of the historically specific conditions that constitute the American mass film industry and, in part, of the way hegemony is constituted, that is, invisibly.

That invisibility is reinforced by the norms we codify and the process by which we codify them. For late-twentieth-century Americans those norms are overwhelmingly cinematic; each time we see a standard commercial film, we perform rapidly and instantaneously a set of normal procedures essential to constructing a narrative out of the rapid interplay of relatively brief—usually between three and fifteen seconds—shots that mix a wide array of angles, perspectives, distances, motions, and object relations. Despite the large number of commercial American films released to mass markets each year, moreover, overwhelmingly the narratives constructed through the use of these procedures focus on a small number of characters who have inordinate privilege. At the end of *Fatal Attraction*, for example, the audience shares with the local police detective kudos for Dan Gallagher and his wife, Beth, who seem nearly gleeful that they have rid themselves of a threatening pest by killing her in their bathroom. If we consider the number of humans, denied faces (not to mention families), whose corpses must be amassed in order to render a character such as Luke Skywalker a hero, we can easily see how, in popular film, large conflicts such as wars become, with the audience's tacit assent, the backdrop for the struggles of the few people whose successes and failures are measured on a rather narrow matrix of romantic values. Photography more than philosophy creates the contemporary *Übermensch* and, with perverted Darwinian logic, frames him hierarchically with his love interest, sidekick, and, in the background, packs of virtually insignificant others against whom to measure or tally his virtue.

A cogent point, to which I return periodically, is that Americans of the 1980s had been extensively and systematically schooled in the norms and conventions of popular film, not only by the themes and decor of their viewing experience but more subtly and more extensively by the formal interpretive processes necessitated by classical cinema. If cinematic techniques such as crosscutting, suture, or close-ups have been commonplace for the bulk of this century, mass exposure to them since World War II has been wholly unprecedented in its scope and saturation. All of President Reagan's electorate has grown up in a world inundated by film and schooled in its codes. The majority of that electorate, having spent most or all of their lives in the presence of television, have seen these codes assume a pervasive role in defining realistic narrative. Although the 1980s added little that was new or radical to the formal aspects of cinematic narrative, the extent of their exposure by that decade was historically significant. Television, as Raymond Williams pointed out with some degree of awe, exposed Americans to "drama" several hours a day instead of the few hours per week, per year, or even per lifetime, as had been the norm in earlier periods of Western history.[10] World War II Americans, moreover, were saturated not only with dramatic narrative but also with the *process* of viewing it cinematically. By the end of the 1980s, this saturation, for all intents and purposes, was total, not because the films of the 1980s used the codes more pervasively but because most Americans under forty had spent all—and those under eighty the majority— of their lives viewing, several hours a day, representations of reality constructed in standard cinematic codes.

Particularly noteworthy in this regard are the powers of framing, the techniques of suture and crosscutting, and ways of representing time. The process of suture (shot/reverse-shot sequences) empowers the cinematic gaze with a totalizing authority that it denies to any subject position with which a spectator can identify. The construction of cinematic narrative thus implies a level of authority endemic to the cinematic apparatus that is superior to anything presented via that apparatus. If suture assumes spatial control, crosscutting assumes temporal control by allowing sequential viewing experience to stand for simultaneous events. Similarly, but conversely, the gaps and jumps that distinguish a story's time span from the film's elapsed time allow film an infinite temporal credit bank.

If this infinite credit system empowers virtually all classical Hollywood film narrative, then perhaps the prolific experience of film—the quintessential American experience of the last fifty years—can promote an understanding of "reality" premised on an infinite time/credit system, authorized by the visual power of the cinematic apparatus. Eliding the boundaries of the screen, these premises have helped construct the political and social "truth" of the Reagan presidency. As Baudrillard so incisively puts it: "Governing today means giving acceptable signs of credibility. It is like advertising and it is the same effect that is achieved—commitment to a scenario, whether it be a political or advertising scenario. Reagan's is both at once."[11]

Like all cultures, President Reagan's America depends on the stories it tells itself, and those stories return repeatedly and pervasively to ideas of class, in the sense that Fussell uses the term, that is, ideas that privilege groups of people by classifying them cinematically, attributing to them roles in narratives that highlight and privilege their actions. To the extent that these narratives allow representation to replace reference, they acquire cogency, for, as Baudrillard points out, "this consensus around simulation is much less fragile than is commonly thought, since it is far less exposed to any testing against political truth."[12]

Because of the consensus around simulation, the audience can trade places with the elite by accepting narratives to which the Reagan presidency lent credibility, implying that class differences are arbitrary. In this light, the Reagan presidency can be viewed as a cinematic effect—a product of cinematic conventions as much as a source of film themes. Extensive evidence shows that Reagan himself made little distinction between serving as president and playing a movie role, just as he often merged aspects of movies with bits of autobiography. The fact that Reagan constituted his identity cinematically was deftly exploited by his handlers to give his performance the seamless quality of naturalness. Thus like a cliché, cinematic or verbal, he seemed perfectly recognizable, comfortably familiar, and hence uncannily credible. Embodying both the perfect movie image and the ideal moviegoer, he made identification easy, allowing the public to see itself as the beneficiaries rather than the victims of the rampant lack of regulation he fostered. Identifying with him, they could project themselves as the heroes of an America that heralded the dismantling of social programs, the collapse of savings and loans, the relaxing of health and safety standards, the spread of influence peddling, the abuse of credit for leveraged buyouts, and the deflection into private pockets of billions of dollars in public funds, in short the demise of its credit surplus and its standard of living.

In the context of substituting narratives for resources, I discuss a number of "death-rehearsal" films that focus on the struggles of the dead to preserve, control, or protect the living, generally urging trust that a dead patriarch will prove a more effective leader and benefactor than his former carnal self. This form of revisionism shares with cinema in general the ability to manipulate the space-time continuum. A fundamental formal trait of film production, it is also necessarily the theme of time-travel movies. In this regard, the *Back to the Future* trilogy is a particularly important product of the era of the Reagan presidency, especially because it depends on extraordinary acts that draw on the time/credit system of cinema to make normative a revisionist version of the 1950s.

Trading Places is one of the earliest films to indicate how much the narratives of deregulation retained their appeal through a process of racial scapegoating. Although the film renounces a form of white supremacist social Darwinism—which it associates with Reaganism—*Trading Places* nevertheless embraces the idea that unregulated wealth can be universally accessible, that the difference in classes is an illusion that relies on the arbitrariness of framing, in the same way that cinematic reality does. The unregulated behavior manifested by the Reagan administration and its cohorts in industry and the financial world become a site of identification. Breaking the rules and the law becomes a class signifier in the film, a form of access that replaces equal opportunity programs.

The same point is made in *Working Girl* and other films that substitute gender backlash for racial scapegoating by validating the heroine's ascent to a predatory relationship with the class from which she has risen. The moral ledger in that film is balanced out by the economic, in a false economy sustained not by production but by faith in the patriarch who, in Reagan fashion, can extend infinite credit so long as his authority remains intact.

Women also suffer extensively in a number of films that concentrate on obsessive-compulsive behavior. These films, which proliferated in the late years of President Reagan's America, unite a variety of genres with common motifs that diminish "motive" as the chief cue for action. The films display unregulated behavior in all aspects of life, from drug use to law enforcement, fantasy to finance, as if this were the logical extension of deregulation. In one more way they level the moral playing field by suggesting that the roles are equal and arbitrary, as they are in sports events. Women, however, turn out to be poorer players and are thus generally punished if they try to escape the role of spectator.

In the sexual arena, however, women turn out to be very dangerous. *Fatal Attraction* is just one of many, many films that suggest the sexual partner, the strange woman who enters the home, the new roommate, may be a killer. These films, I think, refer to AIDS, in a variety of ways using invidious liquids and dangerous strangers to explore anxiety about the linking of sex and death in public discourse, giving rise to several genres of AIDS films, from the lover/killer and evil-double films to the decaying-beloved films and death-as-a-loss-of-innocence (or AIDS pastoral) films.

In contradistinction to these elegy-pastorals, we have the films of John Hughes, who is the filmmaker sine qua non of President Reagan's America. A phenomenal success in the period, Hughes as writer and/or director and/or producer has turned out nearly two dozen films that make concrete the combination of class values and pervasive optimism essentialized in President Reagan's America. In other words, if John Hughes did not exist, Paul Fussell would have had to invent him, for Hughes in his obsession with the distinctions that separate middle from upper-middle class organizes all of American life as the ripples resonating from conflicts at the site of that imaginary boundary. At the center is the adolescent (or the adolescent-like adult) who struggles with the restrictions of his class in a world that is all white and in which homelessness is always a lifestyle decision, never an economic necessity. The resourcefulness of the eight-year-old in *Home Alone* is a function of the infinite resources with which he can battle the burglars. As my eight-year-old son said at the time he saw the film, the reason he wins is because he is rich, or as Fussell said in his assault on Reaganism, "being in the upper-middle class is a familiar and credible fantasy. . . . It's a rare American who doesn't secretly want to be upper-middle class."[13]

Fussell is probably right. At a party a woman told me, somewhat proudly, that she had read *Class* and that everything in it said she was upper middle (with the stress on the "upper"). Fussell points out, however, that "another sign of upper middle class is its chastity in sexual display: the bathing suits affected by the women here are the most sexless in the world. . . . Both men's and women's clothes . . . are designed to conceal, rather than underline, anatomical differences between the sexes. Hence, because men's shoulders constitute a secondary sexual characteristic, the natural shoulder jacket."[14] Fussell has caught his readers between their prejudice toward upper-middle classdom and their affection (perhaps somewhat nostalgic) for their secondary sex traits. This is the crux of President Reagan's America, when seen through the lens of John Hughes.

Although the narratives of President Reagan's America are pervasive, I do not believe that the narratives I discuss are the *only* ones at work in any of the films. Examined in the light of other narratives or approaches, these films will fall necessarily into different groupings, underscore different themes and techniques; "President Reagan's America" may comprise the most extensively deployed set of cultural narratives in known history, but it is not an exhaustive or monolithic set. The films under consideration, I am well aware, are rich with narratives I do not discuss, narratives that in many cases may demonstrate ambivalence toward, or run counter to, the dominant ideology. I feel strongly, in fact, that ambivalence, contradiction, and resistance must be a part of—and therefore can necessarily be found in—any culturally produced narrative in that no narrative can be a seamless and perfect manifestation of its ideological presumptions. At the same time, the purpose of this book is to demonstrate how the dominant narratives take root in the field of dreams, even as at all the edges of the property line, other plots go to seed. Examination of those other plots, however potentially fertile, had to be placed outside the boundaries of this study.

So did many of the period's films that did not best exemplify President Reagan's America, or those aspects of it discussed in this book. And there is certainly room for a book examining the ways in which many films resist the dominant cultural narratives of the period, films such as *The Long Walk Home, Drugstore Cowboy, Enemies: A Love Story, Heathers, Glory,* or *Running on Empty* (to name a few), films like those made by John Sayles, perhaps the most gifted American filmmaker of the 1980s, or Robert Altman, for whom the decade was digression, or Woody Allen, or John Waters, or Spike Lee, films made by countless independent filmmakers. In writing about film, however, somewhat arbitrary limits are necessary to prevent the finished product from reducing to a list of titles and captions. Of the roughly fifteen hundred films I might have discussed, I select nearly one hundred, more than forty of which receive some level of detailed discussion, for the purpose of describing *some* narratives of the period as they are reiterated in many films. For the most part, these films were released between 1985 and 1992. These dates were chosen because the period of economic boom that I have designated "President Reagan's America" runs inclusively from 1983 to 1990, and the lag time between a film's conception and release is usually at least eighteen months.

Within these parameters, what emerges, I think, are numerous narratives about a privileged class, one that can identify with Reaganism, understanding that access to that class is the price of a video rental.

One

Back to the Futures Market: The Cinematic Realities and Trading Places of President Reagan's America

For both of Reagan's foremost biographers, Lou Cannon and Garry Wills, *Back to the Future* provides a particularly privileged cultural product.[1] One reason for its importance is that it constructs a fantasy about the power of cinematic conventions to alter the social world at the historical moment when that fantasy was coming true. This point is particularly stressed by Wills, who identifies an influential triumvirate of technological developments —automobile, radio, television—as endemic to construction of the sensibility codified in and celebrated by the Reagan presidency:

> No wonder that the "time machine" in *Back to the Future*, a film tailored to teen audiences, is a car. The car changed more than an individual's location, moment by moment. Its users became different people because of this tool. . . .
>
> The automobile was just one element in the complex of modern life being woven in Reagan's youth by technological development. Radio changed politics, becoming almost as important to Roosevelt's presidency as television would later be to Reagan's. Movies altered reading habits before television supplanted them. Living an alternative life of continuous fantasy by way of soap operas, genre films, and TV series became ingrained at earlier and earlier years of childhood. Yet this other-life of dreams, opened up by modern inventions, often celebrated outmoded (rather than innova-

tive) codes of behavior. "Home" images were subtly anachronistic, adapting modern life back toward inherited ideals. The new vehicles bore one away from the past as one gazed backward at it. Grandmothers on television are still taken from the Norman Rockwell casting service of the mind.[2]

"President Reagan's America," as I use the phrase, thus refers to a sensibility similar to the one put into biographical perspective by Wills with his title, *Reagan's America*. It is a phenomenon wherein cinema triumphs over economics as the primary producer of social realities, if by "social realities" we mean the narratives (e.g., of class, status, ethnicity, gender, region, religion) that people use as the reference points for their identities. Those narratives acquire and retain cogency through the iteration and reiteration of public performance, in its myriad forms, from TV news to pop novels, congressional debates to phone conversations, films to jokes. Thus at a given moment in the cultural history of a group, community, institution, or society, certain clichés seem natural, as do certain assumptions about virtually everything—what constitutes an edible meal or a serious notion of eternity.

Defining President Reagan's America, therefore, means examining a set of themes that seemed to infect recent popular imagination in the period between two recessions, the eight-year period that started with the third year of Reagan's first term and ended with the first half of the Bush presidency. It also means, more important, examining the process by which those themes acquired the status of reality. That process was one in which, I believe, the themes that were represented cinematically so closely resembled the thematics of cinematic representation that they came to validate each other through the powerful production of a political agenda. President Reagan's America, in other words, was a Hollywood moviefest in which America itself became the theater and television the ubiquitous projector. In 1984, for example, CBS television journalist Leslie Stahl ran a feature contrasting President Reagan's appearance at the Special Olympics with his cuts in federal support for the handicapped. To Stahl's surprise, White House staffer Richard Darmon praised the piece, calling it "a five-minute commercial." "Nobody heard what you said," he explained, "they just saw five minutes of beautiful pictures of Ronald Reagan. They saw balloons, they saw flags, they saw the red, white, and blue. Haven't you figured out yet that the picture always overrides what you say?"[3]

Darmon was simultaneously explaining a number of separate phenomena, the confluence of which focused and popularized the narratives of President Reagan's America. The first was that the popular imagination in contemporary America gives inordinate priority to cinematic representation. Reagan's handlers, moreover, as Darmon makes clear, understood this completely. According to one administration official, Deaver, Baker, and Meese believed that "reality happened once a day, on the evening news. They never read anything. They lived off the tube."[4] Darmon's remarks also call attention to ways that in Reagan the handlers had their ideal subject. As a movie actor and television personality, Reagan understood how moving pictures work on the screen or tube, and as an avid movie watcher, he believed in cinematic and televisual media at least as much as the most credulous Americans. He was the representative American, in other words, less because of his humble origins than his unflinching faith in what he saw on a screen.

If, as Wills puts it, "Reagan does not argue for American values; he embodies them," perhaps this faith in the screen was his most American trait.[5] Thanks to its prolific exposure to television, American culture in this half of the twentieth century has been extensively, continuously, and pervasively educated in reading and automatically translating the codes by which visual media construct reality. It is safe to say that this education has taken place on a magnitude and with a thoroughness unequaled in the history of the world. By Reagan's inauguration day, as Haynes Johnson points out, "the number of television sets being manufactured daily worldwide equalled the number of children born each day. . . . Ninety-nine percent of all American homes had at least one television set, and it was estimated that adult Americans spent nearly seven hours each day before the tube. . . . It virtually ensured that spectacle would triumph over substance."[6] Countless Americans who have no craft or trade, who cannot drive a car or do not know how to read, know how to comprehend the narrative of a movie. They can follow the rapid shifts of scene in a soap opera and integrate temporally the montage of anchors and features, live coverage and edited footage, backshot and insert that constitute the evening news. Many Americans who find themselves confused by the instructions on the labels of common products or lost in large shopping malls have no problem situating a close-up in the context of the establishing shot that precedes it or the medium shot that follows. To put it simply, we have learned to understand conventional presentations of moving images so well that the process seems "natural."

To this sense of the natural, Reagan naturally appealed. Because as a performer he was more or less a natural—certainly not a method actor burdened with a tempestuous unconscious or impeded by introspection—Reagan had a style of delivery that did not disrupt the illusion of naturalness from which television and film media benefit. Not charisma—far from it—but rather Reagan's neutrality made him credible. Whereas charismatic people punctuate space with their presence and thus make us aware of a disruption, Reagan almost always managed to appear seamless with his environment. One of Patti Reagan's childhood friends, in fact, reported that he never knew—in a physical sense—where Reagan came from: "It was like he came in smoke and disappeared in smoke." Speechwriter Peggy Noonan similarly never remembered hearing footsteps,[7] and secretaries in the White House noted his reluctance to give orders. Describing what Cannon calls Reagan's passive style, presidential adviser Martin Anderson said, "He made no demands, and gave almost no instructions."[8] These opinions were widely echoed.

It was this unobtrusive quality that made him such a good spokesperson for General Electric in that he exuded a reassuring neutrality that did not upstage the product. The passivity that made him deft at delivering prepared lines, however, made him equally weak at dealing with unscripted responses. Working from a prepared script, for instance, Reagan handled himself well in the phone call asking for Anne Gorsuch Burford's resignation until she told the president that what he (or the script) had termed "a wonderful agreement" was "the worst agreement possible"; this left him temporarily speechless.[9]

Even his family members and closest associates tended to agree that in those unscripted moments that composed his private life, he was in many ways a loner, emotionally aloof, hard to get close to. Prone to forgetting close associates after the professional association ended, he often did not even know the names of people with whom he was working. At cabinet meetings, even the salutations and small talk were read from cue cards. He related to his job in much the ways stars did in the old Hollywood system, having no real relationships and showing no interest in "members of the crew that did not interact with him or his performance."[10]

To the extent that one might wish to identify with Reagan or to trust his leadership, these characteristics might seem troubling. Acts of identification or trust, however, would mean confusing Reagan with the role he was playing, which is exactly what many Americans did. The themes that tested well going into the 1984 campaign stressed "a strong, can-do approach to leadership," Reagan's pollster Dick Wirthlin explained. "The role was written for a leading man like Reagan—a serene, self-confident hail fellow unburdened by doubt or morbid introspection—and in a thousand Peorias, it played."[11] That Reagan was generally staged, handled, managed, scripted is a commonplace. "He was an actor and he worked from a script," said one White House chief of operations. "If you gave him a script, he would do it."[12] As Cannon points out, "the cinematic approach became so woven into the fabric of the Reagan presidency that subordinates schooled in economics or statecraft routinely used Hollywood terminology to direct Reagan in his daily crafts."[13]

Thus, while many outside the White House feared that his pragmatic staff was not allowing "Reagan to be Reagan," those who handled him, pragmatists and ideologues alike, feared most the situations when Reagan might go off script. His head ascramble with snippets of sundry scenarios from politics and Hollywood, his temperament such that he was likely to be highly influenced by the last person with whom he spoke or the last poster he saw, off script he could, as his staff knew, say anything.

The anecdotes to illustrate this potential have generated one whole book and chapters or sections of many others. A few incidents illustrate exactly what his handlers feared about letting Reagan be Reagan. In 1982 he said, "The Soviets have 945 war heads aimed at targets in Europe. . . . *And we have no deterrent whatsoever*" [emphasis added].[14] In defiance of all known medical science, he declared that "children have been born even down to the three-month stage and have lived, the record shows, to become normal human beings."[15] Although he had never left the United States during World War II, he told Israeli prime minister Yitzhak Shamir that he had filmed the liberation of the Nazi death camps.[16] And in the middle of a meeting in which the Lebanese foreign minister was trying to explain the complexities of the intense factionalized turmoil in Lebanon, Reagan interrupted with the clearly unscripted remark: "You know your nose looks just like Danny Thomas's."[17]

A script was essential and, from Reagan's perspective, desirable, for while other important leaders might have been offended by the insinuation that they were scripted, Reagan could see the description as a tribute to his professionalism. During his acting career, he was a quick study well known for being prepared and reliable. Wills accurately characterizes Reagan's style of professionalism: "He learned his lines; was winning, conscientious, dependable; but did not agonize over character. For one thing, he likes regular hours. He did not like location shooting because it played havoc with his schedule of rest and exercise."[18]

Little indicates that he approached the presidency any differently. It is widely acknowledged that he took little or no interest in the aspects of his job that did not concern his delivering lines. Although he was uninterested in political strategy, as Cannon succinctly points out, "what animated Reagan was public performance. He knew how to edit a script and measure an audience."[19] When not performing, on the other hand, he exuded a very different persona. Interacting with secretaries or advisers, he generally gave the impression that he was a worker getting assistance, not the chief executive taking charge. Even his schedule suggested that he had contracted to work a normal nine-to-five workweek with a firm that had a fairly liberal vacation schedule (not to mention a very liberal housing allowance). It was almost as if Reagan regarded the weekends—frequently three-day weekends—at Camp David or the summer months spent on his ranch (345 days, or the equivalent of 6 working days out of every month he was in office) as time off from being president. Republican campaign consultant John Sears even suggested that this was in fact an asset: "Reagan proved that he could be president, address the country's problems, and still go riding once a week. In a strange way it was a relief to the country . . . People were relieved to find that you could run this very complicated job without having to spend all your time on it."[20] And to some degree, Sears was no doubt correct, making Reagan similar in this respect to the Maitlands in *Beetlejuice*—a film significantly symptomatic of President Reagan's America. For them, taking time off becomes their ghostly job, one that enables them without any labor to acquire the provincial, anachronistic life they had desired.

This is not to suggest that Reagan didn't work, but rather that during those substantial periods of time when he wasn't working he wasn't really president, any more than Clark Gable was Rhett Butler when he wasn't on the MGM set. Reagan's actual work, therefore, had two chief aspects to it, acting and preparing to act. These are the same duties he performed with diligence in Hollywood, and after the studio assigned Reagan to his next film, the lines, the cast, the plot of the previous piece reduced, as it did for most studio actors, to a small residue of recalled phrases, favorite scenes, random plot details, perhaps a sense of the film's "message" or "theme," and occasionally a friendship with one of the cast members.

This description of his acting life very aptly glosses Reagan's approach to the presidency. When he first assumed the presidency, he was daily given much reading material that he studied dutifully each night, sometimes staying up very late, like an actor learning his lines for the next day's shooting. (The workload was lightened after Nancy complained.) Although he had a few basic themes and ideas, like a good actor, he was less concerned with substance than with performance, and being the president was, as Cannon correctly called it, "the role of a lifetime." "The world of illusion suited Reagan," Cannon explained,

> and it was easy for him to portray the good guy in films that were usually sentimental celebrations of America. Portraying a citizen president should have been more demanding, but Reagan also performed this role too effortlessly. Because of his ability to reflect and give voice to the aspirations of his fellow citizens, Reagan succeeded in reviving national confidence at a time when there was a great need for inspiration. This was his great contribution as president. But because he believed in happy endings obtained with too little sacrifice, this revived confidence became an end in itself that Reagan rarely sought to focus on higher goals.[21]

Cannon, of course, is assuming that Reagan might have been able to conceive of goals higher than that of attaining a desired audience response. But if reality is defined by the movies, then there can be no higher goal for a movie actor. Cannon, too, is trying to separate the actor from the role, but when we do so, we find nothing behind that role but a prior role, a compendium of anecdotes that blurs hopelessly the fragile line between fact and fiction, or between alternative fictions. As the record shows, Reagan was equally likely to misrepresent public policy and personal history in such a way that even Cannon points out, "Reagan playing Reagan, in real life as in the movies, established an enormous presumption of credibility that no ordinary politician could hope to duplicate."[22]

If we posit, moreover, that Reagan was not only the ideal movie actor for the role he played but also the ideal movie spectator, then his focus on audience response was not a failure any more than his misstatements were lies. He was merely participating more extensively and more overtly in the same mode of understanding accepted by much of the American public, as his success indicated.

And Reagan was indeed the consummate movie watcher. During the course of his presidency he did more movie watching than *anything* else. He usually watched two movies on each of the 183 weekends he spent at Camp David. In addition, he watched movies just about everywhere else, from the White House to the suites he stayed in when traveling. The night before Reagan was to host the international economic summit of industrialized democracies, in Colonial Williamsburg, James Baker delivered to him an important briefing book covering all the major issues, but the following morning Baker discovered that Reagan hadn't even opened the book. "Well, Jim, *The Sound of Music* was on last night," Reagan explained.[23]

As Wills and Michael Rogin have demonstrated, a significant part of his autobiography as well as many of his privileged themes and anecdotes come not from experiences but from films, particularly ones in which he was featured. His understanding of the Strategic Defense Initiative, for example, bears an uncanny resemblance to a concept from *Murder in the Air*, a film he made in 1940, and even the title of his first autobiography, *Where's the Rest of Me?*, comes from a line he spoke in the film *King's Row*.[24] More striking, however, is how *extensively* movies constituted Reagan's definitive frame of reference. When Tip O'Neill told Reagan, who was admiring his desk, that it had once belonged to Grover Cleveland, the president replied, "That's very interesting. You know I once played Grover Cleveland in the movies," confusing the baseball player Grover Cleveland Alexander with the president after whom that athlete was named.[25] As the anecdotal material and the inferences of many of his closest associates suggest, Reagan's understanding circulated on a narrow plane, delimited at one end by the validity of anything done to create a desired audience response and at the other by the validity of anything to which an audience responded favorably.

Like the Teflon with which he became so widely identified, Reagan was consummately two-dimensional, a trait that could be considered a disadvantage were he not attempting to lead a population the bulk of whom had been schooled daily over four decades in the normative quality of two-dimensional realities. These representations, as I discuss at length in the next chapter, disrupt the space-time continuum by representing time spatially. They provide, in other words, a compilation of instructions, signs, and cues enabling

Figure 1

Ronald Reagan playing Grover Cleveland (Alexander). Photo: Museum of Modern Art/Film Stills Archive.

an audience to construct from a two-dimensional play of light a narrative having depth and temporality. These cues and instructions, moreover, represent themselves, for the most part, not *as cues* but as a part of the very reality that they are directing the viewer to construct.

Films that deal with time travel are thus films that make the temporal problematics endemic to cinema a topic of discussion and an aspect of the film's thematics. The characters in the film face the same problem as the makers of the film and, so it seems, the same problem as the handlers of Reagan: constructing a "natural" effect out of an "unnatural" process. All three—the characters, the makers, the handlers—succeed because they all have the power of cinema on their side. If the history of popular American cinema can be seen as standardizing the production of a dominant style and proliferating its distribution, the economic power of both America and its film indus-

Figure 2

Ronald Reagan as amputee in *King's Row*. Photo: Museum of Modern Art/Film Stills Archive.

try has allowed this style to have profound global impact.[26] And the techno-logical and economic prowess of television has exponentially accelerated and intensified that impact. By simply conforming to conventions of cinema, representations acquire the aura of the natural that those conventions have come to signify. And no one in high public office more earnestly, more ex-tensively, or more credulously conformed to the conventions of cinematic re-ality than Ronald Reagan. Like *Back to the Future*, he proved that tampering with the space-time continuum was not dangerous but beneficial; it was, in fact, as Doc (Christopher Lloyd) and Marty (Michael J. Fox) demonstrate, absolutely necessary for happiness and comfort. It was their means of consumption.

In a phantasmagoria of consumption—made possible by the technology of time travel, that is, by the technology of film time credit—*Back to the Future* enacts the complete separation of acquisition from production. The narrative of production is completely divorced—as in Jean Baudrillard's worst, and thus most American, vision of contemporary life—from the codes of consumption.

It is not surprising, then, that Baudrillard so astutely understands the source of Reagan's power. "Governing today," he explains,

> means giving acceptable signs of credibility. It is like advertising and it is the same effect that is achieved—commitment to a scenario, whether it be a political or an advertising scenario. Reagan's is both at once.
>
> Everything is in the credits. Now that society has been definitively turned into an enterprise, everything is in the synopsis of performance and enterprise, and its leaders must produce all the signs of the advertising "look". The slightest failing becomes unpardonable, since the whole nation would be diminished by it. Even illness can become part of this "look," as for example with Reagan's cancer. By contrast, political weaknesses or stupidity are of no importance. Image alone counts.[27]

Because image alone counts, Ronald Reagan–the–actor is far less important to this book than President Reagan–the–role. Reagan-the-role, who focuses the ideological positions articulated in the scripts written for Reagan-the-actor, is the Reagan of President Reagan's America. He is the set of beliefs and practices valorized in the eight years between recessions, during which time an extension of credit, a production of waste, a fetishizing of details, and a glorification of image—the qualities of the Hollywood film—became manifest as themes in public policy.

To that codification known as the Reagan Revolution, Reaganomics, simply Reaganism—or, as Barbara Ehrenreich termed it in her "Irreverent Notes from a Decade of Greed," the "'Reagan Renovation,' that finely balanced mix of cosmetic refinement and moral coarseness which brought $200,000 china to the White House dinner table and mayhem to the beleaguered peasantry of Central America"[28]—it is now necessary to turn.

The most lasting and far-reaching aspect of Reaganism, of course, was the presumption of limitless credit, a presumption applied to both federal and personal pocketbooks. According to supply-side theory, the immense tax cuts were to have stimulated the economy in ways that would have actually increased overall revenue. This, as Director of the Budget David Stockman made clear as early as 1981, they could not do. Arguably, however, they ought at least to have provided an infusion of cash to the private sector that would reduce the need for additional credit. Quite the opposite was the case. As the national debt tripled, personal and corporate debt also sky-rocketed. In the intricate world of corporate mergers, debt became a kind of capital to the extent that it could be leveraged. In this regard, we can associate Reaganism with a virtually compulsive acquisitiveness.

If the compulsion to acquire went unregulated, so did virtually everything else. Deregulation, in fact, might be the most apt label for the general abuse of public office and indulgence of private excess proliferated by the Reagan administration, much of the corporate and banking world, and a significant portion of the general population. Numerous books have been written detailing this unregulated behavior, and summarizing their findings could easily double the length of this book.[29] A few cogent examples, however, may be helpful.

About military spending, for example, Reagan told his staff, "Defense is not a budget item. You spend what you need."[30] The lack of regulation over military spending was matched by military adventurism of both the overt and covert sort. From the trivial invasion of Grenada to the significant involvement in El Salvador and Nicaragua, the administration pursued questionable goals through dubious means, regulated neither by financial nor legal constraints, neither by honest reporting nor clear accountability. "Within five weeks of taking office," Johnson points out, "Reagan increased aid to El Salvador fivefold. He immediately approved twenty million dollars for shipment of arms and equipment there, sent additional U.S. military advisers to train Salvadoran forces fighting the rebels, arranged for additional millions in loan guarantees, and requested another twenty-five million dollars more for arms purchases."[31] Covertly, the CIA was supporting the most right-wing elements in the Salvadoran government, those responsible for the civilian murders that exceeded the total number of American lives lost in Vietnam and included the torture of women and children and the assassination of priests and nuns.

As the focus of Central American policy shifted from supporting the Salvadoran government to overthrowing the Nicaraguan government—technically an act of war—the administration rejected regulation by congressional oversight, by the United States Constitution, or by international law. Initially, the excuse given for covert activities in Nicaragua was the need to cut off arms shipments to the Salvadoran rebels. The actions that ensued clearly indicated that this was a lie, a lie flaunted in the face of a congressional law that explicitly prohibited the United States from using covert means to overthrow the Nicaraguan government. In blatant defiance of congressional regulation, the CIA secretly mined the harbors of Nicaragua. "Agents who took part in the mining operation," Johnson further notes," included . . . no contra Nicaraguans in whose name the mines had been laid. It was disclosed, too, that a CIA training manual that described sabotage and assassination methods had been prepared and distributed to contra forces."[32] The fact that the administration had simultaneously broken United States and international law in no way had a regulating effect on its activities. In fact, the more Congress sought to regulate the covert activities, the more regulations the administration officials ignored.

This included the infamous shipment of arms to Iran, the profits from which were diverted to the contras. In specifically ordering that this information be withheld from Congress, Reagan participated in what Senator Daniel Patrick Moynihan later termed a "however unwitting . . . effort to subvert the Constitution of the United States."[33] Another attempt to free the executive branch from constitutional regulation can be found in Oliver North's testimony at the special hearings on the Iran-Contra Affair. North, who worked at the National Security Council, had been in charge of executing the deal that brought illegal aid to the contras. Repeatedly he argued that he could not be guilty of a crime because under the separation of powers, Congress could not pass laws that were binding on the executive branch. This novel interpretation of the Constitution by logical extension would create of the entire executive branch—elected and appointed—a virtual aristocracy exempt from the legal regulations that applied to the rest of the populace. Anything mandated by a legitimate lawmaking body—in other words, any legitimate "law"—was illegitimate when it came to Reagan and his appointees, whether that law concerned arming contras or using drugs, committing arson or larceny, evading income taxes or lying to Congress.

We could say that this was Reaganism deregulation ad absurdum, but the absurdity seems to have been lost not only on those involved in the Iran-Contra Affair but across the entire spectrum of the administration. In agency after agency, we find practices regulated by neither ethical nor legal standards. Conflict of interest, influence peddling, negligence, fraud, and perjury became all too common symptoms of an unregulated government. A sign of ethical conflicts came as early as the transition period, during which volunteer transition squads composed of lobbyists helped educate new agency officers. In 1983, Anne Gorsuch Burford and twenty other top officials of the Environmental Protection Agency were forced to resign. Earlier Rita Lavelle, the head of the hazardous waste program in that agency, was dismissed and later convicted of perjury and obstruction of justice.

More scandalous was the situation in the Office of Housing and Urban Development, where the fraud and abuse diverted more than a billion dollars into the hands of large Republican contributors and friends of the administration. James Watt, for example, after leaving his post as secretary of the interior, collected almost half a million dollars for a few phone calls steering his friends in HUD to a company that wanted assistance in constructing three housing projects. Watt justified his fee before congressional investigators by explaining "that while the 'system was flawed,' there was no reason why he should not profit from it."[34] So excessive were the abuses at HUD that HUD secretary Samuel Pierce refused for a long period to appear before Congress, and when he eventually did, he became the first sitting cabinet secretary in American history to plead the Fifth Amendment.

Even some of Reagan's closest associates failed to recognize that they were regulated by laws, ethical standards, or obligations to the public, from Stockman, who "cooked the books" on Reaganomics for ideological reasons, to longtime Reagan associates Meese, Nofziger, and Deaver, whose activities, according to Schieffer and Gates, "left the impression that they had gone to Washington not to serve the country so much as to use their special connection in the White House to promote their own interests."[35] Like more than one hundred other Reagan appointees, these three all suffered serious legal problems. Nofziger and Deaver were both indicted for influence peddling, and Meese spent most of his energies throughout the Reagan presidency defending himself against ethics charges. During the second term, when Meese was attorney general, the Office of Governmental Ethics concluded that he had violated conflict-of-interest rules. Two deputy attorneys general resigned, explaining personally to President Reagan the problems with Meese's continued leadership. In a historically unprecedented act, one of the deputy attorneys general, William Weld, even recommended to the president that Meese be indicted (although, according to Cannon, Reagan may have been dozing during Weld's presentation).[36]

At the other end of the spectrum, unregulated was the increase in home-lessness, the spread of poverty, the erosion of the middle class. In *America: What Went Wrong,* and more recently in *America: Who Really Pays the Taxes?*,[37] *Philadelphia Inquirer* reporters Donald L. Barlett and James B. Steele have collected telling statistics that detail the unregulated decline in wealth, security, and financial prospects among the majority of Americans. Tax systems firmly weighed against the middle class, coupled with subsidies to businesses that create low-wage jobs, rewards for transferring jobs abroad, decreased support and subsidy for higher education, and permission for corporations to trim or eliminate health benefits and pensions—all con-tributed to the unregulated growth of a population that has lost many of its middle-class options, or fallen into the category of the working poor, or, even worse, has joined an impoverished underclass.

From 1980 to 1989, for example, "the total wages of all people who earned less than fifty thousand dollars a year—85 percent of all Americans—increased an average of just 2 percent a year. At the same time the total wages of all millionaires shot up 243 percent a year. Those figures are not adjusted for inflation, which cuts across all income groups but hits the lower and mid-dle classes the hardest."[38] During the same period, there was a nearly 1,000 percent increase in the number of people earning five hundred thousand dol-lars. Noting the graphic difference between the top and the bottom, Barlett and Steele point out that in 1989, "the top 4 percent of all wage earners in the country collected as much in wages and salaries as the bottom 51 percent of the population."[39]

At the same time that they assumed a greater portion of the tax burden, the middle class was, thanks to deregulation, receiving less from the gov-ernment. In addition to the cutbacks in social programs, citizens saw the De-partment of the Interior, under Secretary James Watt, sell off public lands, and, under Secretary of Labor James Donovan, it saw the government with-draw significantly from its role of protecting worker safety. Almost immedi-ately Donovan withdrew numerous health and safety standards put forth by the Carter administration. "With Reagan in office, both the Heritage Foun-dation, a conservative 'think-tank,' and the pro-business U.S. Chamber of Commerce proposed numerous changes in OSHA [Occupational Safety and Health Administration] policy, including the abolishment of OSHA's 'police-man's orientation,' use of cost-benefit considerations to set safety standards, and the transfer of significant enforcement powers to the states. For the most part, these suggestions have been implemented."[40]

The financial industry under Reaganism perhaps best illustrates the cumulative result of several forms of unregulated behavior that characterized the 1980s. The first form was the government's abdication of its regulatory role. With the 1981 appointment of John Shad, the Securities and Exchange Commission for the first time was led by someone whose background was as a Wall Street executive. Johnson concisely summarizes changes in the SEC under Reagan:

> Once in power [Shad] announced plans to cut the SEC's staff and to reorder its operational patterns and priorities. During his seven years as chairman he succeeded in keeping total SEC employment either below its 1981 level or about the same number. In that same period the number of stockbrokers over whom the SEC had regulatory authority nearly doubled. He shifted emphasis for policing Wall Street from the federal government back to Wall Street itself.
>
> Historically, the SEC's enforcement division had been one of the strongest and most effective in the federal service. Shad changed its top priority from overseeing corporate practices to pursuing cheating by individuals. He also succeeded in reducing governmental restraints on stock trading, including in those new speculative stock-index futures. Shad actually believed that a certain amount of speculation was good for the markets: It helped the flow of capital; it made it easier for companies to obtain funds for growth.[41]

Like supply-side economics, deregulation of this sort constituted a borrowing from the future; it used anticipated benefits to permit current excesses, and it thereby justified unrestrained greed. In what Barlett and Steele call an "orgy of debt and interest . . . American companies went on a borrowing binge through the 1980s, issuing corporate IOUs at the rate of $1 million every four minutes, twenty-four hours a day, year after year. By the decade's end, companies had piled up $1.3 trillion in new debt—much of it to buy and merge companies, leading to the closing of factories and the elimination of jobs."[42] For those who thought Reagan should be allowed to be Reagan, it might follow that Wall Street should be allowed to be Wall Street. And under Shad's SEC it was. "During the Reagan years the wave of corporate mergers, takeovers, and restructuring resulted in more than twenty-five *thousand* deals, cumulatively valued at more than two *trillion* dollars."[43] Like much of the Reagan prosperity, this burst of acquisition was financed by credit, but unlike the predictions, the effect was a siphoning up of resources rather than a trickling down. The siphoning worked on the personal level as well as an institutional one. Looking at executive compensation, Barlett and Steele note that in 1953 it constituted 22 percent of corporate profits, while in 1987 it equaled 61 percent. As Galbraith, among others, points out, "in 1980, the chief executive officers of the three hundred largest American companies had incomes twenty-nine times that of the average manufacturing worker. Ten years later the incomes of the top executives were ninety-three times greater. The income of the average employed American declined slightly in those years."[44]

The encouraging of unregulated greed within legal parameters, combined with the removal of many regulations and the reluctance to enforce the remaining ones, was only a small step away from another aspect of unregulated behavior under Reaganism: criminal activity. Just as for Reagan the line between film narrative and life story seemed to dissolve, in the climate of Reaganism, the line between the laissez-faire, the unethical, and the illegal blurred so that on Wall Street, deregulation was often the corporate partner of lawlessness. Although the scandals associated with this lawlessness focused around specific personalities such as Ivan Boesky or Michael Milken, the practices they typified and the examples they set not only contaminated the world of stocks and bonds but also spread in viral fashion to ancillary industries including real estate and banking. The savings and loans debacle was permitted by the removal of the regulations that prevented savings and loan institutions from making risky, speculative investments, at the same time that numerous forms—legal and illegal—of high risk speculation became increasingly acceptable practices.

Risk and speculation are in fact two of the most notable offspring of the marriage of Reaganism to deregulation. Banking on quick returns, on an infinite supply of credit, on not running out of time, on not getting caught—in other words, banking on all of the cinematic powers that facilitate Doc and Marty's adventures in *Back to the Future*—thousands of financiers, traders, speculators, and public officials disrupted the space-time continuum through insider trading and leveraged offers. They went, so to speak, back to the futures.

These are the trading places that make so fluid the ebb and flow of class and identity under Reaganism, a sensibility that the film *Trading Places* captures almost prophetically in 1983, in the first strong rays of morning in America. At the center of the film's plot is a debate over social Darwinism. The Duke brothers, Mortimer (Don Ameche) and Randolph (Ralph Bellamy), a pair of superwealthy commodities traders, attempt to settle an argument about the relationship between heredity and environment by conducting an experiment wherein they destroy the life of their firm's manager, Louis Winthorp III (Dan Ackroyd), and elevate to his position a black street hustler, Billy Ray Valentine (Eddie Murphy).

For the experiment to work, they believe, the switch must be complete. They must cost Winthorp not only his job but also his home, all of his savings and credit, his fiancée, and his esteem in the eyes of everyone he knows. To do this they frame him as a thief and drug pusher; they pay a prostitute, Ophelia (Jamie Lee Curtis), to make him look like a pimp in front of his fiancée; and they arrange to have his assets frozen and his credit cards confiscated. As the owners of his luxurious Philadelphia townhouse, the Dukes have the butler, Coleman (Denholm Elliott), deny Winthorp access to his (former) home and possessions. All of these actions are effected though illegal means. The Dukes have their agent plant the stolen money and drugs on Winthorp. They also use their influence with the police, the banks, and the social clubs to render Winthorp a destitute outcast.

They want to see if he will turn to crime, by which they mean the kinds of criminal activities that they associate with the lower class: assault, armed robbery, drug dealing. This life of "crime" remains completely discrete in their minds from the illegal activities pursued to advance their own interests, whether those interests be conducting a social experiment or obtaining in advance orange crop reports. Class thus refers for the Dukes not only to an economic stratum but also to a kind of criminal activity.

This type of class distinction, Jimmie L. Reeves and Richard Campbell insightfully argue, informs media coverage of cocaine use during the Reagan presidency. In the early 1980s, the media used a "therapeutic" model, they demonstrate, suggesting that the cocaine use was the affliction of "a degenerate element of the economic elite" that was slowly trickling down to "an envious and ingenious middle class that studied and admired the life-styles of the rich and famous—and was consequently vulnerable to their vices."[45] The difference between the elite and the middle class is thus not represented as a qualitative distinction but as a quantitative one. In media coverage, when Dan Rather uses "us," they point out, the group with which he is implicitly identifying, despite his two-million-dollar salary, is "the camp of common-sense Middle America."[46] The danger to that group is not that they see themselves as Other to the wealthy elite but that they see themselves as similar enough to be endangered by contaminating vices. The wealthy elite are thus not criminals who may threaten "us" but ill people who may infect us.

In 1986, the paradigm shifts from one that identifies cocaine as something infecting "us" to something propagated by "them," the racially and economically Other. The therapeutic model, Reeves and Campbell thus point out, is replaced by a "siege" model in which the media represents the threat of crack as emanating not from an uncomfortable affinity with its users but from unsurmountable differences with them. Commenting on a television report about cocaine use that claims what was formally a "ghetto problem" is now moving into the suburbs, they describe an effect that is consistent with what typifies, as I will demonstrate in detail, the cinematic rehistoricizing proliferated in President Reagan's America:

> The ahistorical historical observation [about the move from ghetto to suburbs] plays over a dramatic tracking shot that begins on a mean inner-city street and dissolves into a neat suburban setting. For us, this clever dissolve covers a major case of journalistic *amnesia* regarding the class dimensions of cocaine pollution during the early 1980s—amnesia that *replicates* the ahistoricism and victim-blaming of the new racism.[47]

In *Trading Places*, the class distinctions embedded in the Dukes' construction of what constitutes a crime or a criminal type acquire a racial dimension similar to the one that would shortly appear in the media treatment of cocaine. When Billy Ray Valentine becomes the test case, he does so as Winthorp's pure Other, that is, as the essential embodiment of criminality. As the plot makes clear, the Dukes, having confused the cause with the effect, in a very literal sense, have blamed the victim. Valentine had simply bumped into Winthorp as Winthorp was leaving his exclusive club carrying an attaché case with the payroll. The minute Winthorp saw Valentine's black face, he assumed he was being mugged and pleaded for his life. He refused to allow Valentine to return the attaché case or accept Valentine's confused, albeit truthful, assertions of innocence. Instead he called for the police, who also refused to accept Valentine's truthful narrative over Winthorp's imagined one. Recognizing that he had no chance of proving that he was the victim and not the aggressor in this incident, Valentine tried to escape by running into the club, where after a brief melee he was captured with half a dozen cocked police pistols pointing at his head. Winthorp, all the more convinced of his own version of the event, then insisted on pressing full charges.

When the Dukes have the charges dropped and give Valentine Winthorp's home, property, and job, therefore, we must assume that they are doing so because they are sure Valentine is guilty. Their experiment, after all, depends on changing the environment of a bona fide criminal, and it is thus purely out of self-interest that they set lose someone whom they believe to be a dangerous felon. If they are wrong about Valentine's character, they are not wrong about Winthorp's. They destroy him despite the fact that he had shown every sign of growing up to be just like them, that is, the implicit ideal of white America.

The Dukes, after all, represent all we could wish for: the bastion of family values and proper manners, they quintessentialize the Protestant ethic,

_____ *Figure 3*_____

An innocent Billy Ray Valentine framed by police guns. Photo: Museum of Modern Art/Film Stills Archive.

thinking about nothing but their work and, despite their affluence, perfecting frugality to an art. Although they trade in futures, they represent the past symbolically in much the way that, as Wills has pointed out, twentieth-century media does. They do so, moreover, not only as characters in the plot but also as stars, carrying with them a cinematic history as rich as the financial history that their characters embody. Between them, Bellamy and Ameche have more than a hundred years of film experience, primarily as leading men through almost the totality of the sound era. Perhaps most significant, they were both strongly associated with leading roles in which they played prominent Americans. Ameche's 1939 portrayal of Alexander Graham Bell so identified him with the inventor that it initiated a very long-standing joke (or series of jokes) about Ameche's having invented the telephone, and Bellamy's portrayal of Franklin Delano Roosevelt, a re-creation of his Broadway stage performance, identified him as strongly with American political history as Ameche's role did with American industrial history. Combining industry with politics, capitalism with the New Deal, futures trading with established wealth, movie roles with American history, the Dukes as portrayed by Ameche and Bellamy represent, in other words, the apotheosis of Reaganism.

This point is underscored by the photograph of Reagan on Randolph's desk, distinctively situated where family photos are normally placed. The visual equation of Randolph Duke with Reagan suggests interesting similarities. Both men profess a belief in upward mobility, in the potential of people from deprived origins to succeed as executives. Not only in theory but in demeanor, Randolph evinces generosity, kindness, and optimism. He shows faith in Valentine's potential and is somewhat instrumental in affecting Valentine's opinion of himself. At the same time, however, that he asserts Valentine's potential to become a law-abiding citizen, Randolph turns his back on his own lawlessness. His demeanor does not reflect compassion or ethics; it substitutes for them. In this way style is Randolph Duke's capital, capital that allows him to borrow on the future, evade regulations, and distinguish himself completely from the racially and culturally Other.

One aspect of Reagan's role, of course, was that the public did not identify him with people like the Dukes but with people like themselves. He seemed, in other words, not like the superrich but like average Americans (who merely want to be superrich). This "average" appearance served the interests of the wealthy well as it enabled Reagan to mediate between the aims of the affluent and the desires of the middle class. Randolph Duke, therefore, was less like Reagan than he was like the General Electric directors for whom Reagan performed his public relations tasks. As someone inordinately impressed by wealth, this aspect of his performance also came easily to Reagan. Like Marty at the beginning of the *Back to the Future* series, as we shall see, and like Melanie Griffith's "working girl" or many John Hughes adolescents, Reagan found approval and self-approval strongly linked to affluence. Discussing Robert McFarlane's and Donald Regan's relationships to the president, Johnson noted that what "McFarlane resented perhaps more than anything else was that the President seemed to have a higher opinion of Regan simply because Regan was a millionaire, whereas McFarlane was not a man of means. McFarlane had discovered, as others did before him, that Reagan viewed men of wealth with a respect bordering on awe."[48] When Regan became chief of staff, in fact, Regan bragged to the president about his own wealth. "I've got 'fuck you' money," he said. "Anytime I want, I'm gone."[49] The Dukes thus combined Donald Regan's "'fuck you' money" with the movie version of American history and also with the name "Duke," which was the nickname of John Wayne, the movie actor Reagan most envied.

In this way, the Dukes brought to the futures the full promise of Reaganism: that unregulated trading and investing would give everyone who deserved it "fuck you" money. Their name even suggested the aristocratic superiority to the law that Ollie North would later announce was the privilege of the executive branch, very broadly extending the claim of "executive privilege" earlier—and unsuccessfully—asserted by Nixon. They regard, moreover, the sacrifice of Winthorp to the fictional illegalities of their frame-up not only as above the law but also as serving a higher law, that of science. The power of science and technology is omnipresent in the film but in a context of the sort that, to Wills, typifies Reaganism. Always evoking an earlier narrative of American individualism, the sophisticated high-tech computer that feeds into the Dukes' office and car is used to keep them apprised of minuscule, second-by-second shifts in the market but never to influence decision making. It is simply a faster, more ubiquitous Teletype or foot messenger, completely devoid of the analytical programs essential to sophisticated futures investing. Rather, the decisions to buy and sell are made in the same way Reagan made policy decisions—by substituting an understanding of one's community arrived at anecdotally for any educated expertise or technical analysis.

Similarly, the debate over Darwinism evokes once again the narrative that vindicated the upper class: that the rich are rich because for some reason—environmental or hereditary or both—they are more fit. (No matter which Duke is proved "correct" in this debate, the result can never be simply that the rich are rich because they have more money.) The goal of understanding whether heredity or environment dominates is framed by the implicit understanding that measures positive results by the degree to which the experimental subject is able to emulate the Dukes. Their role as social model becomes the constant against which the variables of nature and nurture measure up.

When Valentine proves he can assume his new role as manager of the Dukes' firm with comfort and that he can do well as a commodities trader, he only demonstrates that the advantages of the rich do indeed qualify them for their commensurate responsibilities and rewards. Now that Valentine has the advantages, he too is qualified, or ostensibly so. To the Dukes, of course, Valentine will remain forever *qualitatively* different, even after the quantitative gaps are broached.

The film is emphatic on this point. When Randolph Duke initiates the experiment, he says of Valentine, "That man is the product of a poor environment. There is absolutely nothing wrong with him, and I can prove it!" Randolph seems to be arguing from a liberal perspective, in contrast to Mortimer Duke's response—"Of course there's something wrong with him: He's a NEEE-gro—probably been stealing since he could crawl"—which seems to argue from a white supremacist perspective of biological determinism. At the end of their experiment, however, their conclusion identifies the Dukes not as natural scientists but as divine interventionists: "We took a perfectly useless psychopath like Valentine and turned him into a successful executive," Randolph claims. "At the same time we turned an honest, hard-working man into a violently deranged would-be killer." The turn of events, in other words, is not the function of environment but rather of social engineering. Although the Dukes have claimed a laissez-faire approach to their experiment, at every stage, as they inadvertently admit, they have rigged the outcome, in the same way that they are attempting to benefit from the laissez-faire conditions of commodities trading by rigging prices through the use of illegally obtained information. The free-trade rules of the futures market are thus a Trojan horse that disguises the immense advantage those rules give to people who can get away with breaking them.

The secret of the experiment, which has been lost on the Dukes, of course, is that they could not have done anything to make Valentine like them, because *they were already like him*. The difference was never qualitative. Valentine succeeds because he is already familiar with the way the Dukes work; he too is a con man, a hustler, figuring the odds, looking for the edge, calculating the most profitable angle, regardless of legal regulations. Valentine identifies the similarity very quickly, responding to the Dukes' explanation of commodities trading by saying, "Sounds to me like you guys are a couple of bookies." Despite their affluence, from Valentine's perspective they are his kind of people. Valentine is thus like the viewer of television news when the "therapeutic" model dominated cocaine coverage. The failings of the elite were a danger to him because he could identify with them too easily. From the Dukes' perspective, however, identification is impossible on racial grounds, if on no other, as they both conclude, regardless of Valentine's success as an executive. "Do you really think I would have a nigger run our family business?" Mortimer asks, to which Randolph replies, "No. Neither would I." The Dukes' understanding of the situation replicates the "siege" model, wherein Valentine, as racial Other, is blamed for being the victim of the Dukes' prejudice, just as in Winthorp's initial collision with him, Valentine was victimized by the assumptions of Winthorp's "siege" mentality.

In another version of this story, a version that has a long-standing tradition in American film and literature, the *conditions* of the Winthorp/Valentine trade might resemble those that pertain in *Trading Places*. The *effects* of the trade, however, would not, for traditionally this kind of plot structure produces an Empsonian pastoral, that is, an outcome in which the low person who is elevated serves to recall the decadent upper class to its traditional values.[50] Think, for instance, of *If I Were King*, in which the rogue poet, François Villon (Ronald Colman), sensitizes King Louis XI (Basil Rathbone), or *The King and I*, in which a middle-class British schoolteacher (Deborah Kerr) reeducates the king of Siam (Yul Brynner). The same is true of *The Prince and the Pauper*, *Mr. Deeds Goes to Town*, or *Little Miss Marker*, to name a few versions of pastoral. In these and countless other examples, the ruling class needs to remember its values, which have become obscured in a complex and decadent social world. The simple figure elevated thus saves himself or herself by simplifying the complex social world so that it may reclaim itself.

Screwball comedy, a film genre that bears a strong kinship to *Trading*

Places, also relies heavily on this formula. The marriage plots around which those comedies revolve all require the reeducation of the upper class so that its unruly but vitally energetic heiress can contribute productively—via marriage—to the reformation of the decadent upper class from which she originates. Because the majority of screwball comedies were products of the depression era, the question of the survival of a class or a social order was far from trivial, a point that gives added significance to the rarely discussed manifestations of naturalism endemic to the screwball genre.

In this light, *My Man Godfrey* can be usefully compared with *Trading Places* for several reasons. The first is that *Godfrey* is a trading places story, in that it contrasts classes through a changing of roles, although in *Godfrey*, the switches from high to low and from low to high are both effected by the character of Godfrey (William Powell), who in a manner of speaking trades places with himself. Godfrey Park, a member of the upper class, has become a "forgotten man" living on a Manhattan dump on the bank of the East River. Initially claimed in a scavenger hunt, he becomes the butler of the Bullocks, a decadent rich family. As their butler, he is able not only to discover a work ethic but also to restore the family to the values of sobriety, responsibility, prudence, and hard work with which it had lost touch. In addition, through a series of plot machinations, he makes investments that save the family from bankruptcy and also allow him to finance a restaurant/housing project. This project converts the dump where he had lived into a source of work and housing for the other homeless men who live there.

In both films the issue of naturalism is significant. Just as a naturalist experiment constructs the plot conditions in *Trading Places*, questions of naturalism—never explicitly articulated—inform the relationships in *Godfrey*, for the film conducts an anthropological investigation from the outset, in which Godfrey, identified as a forgotten man, proves to be more of a missing link in the story of social (as opposed to biological) evolution. Even the title entails a pun that evokes the anthropological question of what it means to be a "man." To be "my man" in the sense of being a servant or possession means to be relegated to a subordinate status, to be property like a dog or a car. To be "my man" in terms of a courtship and marriage relationship is to be in the implicitly superior position of the owner or boss.

The term in the film that mediates these two contradictory roles is *protégé*. Irene Bullock (Carole Lombard) hires Godfrey so that he can be her protégé,

_____ *Figure 4* _____

In *My Man Godfrey*, Carlo imitates a great ape.

drawing explicit parallels between him and Carlo (Mischa Auer), her mother's protégé. Carlo, too, is a potential missing link, noted for his ability to imitate a great ape. Articulating the indeterminacy of Carlo's role in the evolutionary schema, Mr. Bullock (Eugene Pallette) at one point even shouts, "Why don't you stop imitating a gorilla and start imitating a man!" The "protégé," in other words, occupies the same indefinite position on the social spectrum as the missing link does on the evolutionary. Carlo also suffers from depression; although an alleged musician/composer, he is too depressed to work. In this way he participates in the ubiquitous social environment of the film. Both Bullock sisters are frequently depressed, as is Mr. Bullock out of frustration with the profligate ways of his family, a problem he deals with by consuming huge quantities of a depressant, alcohol. Depression (over a failed love affair) is also what drove Godfrey to the dump. In the social environment of the film, everyone is, like Godfrey, down in the dumps. Indeed, the psychological depression functions as a metaphor for the Great Depression—the environment of economic depression that is testing the survivability of American society.

The symbiotic relationship in the film between depression as an economic condition and depression as an emotional state constructs a social Darwinist reading of the Great Depression that makes the rich, rather than the poor, its victims. In this reading, the question of survival is one of revivifying the upper class, ridding it of its depression. This task takes the form of a vitalist search for the right man, that is, one not suffering from (the) depression. Godfrey becomes that man by feeding off the vitality of the screwball heroine, who, like the screwball baseball pitch, has significant energy moving in unpredictable directions. The marriage plot thus becomes a form of natural selection wherein Godfrey returns Irene's energy to her in a directed manner that brings an end to the depression in the family and hence anticipates the end of the Great Depression through the redirection of the energy of the rich as a form of capital.

The social implications, with Darwinian overtones, of this outcome are expressed by Godfrey when he states that "the difference between a man and a bum is a job." The reeducating and revitalizing of the upper class thus impact on the entire species. When my man Godfrey, the property, turns into my man Godfrey, the proprietor (and hence my man, the husband), not just Godfrey or the Bullocks but manhood itself survives, a point underscored when Bullock celebrates his survival by throwing Carlo out. Particularly because of the parallel established at the outset between Godfrey and Mr. Bullock—who also calls himself a forgotten man—the embrace of Godfrey and the casting off of Carlo as unfit become part of the selection process that vouchsafes both men's manhood. Manhood, capital, and the Protestant ethic thus circulate in an economy that survives through an exchange process facilitated by the merger of naturalism with pastoral.

While evoking elements of naturalism and pastoral, *Trading Places* can adhere to neither genre because neither is compatible with the cultural narratives of President Reagan's America. In *Trading Places*, Valentine is both the Godfrey figure and the Irene figure in that he is simultaneously the forgotten man capable of reeducating the decadent society and the dynamic presence capable of energizing its world of moribund butlers and superannuated preppies. The plot cannot proceed in the direction of reeducation, however, because to reeducate the Dukes to their lost values will not redeem them but rather make visible their chronically corrupt state. Nor can the plot evoke in a positive sense naturalist themes, because the energetic savior is not found within the class (or race) of the elite whose values and wealth are the normative objectives in the film. If the savior were of the right class and race, the film could conform to the therapeutic model of cocaine news coverage and, in a fantasy resolution, the therapy would be completed successfully. The energetic potential savior here, however, bears the face of the Other who objectifies for the privileged class its siege mentality. Within the cultural narratives of President Reagan's America, the only appropriate role for the black is to be complicitous with his own invisibility, which, as I demonstrate in Chapter 2, he or she is in films such as *Ghost, Field of Dreams*, and *Beetlejuice*, but he is punished for not being in *Ghost Dad*.

Trading Places is, therefore, a revenge comedy—a story, that is, in which the transgressors are not reformed and redeemed but rather are punished and expelled. As Valentine says to Winthorp after they have uncovered the Dukes' treachery and joined forces, "It occurs to me that the best way to hurt rich people is by turning them into poor people." In the fluidity of class and image made possible by cinema, reflected by 1980s culture, and articulated by this film, the trading of places is no longer between Valentine and Winthorp but between them and the Dukes. The film began with Valentine trying to con the Dukes and being framed by Winthorp; then the Dukes con Valentine and frame Winthorp; then Winthorp attempts to frame Valentine, in a form of racial scapegoating that continues to be a legacy of the Reagan era. Waking up later in his former home after a suicide attempt from which Valentine and Ophelia have saved him, Winthorp summarizes his belief that his financial and social plight can be blamed on blacks: "I had the most absurd nightmare. I was poor and no one liked me. I lost my job. I lost my house. Penelope hated me. And it was all because of this terrible Negro."

In this speech, Winthorp is speaking not so much for the superrich as for the lower-middle-class whites who constitute what has been called "Reagan Democrats." This group indeed suffered a great deal under the Reagan administration. As Thomas Byrne Edsall and Mary D. Edsall point out, during the 1980s for those in the top 1 percent of the income bracket, capital gains grew by 112 percent and salary income grew by 81 percent, whereas for those in the bottom 90 percent of the income distribution, a whole decade of work yielded only a 3.9 percent wage increase (an average of $825), and capital gains for that 90 percent of working Americans "rose by an average of $12."[51] Nevertheless, the Republican party retained the support of the Reagan Democrats by blaming these inequities not on the policies the Reagan administration implemented but on those that Reagan opposed on racial grounds. "Opposition to race-based affirmative action became for the Reagan regime," the Edsalls point out, "a matter not only of principle and of policy, but of partisan strategy. Republicans delineated two competing visions of America: one of individual initiative and equal opportunity (Republican), the other of welfare dependence and anti-egalitarian special preference (Democratic)."[52]

The act of revenge that resolves the conflict of *Trading Places* is one in which Valentine and Winthorp steal the Dukes' information about the orange crop report. They then supply the Dukes with an incorrect report while they use the correct—but illegally obtained!—information to position themselves so as to make a killing at the same time as they bankrupt the Dukes. The Dukes will now occupy the place that Winthorp had occupied after the Dukes' experiment and that Valentine had occupied prior to it. This final trading of places is only possible, however, *because* Winthorp and Valentine had already assumed the place of the Dukes, that is, of criminals who in a thoroughly unregulated manner use stolen information for personal gain. The only reason they were in such a place, however, was that the Dukes had already been in the place to which they designated Valentine and Winthorp, the place of the criminal stealing from the marketplace. To Mortimer's assertion "He's a NEEE-gro—probably been stealing since he could crawl," Valentine might have said about Mortimer, "He's RICH—probably been stealing since he could crawl." But to make such an assertion would be to regulate one's desire for wealth, and nothing could be more of an anathema to all the characters in film, as well as to Ronald Reagan, or most of his administration, or to the principles of Reaganism itself.

At the same time, of course, the association between Randolph and Reagan, and the demand at the end that the Dukes pay the debt they incurred as a result of their illegal schemes and unregulated greed, imply a strong rebuke of Reaganism in general and, more specifically, of its fiscal irresponsibility. In this way, the fate of the Dukes suggests an allegorical reading of *Trading Places* in which the deregulation, criminality, deception, false promises, poor financial planning, and covert racism of the Reagan administration come back to haunt it in a cataclysmic day of reckoning, a day when the unpayable debt on futures comes due.

Although this cautionary aspect of the film is hard to ignore, it is also somewhat problematic for several reasons. The first is that, unlike *My Man Godfrey*, it recognizes no potential either in the realm of legal regulation or in the resources of human character for the system to be corrected. The Dukes are not punished for having *illegal* information but for having *incorrect* information. The actual or attempted crimes are never uncovered, and the Dukes are never branded as criminals. They simply become destitute (which in the lexicon of their culture is the functional equivalent of criminal). Nothing will be done, furthermore, to prevent future abuses; the success of Winthorp and Valentine, in fact, validate those abuses in terms of the world of futures trading portrayed in the film and also in terms of the plot that represents this success as an unambiguously happy ending.

This dramatically differentiates *Trading Places* from films like *My Man Godfrey*. In *Godfrey*, there is also an attempt to brand Godfrey a criminal by framing him with the theft of pearls. He thwarts the attempt by finding the planted pearls and hiding them before the police arrive. From that point on, however, the pearls acquire an almost talismanic power. They serve to discredit the bullying older Bullock daughter, Cornelia, and provide Godfrey with the capital he needs to make investments that save the Bullock family and finance his own business. In finally returning the pearls to Cornelia, moreover, Godfrey is able to construct both an economic and a moral parable. He shows how the proper use of capital, not for pleasure, decoration, waste, or revenge but for judicious investment, turns the pearls into fishes and loaves; it creates an economy of pure surplus and zero loss. Whereas at the outset there were only pearls, now there is economic security, urban renewal, *and* the original pearls. In this regard, Godfrey is also able to renounce the use of fortuitously acquired wealth for personal gain at the expense of others, even at the expense of their vindictive or selfish acts. The moral for the Bullock family is also the moral for the capitalist system in general. The film represents capital as a benefit, the only constant benefit in the film, but one that is constantly undermined by the moral lapses of the capitalist. The Darwinian message in this film has to do with the fitness of capitalism for survival and the conclusion is that the necessary trait for survival in the crisis of the Great Depression is a return to family values of the sort that usually fall under the rubric of the "Protestant ethic." Because the attempted framing allows Godfrey to demonstrate the potential for survival, it saves the rich family.

In *Trading Places*, however, the framing ultimately destroys the family. It creates an economic disequilibrium that can never be righted, and, moreover, it allows the Dukes, even in their own destruction, to set criminality and unregulated greed as the terms of survival. The Dukes fail because they incur the wrath not of people who are more honest than they but of those who are more successfully criminal. For that reason, the kind of resolution in *Godfrey* is impossible in *Trading Places*. Put simply, there is no honesty to revitalize and no honest position from which to revitalize it. In the end, like everyone else, the Dukes have been framed. But framing may be impossible to escape because in the world of cinematic reality, framing constitutes the only definitive margin. Framing in photography and cinematography, as in argumentation or experimentation, is a fundamental inclusionary or exclusionary act, and framing a social agenda or a political platform, like framing a political ad or the shots that compose that ad, constructs an image by controlling its margins.

In acquiring the title the "Great Communicator," Reagan was being lauded for his ability to use the public forum to frame the argument. His opposition was not defeated by his superior information or the logic of his arguments, or certainly by the truth of his assertions. Rather, they were constantly on the defensive by virtue of his ability to evoke specific narratives, imply specific frames of reference.

The administration approach to education provides a good example of this process.[53] The problems in the schools were a question of family values, Secretary of Education William Bennett asserted, claiming that studies showed that students without the proper home environment benefited little from enhanced (i.e., expensive) educational programs. By framing the discussion of education in terms of a conflict between supporting "family values" (a Republican position) and "throwing money at a problem" (the alleged Democratic alternative), Reaganism had successfully defined the problem as the solution. The debate between two forms of *value*—"family" and "tax revenue"—framed the discussion within an economy that excluded almost completely the issue of education. Given studies that suggest as much as 30 percent of all Americans are functionally illiterate,[54] and given the nation's high number of violent crimes, incidents of spousal abuse, and problems with drug addiction, we can assume—since violent criminals, wife beaters, and drug users constitute a share of both the literate and illiterate parental households—that a statistically significant portion of the school-aged population lives in less-than-ideal homes, from the perspective of the studies Bennett used to frame the Reagan administration's position. Framed in that way, the position does not have to address the problem of educating children who come from families with the wrong values.

The "values," moreover, are defined as accruing only narrowly delimited benefits. In *Godfrey*, Godfrey and the Bullocks' acquisition of family values has broad social impact; it is the *source* of a social program, not the *alternative* to one. The rhetorical position of *Godfrey*'s narrative, in other words, is that capitalism is an *inclusive* social order and hence can be measured by the benefits that maintaining a wealthy elite produces for society as a whole. Reaganism, however, like *Trading Places*, frames capitalism *exclusively*, such that family values are equated with economic values. Because the haves are not responsible *for* the have-nots, they possess no responsibility *to* them. The social frame is arbitrarily drawn to define society as those who have value—social, economic, family—and to marginalize those who lack the said "value." The cinematic technique of framing thus creates the social reality that Reaganism was so adept at codifying. It is the reality—with all the racial implications so well demonstrated by Reeves and Campbell—of the siege.

Just as the Reagan presidency was chronically and very carefully framed by the photo opportunity, the issues presented by that presidency were framed by sound bites. This imagistic form of representation, designed for the highly edited style of cinema narrative and television news, defines Reaganism in numerous ways, perhaps the most significant being that framing allows disparate pieces to be edited together to create the illusion of a logical continuum out of bits that are temporally, spatially, and logically discontinuous. In film, if the camera were to pull back, it would reveal that the apparently natural shot was constructed by an extensive apparatus that included lights, reflectors, sound equipment, multiple cameras, and an immense staff of operators and helpers, without whom the illusion of naturalness would falter. Such a reframing or metaframing, moreover, would not only show the individual shot to be contrived; it would also make impossible the implicit continuity of shot-to-shot relations. In filmmaking, control over framing is the first step in establishing the logic on which continuity depends.

That artificial logic creates the credit system, which I examine in the next chapter, out of which films draw the infinite reserves of time and space. So too, through careful control of framing, Reaganism's assertions of opportunity are prevented from contradicting its evocation of racial divisions, its undermining of public education, its practice of blaming the victim, its tilting the playing field in favor of the rich while removing the regulations that keep the game fair. By framing public advocacy groups as "special interests," Reaganism was similarly able to equate the "public" interest with the rampant deregulation that benefited large corporations over small, corporate stockholders over employees, people with capital interests over wage earners, people who purchased public lands over those who enjoyed them.

Needless to say, many people did get rich in an America whose social agenda was framed by Reaganism (although not nearly as many as got poor). It is fitting, therefore, that *Newsweek* followed up its 1984 election coverage with an extended special feature on December 31 that dubbed 1984 "The Year of the Yuppie,"[55] which pointed out that the glamour of this group obscured a more significant trend among their peers toward downward mobility, noting that between 1979 and 1984, the median income, calculated in constant dollars, fell 14 percent for families in the age bracket of twenty-five to thirty-four.[56] But *Newsweek* named the year after the affluent minority who quintessentialized Reaganism's esteem for "'fuck you' money." As *Newsweek* points out, "if Yuppies change the world, it will be through the force of example, not weight of numbers. Their strength is as the strength of 10, because they want it all so badly, a quality that doesn't show up in the statistics."[57] Statistics, like democratic processes and market values, describe majority preferences. But the scale under Reaganism, as *Newsweek* understands, has been tilted perhaps as much as ten to one in favor of the affluent minority who "want it all so badly." They are people privileged by virtue of their similarity to the Dukes, rather than their loyalty to any institutions, people, or principles. "Yuppies are known," says a professor of management at Yale University, "not so much by their willingness to work hard for the corporation, but their devotion to accumulating power and getting rich."[58]

The road to riches, however, was often framed for the general public, just as it was for the members of the administration, not by playing fairly or by recognizing social responsibilities but rather by embodying the hypocrisy and duplicity, or at least the selfish indifference, exemplified by Reaganism.

The yuppies are the implicit heroes of *Trading Places*, and they come from all social strata. At the end of the film the successful coconspirators luxuriate in the Caribbean, in a classless society of the sort only available to the superrich, with Winthorp from the best background and the upper class, Coleman also from the best background but as servant (technically the lower class), Valentine from the black lower class, and Ophelia from the white lower middle class. Thus they represent the cinematic ideal represented by President Reagan's America—that deregulation will pave the way to a classless society in which women, blacks, the servant class will all be able to share in the benefits that were formerly reserved for the elite. Didn't Reagan himself exemplify such a prospect?

Their utopia has been made possible by hard work in a climate not framed by any legal or ethical regulations, hard work, moreover, that does not result in any tangible product. Carefully framed out of this classless society and the narrative that it facilitated is all the labor that makes trade in orange juice futures possible. All those who grow, pick, process, and ship the real oranges are separated from any of the value that the juice acquires when converted into the abstraction "orange juice futures." All wealth in *Trading Places* accrues from the ability to turn that labor into an abstraction, whereby the parasitical connection between futures and agriculture may be completely effaced. Between Winthorp's and Valentine's initial places is a working America whose labor makes commodities trading possible and yet receives no benefits from it. By definition trading places must be symmetrical and value free. The futures trader does not care, per se, whether there is more orange juice or less or how the orange pickers' salaries fare; the futures traders only care how accurately they predict fluctuation. The space of working America is bracketed out of the narrative as it necessarily must be out of the commodities exchange.

In the final shots of the film, Winthorp, shown offshore in his yacht, and Valentine, lounging in his shaded beach chair, exchange champagne toasts, through an interchange of close-ups. The physical distance between Valentine and Winthorp—perhaps a quarter of a mile—make this exchange of gestures, much less words, absolutely impossible in the space constructed by the narrative, but that impossible distance is broached by the conventions of cinematic framing, which trades close-ups as though the intimacy available to the viewer were also accessible to the characters. But, no matter how

_____ *Figure 5* _____

Valentine, lounging on the beach, exchanges a champagne toast with Winthorp . . .

_____ *Figure 6* _____

. . . offshore in his yacht . . .

_____ *Figure 7* _____

. . . through an exchange of close-ups that broach cinematically an un-broachable distance of space and class.

much we accept continuity editing as natural, the illusion of mutual access and of broached distance, the expressions of mutual admiration and equal contentment are purely cinematic, in other words purely the stuff of which President Reagan's America was made.

It is an America, therefore, that finds little to distinguish the prostitute Ophelia from her Yuppie counterparts; like them she is entrepreneurial, upwardly mobile, and has loyalty to little beside money. As a typical Yuppie, *Newsweek* cites Carrie Cook, a twenty-five-year-old ad agency executive who "liked Reagan 'for financial reasons,'" but because of the Republican stance on abortion and other social issues she eventually voted for Mondale. Not that she actually wanted the Democrat to *get elected.* 'I knew Reagan would win easily anyway,' she says. 'If I thought it were a close election, I might not have voted for Mondale. I had the best of both worlds. I could vote my conscience and still come out ahead financially.'"[59] More noteworthy than Carrie Cook's hypocrisy is the way in which she frames cinematically both the political issues and her personal role. The casting of the vote for Mondale contributes to having "the best of both worlds" only if she can construct a context that gives value to casting a vote for someone she wants—and knows is going—to lose. That context implicitly situates her before a camera that records her vote against financial self-interest as something dramatic—as an "act of conscience" in which the pulling of the lever is the final gesture in a cinematic narrative revolving around the conflict between money and morals, social good and personal gain. Appropriately framed and edited (by Carrie Cook), Carrie Cook's conscience appears to have integrity and continuity; in a cinematic sense, it seems natural. Stripped of the narrow framing and continuity editing, it appears more like a fictional construct necessary for a Carrie Cook production of a cinematic narrative that stars Carrie Cook as "a person with a conscience" and even provides, in the classic Hollywood tradition, a happy ending by giving Carrie Cook the financial reward of the Reagan victory she had denied to herself by following her conscience. This is the kind of happy ending we find in the films of President Reagan's America as well as in the consciousness of the president himself, for whom the idea of America precluded unhappy outcomes, unsurmountable problems, or inadequate rewards for the good and virtuous, regardless of the cinematic manipulations necessary to construct the virtues or distribute the rewards, regardless of how Donald Regan's "fuck you" money is attained.

Two

Flatlining on the
Field of Dreams

Throughout the second half of the Reagan-Bush boom years, especially as the cumulative debt that fueled the boom mounted to Gothic proportions, a number of films focused on the struggles of the dead to preserve, control, or protect the living. In *Ghost*, a young stockbroker, murdered so that he would not discover a million-dollar money-laundering operation, is helped by a black psychic to communicate with his girlfriend, and through an act of pure willpower he exerts physical force in the living world to protect that girlfriend and avenge his murder. In *Ghost Dad,* Elliot (Bill Cosby), helped by his motherless children, exerts similar acts of willpower to create a physical presence—an illusion of life—that must last for three days following a car accident, before his life insurance policy goes into effect.

It would be easy to suggest that this illusion—of a living, thinking creature constructed purely out of willpower—refers directly to President Reagan himself. Anyone who has tried to connect the rhetoric with the referent in Reagan's assertions, or to find the kinder and gentler aspects of George Bush's America, or to fathom the ghostly blank in Dan Quayle's eyes as he recites his lines—memorized indeed, as the peculiar caesuras testify, by the *line* rather than by the *sentence*—anyone who has tried these feats will recognize immediately their relation to death-rehearsal movies. One will see a world in which agency is a form of nostalgia, a world in which the pharmakon of language has drugged the audience into an infinite loop of craving and escape, both of which are represented by the promise of meaningful speech, solidified by the father/king/God who is elsewhere.[1]

That patriarch was indeed embodied by Ronald Reagan, whose gap between speech and meaning rapidly became one of his identifying traits. "Reagan had known intuitively for years that it was the punchy line and the performance that 'made the point,' not substance or accuracy."[2] In the 1980 campaign, for example, Reagan's "counterfactual statements," as James David Barber pointed out, "rolled forth so fast the news magazines had to bundle them together as a weekly feature. In a factual sense, be the subject air pollution or nuclear power, farm policy or foreign policy, he literally did not know what he was talking about."[3] Barber's concern, as early as 1982, however, was less over the ostensive ignorance of the nation's chief exccutive than in the way in which Reagan's misstatements were "being defended as a positive good," under the rubric of a patriarchal beneficence that, in the eyes of David Gergen, the president's director of communications, gave his falsehoods an instructional quality: "'These stories have a parable-like quality to them,' Mr. Gergen says. 'He's trying to tell us how society works'— which presumably cannot be done with the straight story."[4] Although in a 1983 meeting with heads of the Big Three auto manufacturers Reagan read from the wrong note cards remarks that "had nothing to do with . . . any . . . relevant subject," Schieffer and Gates point out, "most members of the White House staff came to realize that such lapses didn't matter. . . . The public didn't seem bothered by any of his blunders, so why should they care?" By 1983 they trusted the power of illusion to carry them through the 1984 election.[5]

But the illusion that the president *understood* what he said was part of a more comprehensive illusion that the president even *knew* what he said. As presidential spokesperson Larry Speakes admitted, he manufactured quotes released in the president's name, assuming that he knew what the president wanted to say. The practice was routine in the Reagan White House.[6] As Michael Schaller notes, "Assistant Chief of Staff Michael Deaver (who once declared: 'I am Ronald Reagan. . . . Every morning after I get up I make believe I am him and ask what he should do and where he should go') and Communications Director David Gergen rewrote the rules of Presidential image making. . . . Each morning White House staff set the 'line of the day,' which all high officials were expected to stress in their press contacts."[7]

If the ghost created, therefore, by the fictions of Speakes, Deaver, Gergen, or Peggy Noonan was played most effectively by Ronald Reagan, I want to suggest that his role marks the site of an America haunted by the specter of a much vaster death. It is the death not of a person or of a type but of a national narrative, one that represents America as the successful economic and political model for the world. And, like films such as *Ghost, Ghost Dad, All Dogs Go to Heaven, Chances Are, Beetlejuice, Field of Dreams, Drop Dead Fred, Late for Dinner, Flatliners, Bill and Ted's Bogus Journey*, and *Jacob's Ladder*, this national narrative is basically a domestic story, the story of Dad who is protector, provider, and, as it now appears, dead. But surely it cannot be death, just a death rehearsal. Our founding fathers cannot have abandoned us; we cannot be subject to the poverty, homelessness, economic and emotional scarcity that exists elsewhere, that we know about *only* through television.

Contemporary television, as Daniel C. Hallin points out, is a news medium that distances this world of Others, even in the process of bringing them into American homes. Particularly with Reagan's landslide reelection, Hallin argues, the network news programs have worked to contextualize threats, crises, disasters, or instances of deprivation as aberrations within the normative world of people who exemplify Reagan's version of American life: optimistic, patriotic, and definitely housed and employed.[8]

Even when the television represents these figures as close to home, the discourse of President Reagan's America reads them as the outside, the alien, the anomaly. With a domestic setting as the normative frame of reference, the homeless by definition do not fit in any more than the migratory, the illegal immigrant, the hospitalized, or the incarcerated. Inside the national boundaries, moreover, the national narrative redistributes space in much the way that the Gothic novel does, to create a haunted domesticity, a gridwork of shadow and corridor divisecting the lighted sites where domestic conversation proliferates. In the Gothic tradition, the shadows contain evil, and even the domestic hearth and candle are suspect in comparison with the natural light of the countryside, the timeless place without walls or history.

In a stark inversion of this Gothic paradigm, however, in these death-rehearsal movies the walls of the manor protect instead of entrap the family, and the ghost is not the threat but the savior. Having failed to secure the home during the tenure of his recent history, he returns in diminished form to echo a past—often that of the Cold War 1950s—that will affirm domestic security through a series of strategies all of which rely on a central act of faith:

that we trust the patriarch to accomplish in death that which he failed at in his vitality.[9]

Such an act of faith provides a central theme in *Field of Dreams*. The film's "exhortation of a purer, more innocent America . . . is very close," Stephen Holden points out, "to the mythic American past invoked by that quintessential conservative Ronald Reagan."[10] Faced with certain foreclosure of his Iowa farm, Thomas Kinsella (Kevin Costner) can only plant dreams in his cornfields. With total faith in the ghostly patriarchal voice that says, "If you build it, he will come," Kinsella, following what is in effect the basic premise of Oral Roberts's theology—"plant a seed of faith and grow a miracle"— constructs a baseball field that is then visited by ghost baseball players. When confronted with the economic ruin that he faces when his debt exceeds his revenue, he emphasizes his commitment to the ghosts of baseball past with the phrase "Read my lips!"

The impotence of this bravado would be laid bare were it not for the intervention of Kinsella's daughter, who has a vision thing that Americans will flock by car to this mystical field and, entranced, will gladly hand over twenty dollars to watch the baseball of America's isolationist heyday, the Republican boom era that led to the Great Depression. When the daughter immediately thereafter has an accident and is saved by one of the ghosts, the event has a miraculous effect on the creditors, who also opt for ghosts over food, play over work; they pave the way for the fulfillment of the child's vision, at the end of the movie as a thousand points of headlights trail off into the infinite horizon, signifying the private sector's willingness at twenty dollars a head to subsidize ghosts rather than farms and thereby purchase back a piece of their own lost childhood.[11]

Before the cars can begin their pilgrimage to this hallowed field, which the film dubs "Heaven," "the place where dreams come true," Kinsella has to go through two final rituals. First he must bid farewell to the surrogate black patriarch, Terrance Mann (James Earl Jones), who has served as a reluctant convert and then beneficent inspiration to Kinsella's vision. The conversion has been so complete, in fact, that this former black radical has become an unqualified fan of professional baseball in an era when black players were prohibited. "Despite Mann's presence," Viveca Gretton accurately points out, "the reality of racism in America, and in baseball, is neatly evaded. . . . Provided with the reassurance that Mann's politics are unthreatening and that he is a

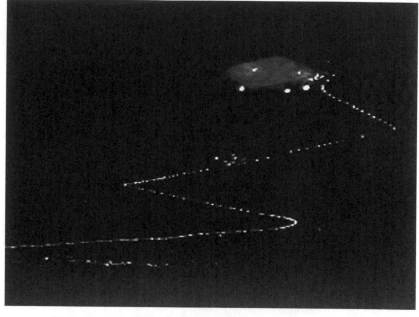

_____ *Figure 8*_____

At the end of *Field of Dreams,* a thousand points of headlights trail off into the infinite horizon, signifying the private sector's willingness at twenty dollars a head to subsidize ghosts more than farms.

secret fan of the game, Mann's 'radical' status evaporates with his complicity in Kinsella's fantasy. (Mann literally disappears into Kinsella's cornfield.)"[12] Parting with this converted black surrogate, Kinsella can then be reunited with his own dead father, the masked man behind the plate, the real "he" behind the voice and the vision. In recognizing that the field of dreams was an altar built to the sacrificed father, Kinsella completes the Grail quest by resurrecting the patriarch, in this case, since Iowa is landlocked, not as Fisher King but as Corn God, whose Spring vegetation rites thus become Spring training.[13]

In many ways, this dead patriarch movie is paradigmatic, containing all the elements of the cultural narrative I am discussing: the house at risk, the daughter in mortal danger, the patriarchal ghost, the benevolent and complicitous black, the reversion to an earlier moment in American history combined with the recognition of a concomitant amnesia. Even as quirky a production as the animated film *All Dogs Go to Heaven* has a young girl orphan at risk, saved by a patriarchal dog who has returned from heaven on borrowed time. And in *Drop Dead Fred* a spirit who is both real and imaginary returns from a young woman's childhood to save her from a bad marriage. Although technically neither dead nor a patriarch, he is named "Drop *Dead*" and is played by the same actor who plays in flashback the woman's deceased father.

In *Ghost*, the endangered woman, Molly (Demi Moore), is caught between two patriarchal men; one is her live-in lover, Sam (Patrick Swayze), and the other is their best friend, Carl (Tony Goldwyn). Both Sam and Carl work on Wall Street, where Carl, unbeknownst to Sam, has been using client accounts to launder underworld cocaine profits. When some of the money gets tied up in computer files to which only Sam has the password, Carl arranges for a criminal to steal Sam's wallet at gunpoint. What is supposed to be a simple mugging, however, runs amok when Sam is fatally shot while struggling for the mugger's gun. Since the objective was to obtain Sam's computer password, the hired mugger subsequently breaks into the loft apartment that Sam shared with Molly; from there Sam's ghost follows him back to Brooklyn, where he hears a phone conversation that discloses the mugging to have been a setup and, more significant, reveals that Molly is in further danger because the mugger plans to return once more to the apartment.

At this point in the film, the objective again is to protect the "daughter" in danger, and to do so again the patriarchal ghost will enlist the aid of the beneficent black. Like Terrance Mann, the black in this case, Oda Mae Brown (Whoopi Goldberg), is at first reluctant to assist or even to acknowledge the supernatural power with which she is confronted. Eventually she becomes a convert who serves as medium between Molly and Sam, convincing the skeptical Molly but at the same time leaving her helpless, as the police refuse to take her seriously. She then turns to Carl, who has been serving as her patriarchal adviser after Sam's demise, indicating that Molly, left to her own devises, cannot differentiate between legitimate authority and bogus authority. Because of Oda Mae's police record, she rejects Oda Mae and therefore Sam, relying instead on Carl, unaware that he was behind Sam's murder. Salvation for Molly, as it does for Kinsella, must come from a blind faith in a ghost.

As in *Field of Dreams*, the ghostly instructions and support of the beneficent black must be supplemented by physical intervention. In this case, Sam is taught to make his presence felt in the living world by a ghost who haunts the subway. "You can't push [that dime] with your finger," the ghost explains.

> "You're dead. It's all in your mind. The problem with you is you still think you're real. You think you're wearing those clothes. You think you're crouched on that floor. Bullshit! You ain't got a body no more son. It's all up to you now. You want to move something, you gotta do it with your mind. You gotta focus. You gotta take all your emotions, all your anger, all your love, all your hate, and flush it way down here in the pit of your stomach, and let it explode like a reactor."

The ghost's instructions insightfully gloss the predicament not only of the ghost patriarchs but also of American power and influence in the era of the Reagan presidency. It clearly distinguishes between image and presence, while arguing that success will come from a conversion of the former into the latter. The mode of conversion, however, according to this sage—if also violently psychotic—ghost, who calls Sam "son," lies in tapping emotions and prejudices: "all your emotions, all your anger, all your love, all your hate." Power must come, in other words, from drawing on the cultural narratives of an audience, the stories it tells itself about its loves and hates. The ability to do so, as we have seen, was the forte of the Reagan presidency. Reagan was able to convert, as these ghost patriarch films do, the matter of death into the image of success.

That conversion, moreover, is closely linked to the creation of an appropriate living space for those who trust the ghosts of America past. In *Field of Dreams*, it is a farm with major league baseball in the front yard instead of crops. In *Ghost* it is the converted loft living space in lower Manhattan for the yuppified couple who combine art (Molly is a sculptor) with finance, urban taste with unpretentious style, the love of interior decor with the appreciation of open space. Notably the first scene of the film shows Molly, Sam, and Carl, each with sledgehammers, triumphantly knocking out the old interior floors to create the light and space appropriate for Molly and Sam's new lifestyle as yuppie cohabitants. Violation of Molly's living space, therefore, becomes an organizing motif in the film, with the mugger breaking in once and threatening to return, with Oda Mae on separate occasions being denied access by Molly. Carl constantly visits Molly's loft with increasingly more threatening schemes. At first he hopes to attain the address book that contains Sam's computer password by helping Molly sort his belongings. Then he returns to make sexual overtures toward her, and finally, he comes there to kill her. His final defeat at the hands of Sam's ghost, moreover, leaves him impaled amid the rubble of a neighboring loft, the renovations of which are not yet complete. Sam's ghostly interventions save, in other words, not merely Molly's life but also her living space, her lifestyle.

The final disposition of the ghostly spirits further underscores the spatial division of good and bad along color lines. The good spirits in the film, such as Sam, are taken upward by amorphous entities in the form of white light; the bad spirits in the film, such as Tony, are drawn downward by shadowy black blobs. Heaven, in other words, means living in a white neighborhood, and Hell means, regardless of race, having to live in a black one.

In *Beetlejuice*, as in *Ghost* and *Field of Dreams*, the house is threatened with ruin, although the threat comes this time not from bad finances but from bad taste. Alec Baldwin and Geena Davis play the Maitlands, a quintessentially conservative couple, so in love with the past that they have dedicated themselves to restoring their home in a small Connecticut town by replicating to the most minute detail its turn-of-the-century appearance. They are so opposed to change that they have built in their attic an exact replica of the house and town, attempting to preserve its rural charm in microcosm, eternally. This couple is conservative with a purity that transcends party lines or even politics itself. They want to preserve, as the apotheosis of American values, the small town mythologized by moviemakers like Frank Capra and movie watchers like Ronald Reagan.

Lou Cannon, in fact, appropriately describes Reagan in terms of one of Capra's most famous movies: "He was the wholesome citizen-hero who inhabits our democratic imaginations. . . . It was a role in a movie—personified by Reagan's friend Jimmy Stewart in *Mr. Smith Goes to Washington*—in which homespun American virtue prevails over the wily and devious 'special interests' that rule the nation's capital."[14] He claimed, in fact, that he grew up in a world like that of Huck Finn and Tom Sawyer. Reagan was, of course, far from the first person to filter out Twain's dark side. Noting this, Wills astutely explains the specific distortions that comprised the sense with which Reagan identified himself as a product of Twain's world:

_____ *Figure 9*_____

In *Beetlejuice*, the Maitlands kiss in their attic, behind them the town preserved in its highly condensed version.

Reagan, by the roles given him—as the voice of midwestern baseball, as the best friend of the star, as the plain-spoken hero of horse epics—was also repeating an American instinct to reclaim a simplicity his circumstances belie, to remain with the innocent at home, even as he escaped home. With Twain, the pretense was artful, highly conscious, used for cultural satire. With Reagan, the perfection of the pretense lies in the fact that he does not know he is pretending. He believes the individualist myths that help him play his communal role. He is the sincerest claimant to a heritage that never existed, a perfect blend of an authentic America he grew up in and that of America's own fables about its past.[15]

In such imaginary places, the poignant scene constitutes the basic unit of social motivation and the anecdote its fundamental historical record. Not surprisingly, as Lou Cannon points out, "anecdotes were Reagan's fundamental form of communication"—so much so that members of the cabinet, much like movie agents proffering scripts, "responded to Reagan's need for stories by competing among themselves to find anecdotes that pleased the president."[16] This proclivity for the anecdotal—for the simple and vivid over the complicated and abstract—goes hand in hand with a preference for the small town. As has been widely noted, "Reagan often talked as if he preferred a simpler society."[17]

In *Beetlejuice*, the town in microcosm is indeed the Maitlands' world preserved in its highly condensed version, in other words, as an anecdote. This explains why the couple divide their time between restoring the house and creating the model—the anecdotal representation—of its environs. The house must contain the town, just as its restoration must help conserve it. Small-town America, in other words, has become a simulacrum possessed by the appropriately conservative household; it has become, in fact, its prized possession, the one that validates its enterprise by giving it an anecdotal representation of itself.

When the Maitlands die in an auto accident, they find themselves confined to their home, surrounded by a sea of dunes and giant sand monsters. Since they had chosen to spend their vacation time in the house anyway, this is not so much a penalty as an almost comfortable recognition of the diminished range of their power and influence. The Gothic scene again is inverted, with the ghosts epitomizing decency and the manor protecting that decency from the evils outside. In the glaring sunlight, about which they can do nothing. They are entrapped, in other words, not by the house but by the countryside and the dangerous Others who lurk outside their—and Ronald Reagan's—version of domesticity. The threats encroach when the Dietzes (Jeffrey Jones, Catherine O'Hara, and Winona Ryder), an affluent and dysfunctional New York family, acquire the house and renovate it according to a contemporary aesthetic. The specter of this family and all it represents haunts the home far more than the benign Maitland ghosts; only when the Dietzes take possession is the house truly possessed, a point emphasized by the ghostly white makeup that renders O'Hara and Ryder far more eerie than the robust-looking Davis and Baldwin.

But what is most troubling about the Dietz couple is their taste, which equates, on the one hand, with its values and, on the other hand, with its urban—specifically New York City—origins. The Dietzes, a composite of vulgar excesses, announce their redecoration plans by marauding through the house with spray paint, like graffiti vandals. At the same time, however, they

_____ *Figure 10*_____
The ghostly white makeup that renders Winona Ryder far more eerie than the robust-looking Davis and Baldwin.

also articulate pretentious ideas about interior design, like the decadent nouveaux riches. Although moving to the house to escape New York, moreover, they continually measure its shortcomings by the yardstick of the city. And while they attempt to make their lives bearable by making the home emulate the city dwelling they have just left, they also attempt to make a huge profit by attracting investors who will help them remake the rest of the town in the image of their ersatz urbanity.

None of this, of course, makes the Dietzes happy or able to function as an affectionate family unit. The shrewish stepmother, Delia (O'Hara), and the mordant teenaged daughter, Lydia (Ryder), are openly hostile to each other, and the wimpish father allows his wife to dominate in domestic matters as she does with her interior designs. She is also an artist—or at least has pretensions along those lines—and even angrily chides the movers to be careful with her grotesque sculpture: "That is my art and it is dangerous!" The sculpture—some of which resembles the huge sand monsters that confine

_____ *Figure 11*_____

The Dietzes announce redecoration plans by marauding through the house with spray paint, like graffiti vandals.

the Maitlands—is dangerous not only because it literally becomes an out-of-control battering ram that penetrates and tears the clapboard walls but also because it figuratively represents the intrusion of New York City on small-town America, an intrusion traditionally derided by political conservatives as fostering on average America the domination of the affluent "Eastern Establishment" and/or the problems of the impoverished "inner city."

This can be seen, for example, in the way that the allegedly corrupt nature of the large city in general and of New York in particular provided a subtext for the community-standards debate in pornography trials and would constitute one of the issues at stake in the Mapplethorpe controversy or the attacks on the National Endowment for the Arts. In the rhetoric of the film, the Dietzes' aesthetic values are causally related to the deterioration of its family values, and saving the architecture of the house is inextricable from saving the family.

Because the Maitland ghosts are too kind and gentle to haunt their own house, they call on Beetlejuice (Michael Keaton), whose lower-class crudity is equal and opposite to the intruding family's upper-class vulgarity. Beetlejuice, a degenerate most notable for his lechery, lives in the cemetery located in the *model* of the town. He is, in other words, the ugliness buried at the center of the microcosmic small town whose anecdotal authority empowers the Maitlands' renovations. Thus their first encounter with Beetlejuice takes place inside the model town; they are brought down to his level, where they discover the ugly and dangerous aspect of the model American town they have constructed. His numerous attempts to molest Barbara Maitland are halted only by the discovery of a bordello in the midst of the (model) town, placed there not by the Maitlands but by Juno (Sylvia Sidney), their other-worldly case worker, as a way of diverting Beetlejuice. Their own subsequent attempts at haunting, moreover, by forcing the Dietzes and their dinner guests to float above the table singing calypso in the voice of Harry Belafonte prove more fascinating than horrifying to the intended victims. When the Maitlands finally enlist Beetlejuice's services, however, his violence is more than they will tolerate. The Maitlands, who epitomize middle-class humility and decency, are thus caught between the untempered pride of the upper class and the unbridled lust of the lower, receiving inadequate assistance from an otherworldly bureaucracy full of overburdened case workers and unintelligible manuals, a red-tape bureaucracy of the type Ronald Reagan promised to abolish with his oft repeated political slogan "government is the problem."

When the New Yorkers, in the interest of commercializing on their haunted house, verge on destroying the Maitlands as well as their home, Lydia summons Beetlejuice again, and he exacts as payment for the inverse exorcism marriage to Lydia, which in this case means both rape and death. Once again the crisis focuses on the daughter at risk, and once again her rescue comes from beneficent ghosts whose conservative middle-class values form the only acceptable alternative to the vulgarities of the impoverished and the elite. The ghosts are assisted by the benevolent black singer, heard but not seen, whose music summons up an earlier period—the 1950s/Cold War era—in ways that make it so appealing that it wins over both parents and child to the values of their ghosts, such that the family restores the home exactly as the ghosts would have, and the daughter exercises educational choice by enrolling in a private school, complete with a uniform and beanie.

They all happily form one family unit that conforms to the anachronistic and isolated vision that the ghosts only imagined when they were alive.

In fact, their state is preferable to the one they envisioned, for as living creatures, the ghosts had to divide their time between house and work. In death, the restoration is completed and the house saved through a fortuitous influx of labor and wealth not their own; infertile in life, they even acquire a surrogate daughter without going through labor. In this way, both *Field of Dreams* and *Beetlejuice* revise the "save the farm" films of the mid-1980s in which adversity is met, not always successfully, with hard work.[18] As if in recognition that the task of fulfilling one's dreams is greatly in excess of the labor available for that task, these Reagan-era movies look to a coalition of benign ghosts and benevolent blacks, with an inexplicable voluntary infusion of cash from the private sector. The energies and the cash will be targeted on a few privileged pockets of need, ones that have the correct conservative values and are properly isolated from the large world of scarcity and deprivation.

This is particularly clear in *Bill and Ted's Bogus Journey*, a ghost story in which Ted and Bill—rehistoricizers so excellent as to realize that all history is anything that one imagines it to be—die and then win a series of contests with Death (William Sadler), who subsequently becomes their friend, cohort, and a popular rock star. The principals, Bill (Alex Winter) and Ted (Keanu Reeves), epitomize the scarcities that follow from America's diminished powers. Untalented, uneducated, undisciplined, they come from dysfunctional middle-class families, in which the mothers are missing and the fathers have taken turns marrying the same teenager. The film, which ends with the song "God Gave Rock 'n Roll to Everyone," reconfigures rock music as the basis for history, science, philosophy, religion, and politics in the future, and it makes Ted and Bill its prophets, despite their inability to learn how to play guitar or sing. At the crucial moment, through the miracle of time travel that is as easy as using a Touch-Tone phone, they disappear for eighteen months of intense music study—coupled with honeymoons and the birth of their children—and return to the exact moment of their disappearance, miraculously converted, as if no time had elapsed. Time itself thus becomes the limitless capital that can erase the scarcity of the present moment by infusing it with the full plenitude of history's resources. Since this refers to future history even more than past, the limitless infusion is not of capital but of credit. Those backing up the band include Death, on bass, and a pair of Martian monsters who can merge into one or redivide at will. The monster(s)—given to Ted and Bill by God to help them out—is supposed to be the greatest intellect in the universe, although it appears to have a one-word vocabulary; as the boys point out, however, this duplicitous creature is "the dude who can make one word mean anything." Death, duplicity, evasive rhetoric thus become the benign accomplices in proving the truth of Ted and Bill's pronouncement—or philosophy—that "the best place to be is here; the best time to be is now." Although this might suggest, on the one hand, "carpe diem," or on the other, that "this is the best of all possible worlds," either of these options would remove exactly what is central to the assertion—its historical specificity, for I think that the film is very much about the present moment in which the paucity of present resources has caused a debt to the future that can only be avoided through evasive rhetoric, duplicity, or death.

In two of the films, *Chances Are* and *Late for Dinner*, this evasion takes the form of amnesia. In *Chances Are*, Corinne Jeffries (Cybill Shepherd), while pregnant in 1963, loses her husband in a car accident. Frantic about his abandoned wife and expected child, the husband harries the angels into an immediate reincarnation before he is given his requisite shot of amnesia. In the mid-1980s, through a series of coincidences, the reincarnated version of Dad, Alex Finch (Robert Downey Jr.), finds himself as a recent Yale graduate back in the Washington townhouse he had owned in his previous life. It is still occupied by Corinne, who is a curator at the Smithsonian. She has neither remarried nor altered one detail of the house in the twenty-three years since his death. Exactly like the ghostly couple in *Beetlejuice*, in other words, she has turned the house into the model of the past that is supposed to stand as the idealized version of the present. She also has barely added a wrinkle to her face, but she has added a twenty-three-year-old daughter who finds herself falling in love with Alex, unaware, of course, that he is her reincarnated father. In the wings is the father's former best friend, Philip Train (Ryan O'Neal), who has acted as a surrogate father to the girl and remained in love with Corinne throughout the years, despite his three successive marriages, all of which ended in divorce. When Alex returns to this unchanged world, frozen in the last year of John Kennedy's life, before Martin Luther King spoke at the Reflecting Pool, he gets flashes from his past and succeeds in convincing Corinne and Philip of his former identity, in having a brief romantic interlude with Corinne, and in barely forestalling the affections of the young woman whom he now realizes is his daughter. He also recalls evidence he had uncovered prior to his death that leads to the indictment of a corrupt judge. But eventually the angel who missed him the first time succeeds in giving him his overdue shot of amnesia, so that he can acquire his daughter as wife and allow Philip, who plays the sappy second-banana role that typified much of Ronald Reagan's career, to become, after all these years of waiting, the romantic leading man by winning the beautiful leading lady.

Besides making incest both permissible and cute, this film fetishizes the past by making it the Other of history, if history is the narrative of change. Frozen in time, Corinne, her job, her home all represent the unchanging past as a version of the present. So the problem of the film is not one of being cut off from the past but rather of remembering that the past is implicated in the process of change and in the specific changes that differentiate then from now. The film's problematic comes neither from Corinne's intransigence nor from the threat of incest, but from the consciousness that can connect this moment with its historical antecedents. So long as Alex maintains this consciousness—from the point at which he recognizes Corinne as his wife to the moment when he is forced to forget this recognition—his position is untenable.

Once again, the Gothic site of the family house arrested in the unchanging past is not the source of horror but of comfort and rejuvenation, inverting the traditional implications of the Gothic, as typified by, for example, Miss Havisham's house in *Great Expectations*. The horror, as in *Beetlejuice*, resides outside the house, in this case taking the form of the Washington landscape memorialized by countless anti-Vietnam protests, and the realm of the *Washington Post* explicitly associated in the film with Watergate, Woodward, and Bernstein. In a Washington, D.C., devoid of blacks, the film indicates that we can have things exactly the way we wanted them in 1963. All we need is a big enough shot of amnesia, and all those we lost during the Vietnam years can return to live happily among us. The daughter at risk is saved from incest not by avoiding the act but by avoiding or covering up records in the popular memory so that there can be no evidence and hence no transgression. Thus, with enough amnesia even incest is possible. Perhaps even more remarkably, these lapses allow (at last) the romantic lead to be played by someone acting like Ronald Reagan, for part of Philip's benign sappiness, significantly, is expressed in his not divulging what he knows. Although privy to Alex's secret identity, he knows that his own success—and, as the film represents it, everyone else's—depends on his keeping his mouth shut. Even without his shot of amnesia, he must act the amnesiac so that he may move into the role of benevolent patriarch.

In this way, even more than in his second-banana status, Philip replicates the patriarch who made lapses and denial into a form of performance art. Consider, for example, Reagan's claim that he did not have cancer: "I had something inside of me that had cancer in it and it was removed."[19] This fantastic inability to recognize cancer rivals his failure to recognize his own son, Ron, at Ron's high school graduation, or his completely forgetting the name of national security adviser Robert (Bud) McFarlane. Perhaps the most infamous lapse of this sort took place when, after having presided over cabinet meetings for six months, he referred to Secretary of Housing and Urban Development Sam Pierce as "Mr. Mayor" at a White House reception.[20]

These signs of personal indifference, however, are overshadowed by commensurate lapses about policy, about knowledge of world affairs, and about the memos he signed or the orders he gave, as most extensively typified by his complete inability to remember his role in the Iran-Contra episode. In response to the embarrassments surrounding Iran-Contra, as he did about his cancer, Reagan went into denial. "'He just denied everything,' a senior aide later said. 'It was strange—I mean really strange. He couldn't confront anything. He was living in a dream world.'"[21] Similarly, he justified his policy toward apartheid South Africa by declaring in 1985 that South Africa had eliminated segregation of hotels, restaurants, and places of entertainment,[22] claimed that trees produce more pollution than automobiles, and that "'the finest oil geologists' had told him that the United States had more oil reserves than Saudi Arabia."[23] Cannon identifies Reagan's problem succinctly: "His biggest problem is that he didn't know enough about public policy to participate fully in his presidency—and often didn't realize how much he didn't know."[24]

Frequently, as I have noted, he filled his gaps with excerpts from films. This practice gave Reagan a peculiarly derivative sense of history in which remembering films became a way of unremembering the events to which the films alluded, often with Reagan himself inserted in events that never occurred. The earliest version of this practice concerns the construction of an autobiographical self who enjoyed a pastoral childhood greatly different from the itinerant life impelled by the financial failures of his alcoholic father. Later, as a radio sportscaster, he not only embellished the events of a game but also punctuated the narration with invented stories about his own life. He also had an invented sense of world history, a point illustrated, for example, by his 1979 radio broadcast, in which he explained, "The North Vietnamese . . . conquered an independent neighbor, South Vietnam. The Vietnam war was not a civil war. They have been separate nations for centuries."[25] This wholly invented history—the division between North and South was created by the Geneva Accord of 1954 and at the time was intended to be temporary—may have been the basis for Reagan's later assertion that for America the Vietnam War was a noble effort. Coming to such a position, however, requires not only inventing a new history of Vietnam but also actively forgetting the history of the war itself. It requires a shot of amnesia similar in its target and scope to the one finally administered in *Chances Are*.

In a similar mode, *Late for Dinner* skips over almost exactly the same set of years that *Chances Are* actively forgets, chronicling the story of Willie Husband (Brian Wimmer), a young, lower-middle class man in 1962 being swindled out of his meager home by a ruthless real estate developer. Wounded in a confrontation with the developer, in his escape he finds shelter with a scientist who freezes his body, along with that of his retarded brother-in-law. When he thaws out twenty-nine years later, after receiving medical help for his brother-in-law from a black doctor and discovering at a fast-food restaurant the levels of inflation, he returns to find his daughter grown and married, his wife a successful artsy entrepreneur, and his old home not only saved but converted into a lucrative business site. The film, which has very little plot, concludes with a series of reunions in which the father meets a daughter who is his age and a wife who is old enough to be his mother, and they agree to live happily ever after.

As in *Chances Are*, the problems were overcome by a loss of consciousness, a narrative that unremembers the Vietnam and Watergate eras. If "consciousness raising" was thought to be the salvation of the mother's generation of women, loss of consciousness instead saves this newer generation. If consciousness-enhancing drugs and heightened political awareness helped create a generation gap, that gap, these films suggest, is closed with a consciousness depressant, a soporific, an injection of amnesia, that purges America's political turmoil from memory. The self-serving quality of such a cure (or placebo) is made clear by the incestuous overtones of *Chances Are* and *Late for Dinner*, which valorize a self-sufficient community, entire unto itself, self-satisfied.

Selective forgetting, then, was not just one of Reagan's personal strategies but rather a cornerstone of national vision he projected, an essential aspect of his political philosophy. "For Reaganism, the decade of the 1960s was midnight in America—and the 1980s its new morn," Reeves and Campbell accurately explain. "The nostalgic orthodoxy of Reaganism vowed to 'take back America' in a double sense. . . . It promised to take all of American back *to* the gilded age of a pre-Fordist, Horatio Alger enterprise culture [and] it promised to take America back *from* the color- and gender-coded 'special interest groups' of the Keynesian welfare state."[26] This process of taking America back *to* and back *from* is suggested by the title of the first chapter of Cannon's *President Reagan: The Role of a Lifetime*: "Back to the Future." And, as I have suggested in Chapter 1, perhaps no film more quintessentializes the imaginary command of the past, the historical gymnastics, the arbitrary turnabouts of the Reagan Revolution. Wills also sees the uncanny way in which *Back to the Future* glosses the Reagan phenomenon:

> Reagan gives our history the continuity of a celluloid Mobius strip. We ride the curves backward and forward at the same time, and he is always there. There is an endlessness of surface that becomes a kind of depth, a self-reflecting omnipresence in the cultural processing of Americans over the second half of the twentieth century. This inescapability of Reagan was a joke in the movie about time travel, *Back to the Future*, which Reagan quoted seriously in his 1982 State of the Union address. Then to complete the loop, Reagan's real son played Reagan in a television parody of *Back to the Future*, the film with which this sequence began. Reagan's image precedes us as we ride forward or backward in time, anticipating our reactions, reflecting us back to ourselves, stirring "memories of the future." Reagan is part of the process that forged our self-awareness, at a time when movie imagery, broadcast immediacy, and highway mobility entered Americans' lives—or, rather, when Americans entered the new atmosphere created by those inventions. This was the past that most vividly created our future.[27]

If *Back to the Future* suggests the ways in which his version of the past made it hard for us to tell if Reagan was coming or going, *Late to Dinner* suggests the ways in which he was historically out to lunch. Exactly because the residue of the Vietnam era constitutes the extended lunchtime in Reagan's America, the *Late to Dinner* climax to this hiatus takes the form of poignant reunion scenes in which daughter and mother see—as they always dreamed they would—the father/husband who disappeared in the 1960s, not as he is today but as they remembered him then, as they fantasized having seen him at a wedding or a birth. The film, in other words, no doubt re-creates the fantasies of numerous families of Vietnam fatalities and MIAs. It completes their dream not only by restoring the missing patriarch but also by erasing the conflict that removed him.

With the benign Gothicism of Reagan's America reconfiguring the haunted mansion as the source of comfort and security, the threat from outside, from nature and the "natural," is the Gothic sublime of Vietnam. What these films are attempting to forget through amnesia, nostalgia, retreat from the present—or, as in the case of *Bill and Ted's Excellent Adventure*, a wild scrambling of time and its artifacts—is the 1960s in general and Vietnam in particular. If moving from the world's largest creditor nation to the world's largest debtor nation has rendered America an economic ghost of itself, just as moving from the opposers of fascism in World War II to the opposers of self-determination in Vietnam has rendered it a moral ghost, the fear in the public imagination, in the political unconscious, of existence in this state is converted into a benevolent Gothicism that divorces diminished power from diminished expectation.

Three death-rehearsal movies, *Flatliners*, *Ghost Dad*, and *Jacob's Ladder*, confront what we could call the anxiety in the political unconscious over the consequences of America's disempowerment using the same elements as the other films—the ghost patriarch, the black accomplice, the house and child at risk—but reconfiguring the relationship of these elements to construct alternative cultural narratives.

Flatliners constructs a world of sons and daughters at risk—medical students who have distinguished themselves as the brightest and the best in an environment that, the film repeatedly emphasizes, is highly competitive. Announcing the curve prior to an anatomy exam, a doctor stresses, "Once again, as in life, you are not in competition with me, yourself, or this exam, but with each other." A group of these students put themselves at further risk by experimenting with death under controlled conditions that they believe will allow their resuscitation (or resurrection). Throughout the film they take turns going through the death-and-revival procedure, each extending the amount of dead (or flatlining) time, with the first death rehearsal lasting under two minutes and the final one in the vicinity of ten.

In many ways these resurrected students are also ghosts, in both their visual representation, colored by a pale blue light, and their uncanny connections with the spirit world. As such, they are not the ghost patriarchs but the ghost progeny, those who will inherit the legacy of the dead fathers. If they are the ghosts of America's future, however, they are haunted by their own past. Nelson (Kiefer Sutherland), when he was nine years old, tormented an outcast boy; Joe (William Baldwin) secretly videotaped his sexual encounters with numerous women to whom he was indifferent; David (Kevin Bacon) in elementary school mocked and harassed the black girl in his class; Rachel (Julia Roberts) believes she caused her father's suicide. After they have flatlined, this generation is forced to remember what the other death-rehearsal films—and Reaganism—insist on forgetting: the errors and indiscretions of the preceding twenty years. In the film's narrative, this becomes a pointedly generational difference, "something to upstage the fucking baby boomers."

The consequences of this upstaging in death, however, become horrifying. Nelson is attacked and beaten several times by the ghost of Thomas Mahoney, who died when he fell from the tree into which he had been driven by rock-throwing tormentors. Joe is sexually harassed by women on the streets, and he sees on screens everywhere the interrogating faces of the women whom he has videotaped. David is verbally abused by a child incarnation of Winnie Hicks, the black girl in his elementary school, and Rachel is haunted by the corpse of her dead father.

These problems are, it turns out, solvable, but not for the most part without great pain and humiliation. Joe must sacrifice his engagement to the only woman he actually loves, and David must seek out and apologize to the adult Winnie Hicks. Since Thomas Mahoney is dead, Nelson must flatline a second time—that is, attempt suicide—in order to tell Mahoney he is sorry, but that entails as well forgiving himself for his childhood errors. And Rachel must revisit the last minutes of her father's life. He had just returned from military service—we can assume in Vietnam—and as a child Rachel burst in on him in the bathroom. Her mother screamed angrily: "You're not supposed to go in there!" after which the father ran past the bewildered child,

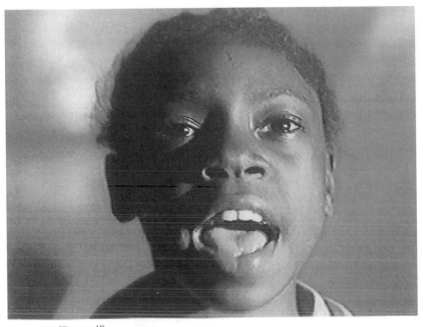

_____ *Figure 12* _____

In *Flatliners*, David is verbally abused by a child incarnation of Winnie Hicks, the black girl in his elementary school

out to his car where he shot himself. The repressed scene from Rachel's childhood, resurrected by her flatlining experience, evokes a sense of guilt for her father's death—it was caused she thinks by her going where she should not have gone. Like the other flatliners, she is encouraged to seek her father's forgiveness; as in *Field of Dreams*, the film presents the daughter at risk and emphasizes the need to forgive the dead father. Rachel's interest in flatlining is motivated, in fact, like Kinsella's construction of the farm baseball team, by voices from beyond.

When her apartment turns into the site of her childhood home, she again walks toward the forbidden bathroom door and again sees her father sitting with his back to her. With her mother not there to stop her, she approaches her father and sees that he is shooting heroin. As she tries to ask for his forgiveness, he instead asks for hers. In an inverse way, the baby boomer returned from Vietnam has upstaged her, acknowledging his guilt and at the same time forcing her to face with him the errors of the Vietnam years. This refusal to *un*remember Vietnam reconfigures the same plot elements—suggesting the same social and cultural fears—of other death-rehearsal movies and relieves those fears through an impossible union of living and dead. And as in those movies, the union is facilitated by the beneficent black, for only after David receives forgiveness from the adult Winnie Hicks can he counsel Rachel and the others on how to deal with the voices and visions that haunt them.

The economy of the relationship established by this convention is telling. The films create an exchange based on seeing the consequences of America's history of racial discrimination and abuse as being balanced out by simple expressions of regret. David has no obligation to Winnie other than asking her forgiveness; that request allows her to free him of his guilt and all the ugly manifestations that the guilt has taken since he flatlined. She facilitates the rest of his life in a manner that is separate and unequal to the way in which he facilitates the rest of hers.

Ghost Dad confronts implicitly the issue of reciprocity by inverting the racial situation that typifies the death-rehearsal movie. Instead of a white family, it presents a black family in crisis, helped by a benevolent white man. Not a ghost or a psychic, the white man is a scientist who seeks and ultimately finds a "rational" explanation for Elliot's apparently ghostlike condition. As such he represents the call to reason, the privileging of reality over the uncanny. But the reality is that this ghost dad, in discovering that he is not a ghost, also discovers that he lacks not only the powers manifest by his ghostly counterparts in the other films but also those of his nonghostly white peers. On the verge of achieving the economic comfort enjoyed by all the ghosts (with the exception of the vilified Beetlejuice) and all their white friends and lovers, in most cases from the outset, and always by the end, Elliot discovers that these expectations—albeit based on fairness and merit—were illusions. For obvious reasons, moreover, black Americans cannot solve the problem with a miraculous return to a simpler period in American history, because the oblique whiteness of the dominant cultural norms in those earlier periods—the obliviousness to the complexity of social injustice, the blindness to racial difference—is exactly what rendered those periods "simpler." The ghost of America past that saves the farm—or preserves the townhouse—in the other films can represent itself as kinder, gentler, simpler because of its claim to white homogeneity. For Elliot to choose the ghostly over the living is thus to choose total erasure.

Elliot therefore finds himself not dead but diminished, and he still decides that life is preferable to death even though it leaves him on the verge of economic ruin. The film ends restoring a single-parent household, with that parent unemployed, aware that all of the progress he has made during the last fourteen years was wiped away by a small bit of ill fortune and the unsympathetic ire of his white boss.

In choosing life over death, this film becomes a version of *It's a Wonderful Life*. But with the hero lacking a community whose resources can come to his financial support or the history of integration in that community upon which to draw in time of crisis, he discovers that it may be a life, but not necessarily a wonderful one. And the Capraesque ending becomes possible only if we choose the "wonder" over the "life," a point made clearer if we also compare *It's a Wonderful Life* with *Beetlejuice*. In their simplicity, their praise of small-town values, their rejection of the high- and low-brow taste, the ghost couple in *Beetlejuice* come closer to being Capra creations than probably any other film characters in the last two decades. They are so decent that they can't crush a spider and, quite literally, would rather die than hurt a puppy. *It's a Wonderful Life* is also a ghost story of sorts, in that Jimmy Stewart, playing a man on the verge of suicide, gets supernatural assistance to see what the world would have been like had he never lived. This act of rehistoricizing, however, is drastically different from the escape to an idealized past represented in these death-rehearsal movies, for Stewart's death rehearsal marks his agency as living person, while these death-rehearsal films resolve economic, moral, and aesthetic problems by empowering death with exactly the agency that life had failed to provide. Instead of the plea to choose the success of life, however modest, over the failure of death, these films represent death as a more successful and benign complement to life.

In this light, we can see *Ghost Dad* as glossing the other death-rehearsal movies by foregrounding the plight of the marginalized black whose beneficence they presume. Totally erased by bright light, the dark shadows of his home do not hide Elliot but reveal him, but when he emerges from the shadows, Elliot becomes literally the invisible man made famous by Ralph Ellison—doubly troped by the fact that he at one point adopts a costume replicating Claude Rains's costume in the film version of H. G. Wells's *The Invisible Man*—as he attempts to win recognition and acceptance from the white bankers and corporate heads. The fear at the center of this film, then, is not of his ghostly incarnation but rather that as a living presence, he has no place in the American Dream, that the Dream has grown too meager to admit him, that America has failed to grow at a rate commensurate with the growth of its minorities and has lost the power to repair that failure.

Explaining the ways in which Reaganism reclaims racism, Reeves and Campbell gloss many of the issues raised by *Ghost Dad*:

> In practice, though, many of the barriers guarded by the new racism are the ones erected by old-fashioned white supremacy to safeguard traditional sanctuaries of white power: the segregated neighborhood; the segregated school; the segregated country club; the white-owned business directed by nepotism; the white-dominated profession regulated by discriminatory qualifications; the "core curriculum" monopolized by Eurocentric (and chiefly masculinist) knowledge; and the legislative body governed by male incumbency. The transgressing forces (or "special in-

_____ *Figure 13* _____

In *Ghost Dad* Elliot adopts a costume replicating Claude Rains's costume in the film version of H. G. Wells's *The Invisible Man.*

terests"), in this scheme, become any group or coalition that undermines the sexual and racial power relations or challenges the perpetuation of white male dominance in the college seminar, the workplace, and the political arena. In other words a siege metaphor frames not only the nationalist response to a hostile international environment, but also describes the moralist panic of the ongoing crisis in white and patriarchal prestige on the "homefront."[28]

If *Ghost Dad* provides a comic gloss on the death-rehearsal movie that suggests it is about the failure of the American Dream, *Jacob's Ladder* represents the death rehearsal not as a failed dream but as a literal nightmare, motivated by America's self-destructive engagement in Vietnam. The film appears to recount the plight, sometime in the 1970s, of a Vietnam veteran named Jacob, who is suffering from severe postdischarge trauma that takes a variety of forms. It seems to have resulted in the dissolution of his marriage and his inability to pursue his career: he is a Ph.D. now working in the post office.

More immediately, Jacob is having recurring flashes back to being wounded in a traumatic battle in Vietnam, visions of strange ghostlike figures, the feeling that he is the victim of an ongoing conspiracy, close calls with death on the streets of New York, fevers, chills, and depression. When he discovers that other members of his unit are having similar experiences, he tries to take legal action to initiate an investigation, but his lawyer and the black vets, apparently intimidated by government authorities, refuse to help him. Finally he discovers that the whole unit had been given an experimental dose of particularly virulent LSD in hopes of making them more savage fighters. In a fit of delusional terror, however, they unleashed the savagery on one another. Jacob is also haunted by dreams of his young son, who was struck and killed by an automobile prior to Jacob's Vietnam service. The final twist of the film comes when we learn, as Jacob goes to join his dead son, that the ostensive flashbacks to Vietnam were the actual experience, and all of the rest was a dream. We have been viewing the nightmare that occupies the last two hours of Jacob's life, following a bayonet wound to his stomach inflicted by one of his fellow soldiers.

Jacob is thus a ghost in the post-Vietnam world that the film presents. As a woman reading his palm at a party tells him, "You're already dead." But Jacob is blessed neither with the amnesia of some of his film ghost counterparts, nor the aid of benevolent blacks, nor the retreat to a pastoral time or place. Most significant, unlike them, he is completely disempowered. He cannot undo the past, or save the child, or provide for the future, or protect his family, or right the injustices of which he is aware. In all of these ways, and most particularly in that he cannot escape the historically specific events that have disempowered him, that have rendered him a failed patriarch, he manifests exactly the condition that these other death-rehearsal movies are constructed to deny.

Especially in constructing the temporal plane of its reality as one continuous event, *Jacob's Ladder* challenges the ideological presumptions of those films, for we normally do not and need not see every moment of action in chronic continuity to assume that a film is "realistic." The principles of editing, upon which standard film narrative depends, allow us to move through a series of events separated by minutes, hours, days, weeks, or (with the proper cues) even months or years. But this is, of course, an illusion that demands a limitless credit bank of time, an illusion that can with total credibility infuse a twenty-fourth of a second with as much time as the narrative requires. This credit system, foregrounded by both *Bill and Ted* films, is the credit system requisite for standard film narrative. It is the system that differentiates a "film" from a "dream," which is not a story represented in a cinematic code but an experience from which nothing is omitted. In discovering that what seemed to be a film narrative spanning several years of a man's life, and concentrating on roughly a three-week period, is actually a completely continuous dream—the uninterrupted flow of images in the last two hours of his life—we are discovering that time is limited to what we see, that the credit system is bankrupt.

Realizing that the film we have been watching implies no reserve of time, moreover, we are confronted not only with the relationship between time credit and film narrative but also with the relationship between credit and time itself, for credit in any of its forms can be defined as the reifying of time so that it may participate in a system of exchange. Credit is the theoretical mechanism by which time is turned into surplus value. To run out of time is to run out of credit, and to acquire credit is to gain time. Credit is thus the means by which exchange converts into narrative, and it is also the means of exchange that creates the differences upon which all narrative depends. Constructing temporal differences, narrative chronicles change through an imaginary temporal space, constructed metonymically by the privileging of a finite number of represented events. In the film medium, the technology of the cinematic apparatus makes these events vividly present, while the codes of cinematic representation convert the illusory present into an implicit temporal organization.

It seems to me no coincidence, then, that the principles of Reaganomics rely on the same exchange system as do traditional film narratives, both illusions constructed by drawing on a limitless credit bank of time. In explaining the ways in which Reagan's policies fed what he calls "the culture of contentment," John Kenneth Galbraith points out that a crucial aspect of that culture "is its attitude toward time. In the briefest word, short-run public inaction, even if held to be alarming as to consequence, is always preferred to long run action."[29] Thus when Reagan "presented Congress with what proved to be the most wildly inaccurate economic forecast in American history,"[30] which not only cut taxes by 30 percent and drastically increased defense spending but also promised a balanced budget in three years, he was merely feeding the culture of contentment by applying a cinematic solution to a fiscal problem. The movement toward a balanced budget was, of course, illusory, just as is all the motion in a motion picture, since cinematic motion is the subordination of temporal trajectories to the illusion of a space-time continuum. This illusion, furthermore, is counterintuitive in that the viewer's elapsed time differs greatly from the time represented by the film's narrative. Nevertheless, in the interest of short-term enjoyment, the viewer gives credit to the illusory and illogical space-time continuum.

Reagan's team was well aware, as I have already noted, that illusion was far more important than substance, or than accuracy, or for that matter than anything else. During the 1984 election campaign, in reference to the deficits and second-term tax plans, one administration official said, "On Mondays, Wednesdays, and Fridays, I think that President Reagan will wind up as Herbert Hoover—with a total economic failure on his hands. The other days of the week, I think he will somehow luck out or muddle through."[31]

What makes this remark so interesting is that it occurred three years after Reagan's budget director, David Stockman, had publicly indicated that Reaganomics was a sham and that he had knowingly cooked the books to indicate a favorable outcome to the tax cut/military buildup combination, which he knew was impossible. "For an administration dedicated to the politics of illusion," Cannon points out, "the article [in *Atlantic* quoting Stockman] came as a heavy blow."[32] By 1984, however, despite extensive evidence that Stockman was telling the truth, the power of illusion had again triumphed, bolstered by the contentment purchased by drawing on time as though the economy were a movie.

The supply side of the cinematic credit formula can be seen in those instances when the same technological code can be used not to escape the limitations of "real" time but to infuse real time with an artificial surplus, a false simultaneity that slows down the clock. At the end of *Back to the Future*, for example, Marty (Michael J. Fox) is told by Doc (Christopher Lloyd) that he has less than four minutes to drive out of the town center in the time machine and return—driving exactly eighty-eight miles per hour—at the moment when the lightning strikes the clock tower. Crosscutting between the car and the clock tower, we split the sites of the movie and expand the four minutes to five. This cut—like the Reagan tax cut—allows us to spend more without taxing the system. All we have to do as viewers is subordinate our experience to the assertions of the narrative; we can accept the rest on credit.

Important here is another quality of *Back to the Future* that makes it so symptomatic of the Reagan era: the credit need never be balanced with the debt, so long as the narrative remains convincing. The world of *Back to the Future*, like the world of President Reagan's America, in other words, relies on a double-entry bookkeeping system in which the dual columns of debit and credit never reconcile. This indeed describes perfectly the thematic structure of the *Back to the Future* series and is articulated explicitly in *Back to the Future II* when Doc warns Fox of the Armageddon that will occur if he ever meets his double directly.

Even in the first film, when such a phenomenon is virtually impossible, the entire crisis of the plot depends on a pervasive doubling of irreconcilable systems, the world of 1955 and the world of 1985, both of which contain Marty as a teenager. He thus has two sets of parents who must not know about each other. Although this double system is represented through the device of time travel, it is present even before the souped-up DeLorean cruises onto the scene, as Marty's attitude toward his parents, who are for him negative versions of the parents he imagines that he wants. His travel into the past thus draws on film's time-credit system to construct the parents he imagines through a massive act of rehistoricizing. The outcome is that he turns his 1985 parents into people he can like, into people who do not make him ashamed, into people, in other words, who are affluent.

Early in the film when the oppressive high school teacher warns Marty that he hasn't got a chance because he is too much like his old man and Marty responds that history is going to change, we already know, even though he doesn't, that he is right, not because he is going to change the future—make history—but because he is going to change the past—remake history. This creates a novel reversal of the American myth of individualism. In that narrative—identified, for example, as the story of the American Adam—the new American succeeds by working to be different from his ancestors, by making the world anew. In this version, one remains forever a product of those ancestors, and success comes from reworking *their* story. Marty thus turns his father—a Peeping Tom, performing a petty act of 1950s surveillance (an elaborately explored theme in *Rear Window*)[33]—into a hero who knocks out the town bully and shoves another rival over on the dance floor.[34]

In the process of remaking his parents, Marty also changes the role of the town bully, empowers the future black mayor, and changes the shape of rock and roll by introducing Chuck Berry's cousin to the sound that Berry will claim. In this light, we can understand the benevolence of the black figures in the death-rehearsal movies as repaying the debt they owe to this white boy for their political gains and for their music.

Although the film voices legitimate fears about this rampant tampering with history—at first Doc says, "We've already agreed that having information about the future can be extremely dangerous, even if your intentions are good. It can backfire drastically"—the film constantly makes clear that the bigger danger lies in *not* tampering. Marty's very survival, and later Doc's, depends on it. When Doc is confronted with his own principle, after he has used information about the future to save his life, he simply responds, "I figured, what the Hell."[35]

In *Back to the Future II* this theme surfaces repeatedly because there has been a further doubling of images, so that the debt to the impossible (i.e., cinematic) manipulation of time has accumulated exponentially. The film's credit, which equates with the narrative's credibility, is sustained by a coherent image, the idea of a central character whose goals and aspirations focus those of the audience. As has been well noted, this focus on the individual's ability to achieve his or her goals has long been among the quintessential characteristics of the classical style of Hollywood cinema. Marty fulfills this function by representing the bridge between the small-town values typified by *Beetlejuice*'s Maitlands and the hip affluence represented by *Beetlejuice*'s Dietzes. He does so by doubling himself so that he can construct a revisionist history of the Maitlands' idealized past that will make it consistent with the Dietzes' 1980s materialism.

And thus at the end of his first adventure, Marty wakes up to Morning in America, at the same address, in the same bedroom, in the same middle-class development. But he finds new decor in the old living room, his family wearing designer clothes, and the garage adorned with a BMW and a sporty Jeep. He has, of course, paid for this new affluence with his life. Whereas he has now acquired parents he can like, a lifestyle of which he can be proud, he remains the product of the life and family he rejected. And it is the potential contradiction implicit in these split lives that threatens exposure in the possible collision of the two images. At all costs, therefore, the McFlys who existed during the thirty years preceding Marty's intervention must remain buried, no matter how much their specters haunt the revisionist Marty. Throughout *Back to the Future II* and *Back to the Future III*, the revised version of history thus becomes normative, and the numerous duplications of image and situation, in other words the formidable powers of the cinematic apparatus, all work to retain those revisionist narratives.[36]

This is a difficult and dangerous task. Early in *Back to the Future II*, when Marty's girlfriend, Jennifer (Elizabeth Shue), risks meeting herself in the future as Marty's wife, Doc worries that "the encounter could create a time paradox the result of which could cause a chain reaction that would unravel the very fabric of the space-time continuum and destroy the entire universe." Although he proves wrong about the film's events, Doc's warning accurately glosses the universe of cinematic narrative, a universe completely dependent on the artificial construction of a space-time continuum. The basic illusion of the cinematic gaze is that it provides a coherent viewpoint on a coherent, causally related set of events that take place within a definable space, over a finite and continuous period of time, with a discrete beginning and end. But this coherence is an illusion created by editing techniques employed in accordance with the codes of cinematic representation. In standard Hollywood-style cinema, in other words, as in the plot of the *Back to the Future* series, the space-time continuum is technically constructed, not inherent in nature.

Collisions with the other version of the self therefore risk the danger of revealing the constructed quality of history, for the power to control history depends on the ability both to manipulate its narrative and to represent the manipulations as "natural." The audience might otherwise identify itself as historical subject rather than as the ego ideal that unifies the narrative, that is, as the manipulated rather than the manipulator. As Doc says, "I sure hope we find Jennifer before she finds herself." Although Jennifer remains unconscious during most of *Back to the Future II* (and *III*), the fear about her consciousness, about what version of the future will inform the "past" of her personal history, dominates the film. She has been taken into the future with Marty to prevent a crucial event that will destroy the life of their teenaged son, but as Doc makes clear, the work of tampering with history is really a man thing, about which women should be kept in the dark. Hypnotizing her, he states, "This way when she wakes up she'll think it was just a dream. Don't worry, she's not essential to my plan." "No one," he further explains, "should know too much about their own destiny."

The crucial destructive event will take place in "The Cafe '80s" "Where it's always 'Morning in America.'" Someone from this eighties generation, in other words, must save future generations by undoing the consequences of a mistake made in the place designed as a tribute to President Reagan's America. Although the tampering is successful, an aged Biff manages to steal the time machine so that he can give to the 1950s version of himself a record book that will enable the younger Biff to become a multimillionaire by gambling on sports events, an option Doc angrily rejects: "I didn't invent the time machine for financial gain!"

Like many of Doc's pronouncements, this will not survive close scrutiny, for financial gain is indeed not only the beneficial outcome of Marty's initial tampering but also the goal to which his further interventions must be directed, not out of unbridled greed but rather out of a fear of any other possible consequence. Marty and Doc must once again travel back to the crucial night, November 12, 1955, to undo the transaction between Biff and himself. Unlike Marty, Jennifer, and Doc, who must tenaciously avoid confrontation with their historical selves, Biff faces no risk, the implication thus being that virtue depends on ignorance in a way that evil does not. In any case, no explanation is given for this meeting of Biffs that apparently contradicts Doc's admonition to Marty: "You must not let your other self see you. The consequences could be disastrous."

But in fact Biff is not the only one who contradicts Doc's warning. Doc himself is seen by his other self, whom he even assists in preparing some wiring. And all of Doc's injunctions about knowing too much about one's future or tampering with the past are violated both by Marty and by Doc with ever increasing alacrity in *Back to the Future II* and *III*. The point clearly is that whatever the dangers of tampering, the dangers of not tampering are worse. Doc and Marty must make a second trip back to 1955, for example, because the alterations brought about by the Biff-to-Biff summit have rendered the McFlys and their entire community far worse off than they were prior to the initial intervention. The middle America typified by Hill Valley now resembles America's centers of urban blight, characterized by crime,

_____ *Figure 14* _____

In *Back to the Future*, Doc himself is seen by his other self, whom he even assists in preparing some wiring.

vice, and violence. The school has burned down six years earlier, and the old McFly neighborhood has drive-by shootings. Gambling has been legalized, and Biff rules over a Las Vegas–like empire, populated by thugs, body guards, corrupt politicians, and policemen on the take. Marty's father has been murdered by Biff, who subsequently coerced Marty's mother into marriage and now is Marty's violent, physically abusive stepfather.

There is a strong kinship between this version of America and the one portended by the marriage of Beetlejuice to the teenaged Lydia: The impotent patriarch is replaced by his crude, violent alter ego, again a monster with his origins in the small town; the economic, and concomitant social, collapse that seems like a nightmare (in fact, it all takes place while Jennifer is asleep) for the citizens of Hill Valley is a way of distinguishing Hill Valley from other parts of America. Put most simply, Hill Valley is the kind of place that is supposed to benefit from the rewriting of history and economics—the "Reagan Revolution"—that supported the credit system of the 1980s, not the kind of place that is supposed to suffer from it. Both recognizing and suppressing their debt to tampering with the past, Doc explains that "the time continuum has been disrupted, creating this new temporal event sequence resulting in this alternative reality. Somewhere in the past the time line swerved into this tangent creating an alternate 1985, alternate to you, me, and Einstein [his dog], but reality for everyone else."

Doc is contrasting the alternative reality, however, not to some unaltered original but instead to the revisionist reality created by the prior intervention. The revisions made in 1985 have now become normative, and the survival of American culture, as epitomized by a merger of big-city affluence and small-town values, depends on preserving the normative status of those revisions at all costs. Thus when Doc, decrying the misuse of time travel, says that "the time machine must be destroyed after we straighten all of this out," he means after they take appropriate measures to restore the version of the past that made Biff poor and the McFlys rich. He even explains to Marty that they can let Jennifer sleep through this entire episode because once they have completed their task, everything "will be changed back into the *real* 1985" (emphasis added).

Restoring the real 1985 means maintaining the retrospective alterations of the 1950s, a task they accomplish, but only at the cost of deferring the alterations to an earlier site, 1885, where Doc has landed after a bolt of lightning struck the time machine. *Back to the Future II* thus ends with the privileged version of history in place but with the film's principals completely displaced. Doc is stranded in 1885 and Marty in 1955. *Back to the Future III* begins with Doc's warning to Marty: "Do not come back to get me—further unnecessary time travel only risks further disruption of the space-time continuum," suggesting that the myth of the space-time continuum must be preserved despite the fact that the continuum is belied by the presence of two Docs, one in 1955 and one in 1885.

Just as cinematic convention will not tolerate such a disparity, Marty cannot heed Doc's prohibition. By this point, both he and the 1955 Doc know that tampering is their obligation and that the past must be altered as much as is necessary to achieve a desirable present. At the end of his western escapade, Doc parts with Marty, telling Marty that his future "hasn't been written yet. No one's has." Doc then leaves for further time travel in the railroad engine time machine with which he has replaced his car time machine. Doc preserves the continuum on which his time travel continues to depend at the same time as he frees Marty from the implications of existing in such a continuum.

Marty's freedom, however, comes from a privileged base of wealth and power derived from his ability to manipulate the continuum to his own ends. Having constructed out of uncannily cinematic technologies an uneven beginning for himself, he can now relish in wiping the slate clean. In this way he replicates the Reagan approach to racial inequities, cogently summarized by Reeves and Campbell: "Indeed, part of Reaganism's symbolic power was its ability to celebrate opportunism while undermining equal opportunity— or, at the least, redefining equal opportunity in terms of reverse discrimination. Collective middle-class (and journalistic) identification with the wealthy during the Reagan era meant that prosperous entrepreneurs were once again widely perceived as like Us, only luckier, smarter, and more daring."[37] Similarly, Marty, perfectly content to deny the ways in which he has uniquely appropriated the past, happily faces the separate but unequal future. Having the full advantage of history on his side, he is ready to compete on an equal basis with the historically disadvantaged.

The same is true of Bill and Ted, who undertake their excellent adventure to avoid failing out of school. Although for them, as for Marty, the future is a rosy place, the present is not particularly pleasant. They are sent on the "Excellent Adventure" that precedes their "Bogus [death] Journey" by the powers seven hundred years in the future, who regard them as the Great Ones, upon whose rock music future politics, philosophy, and culture are based. These Great Ones, however, are in danger of flunking out of high school if they do not get an A+ on their history oral presentation. Rufus (George Carlin), an emissary from the future, is therefore sent back to give them a time machine (in the shape of a telephone booth) that will allow them to gain historical knowledge superior to that contained in the books they had in any case neglected to read, preferring instead to ask random questions of random strangers in convenience stores and strip malls. Although dubious about Rufus's offer, they are reassured by a surprise visit from themselves, already in the midst of their journey. "Why," they wonder in a quandary that encapsulates the essential enigma of President Reagan's America, "would we lie to ourselves?" Thus they embark on a rapid-speed, multistop journey in which they round up Napoleon, Beethoven, Socrates, Billy the Kid, Joan of Arc, Genghis Khan, Sigmund Freud, and Abraham Lincoln, all of whom help Bill and Ted with a presentation of "history" in the school auditorium.

The first thing to note is that although the genre is more absurdist than *Back to the Future*, and hence the time travel more excessive and the acts more outrageous, Bill and Ted's adventure ultimately serves the same goal as Marty's: to appropriate the past in order to handle the quotidian problems of suburban teenagers. The self-serving attitude is manifest even in Bill and Ted's assignment, which is to explain what great historical figures would think of their town, San Demis. The parade of figures on the stage of the high school auditorium, therefore, all give their approval to the present—the place of waterslides, electric organs, aerobics, and shopping malls—rather than provide any information about their lives and times, about anything that makes them *historical*. This is, of course, only a more subtle version of the message suggested by the *Back to the Future* trilogy, which uses the same actors and similar situations to represent four different periods, implying that each of these periods is simply a thinly disguised version of the present.

In their appropriative attitude toward history, Bill and Ted treat it as no different from anything else in their lives, as a desirable to be consumed without effort or worry. The time machine thus legitimizes their refusal to treat the present as a place with consequences, for mastery over time is, indeed, mastery over consequences. The film's narrative, moreover, makes them the focal point for everything that has preceded and as well for everything that will come. They are the repository of the past and the leaders of the future, the apex of all time.

What is particularly vexing about this position is that it seems to impose no sense of responsibility on them. In this way they unwrite the message in John Kennedy's inauguration speech, which asserts the huge, historically specific responsibilities of a generation called by the weight of its past to shape the future for coming generations. Bill and Ted get *credit* for shaping the future when in fact the future takes responsibility for shaping them. The film constructs, in other words, a perspective from which their greatness is already a historical fact, one that validates their current tastes and choices—rock music and partying—as definitive virtues, the same virtues lauded by the historical figures. Lincoln concludes the school presentation by telling the audience that "these two great gentlemen are dedicated to a proposition that was true in my time just as it is today: Be excellent to each other, and party on dudes!"

In this way, they articulate what Reeves and Campbell accurately describe as Reagan's theological philosophy:

> Where Carter's presidential ministry was a jeremiad of long-suffering, sacrifice, and charity, Reagan's was a carnivalesque tent revival where moneychangers and astrologers were welcomed into the fold, indulgences were sold by the truckload, and Jesus was privatized as a "personal savior." Therefore, bound up in the negatives of the backlash politics of Reaganism are a whole host of affirmations: to enjoy the good life; to consume wholeheartedly; to take great pleasure in privilege; to indulge without guilt in the fruits of inequality; to stand tall and take pride in being "a winner"; and, above all, to see economic advantages and good fortune as the just deserts of those chosen by God to succeed in His holy marketplace.[38]

In this case, our heroes were not chosen by God but by destiny—by the future—the omnipotence and omniscience of which is manifest through the eternal light of the cinematic lens.

The film also comes to a very shrewd understanding of the way the time travelers' appropriation of history functions in the present. Needing the keys to the jail cell in which the historical figures have been placed for disrupting a shopping mall, they reason that they could set the time machine for two days earlier and hide the keys where they need them. This idea produces the needed keys in the needed place, obviating the need to go through the "technicality" of actually using the time machine. Time travel, in other words, becomes the pure product of the imagination. The technology that makes time travel possible is also the technology that renders it unnecessary; once cinematic reality replaces the space-time continuum, the illusion of that continuum can be whatever one imagines. *Bill and Ted's Excellent Adventure* thus establishes history not merely as a fiction or illusion but as a cinematically constructed one, thereby equating control over history with control over the codes and technologies of cinematic representation. Cinema provides an inexhaustible line of credit.

In refusing to draw on that credit, *Jacob's Ladder* reveals the fallacy of the system, just as in refusing to turn its back on Vietnam, it rejects the wholesale selling of time in *Chances Are* and *Late for Dinner*. The ghost patriarch in *Jacob's Ladder*, rather than acquiring power, is confronted over and over by the ways in which the war has deprived him of it. Instead of returning to the simpler past, he is rent from it. Instead of haunting the present, he is haunted by it. Incapable of buying time, he is reminded repeatedly that his time has run out. Instead of saving the child in mortal danger, he joins him in death.

The director of this film, Adrian Lyne, who reshot the ending of his previous film, *Fatal Attraction*, did not provide *Jacob's Ladder* with an artificially happy ending, for this film is critiquing exactly the practice of drawing on the credit bank of time to tell the audience the story it wants to hear, the story that its credit and power are inexhaustible, that the future will be a version of the past, that the next generation is safe under the protection of the dead patriarch, that it's a wonderful death. It is critiquing exactly the cinematic devices, in other words, that could make some movies the perfect vehicles for Ronald Reagan.

Three

The *Pretty Woman*, *The Little Mermaid*, and the *Working Girl* Become "Part of That World"

If the death-rehearsal films all valorize patriarchy, they do so not by excluding women but by allowing them a crucial role in the affirmation of the dead patriarch. In *Field of Dreams*, for instance, the immediate chain of events that allows Kinsella to reconcile with his dead father is initiated by the visionary daughter who articulates the salvation of the field of dreams and then nearly chokes to death on a hot dog. In *Beetlejuice*, the exorcism of the house and the reformation of the parents are effected by Lydia's offer to sacrifice her own life to become the bride of Beetlejuice, and in *Flatliners*, Rachel allows herself to bear the guilt for her father's suicidal involvement in Vietnam. In *Chances Are*, Corinne puts her own life in suspended animation until the return of the dead patriarch.

Important to understanding these women is the character to whom I gave little attention in my discussion of *Trading Places*, the prostitute, Ophelia. What makes her unique in the film is her absolute lack of uniqueness. Neither the "Belle Dame Sans Merci" nor the whore with the heart of gold, she is just another merchant in trade. Like Billy Ray Valentine, she already resembles the Dukes, in that she has mainstream values, a sense of frugality, and a faith in investment planning; she is also doing something technically illegal.

She differs from the Dukes not in kind but in class. This is the same thing that differentiates her from Winthorp's fiancée, Penelope (who is also the

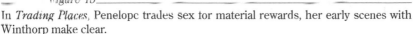

Figure 15

In *Trading Places*, Penelope trades sex for material rewards, her early scenes with Winthorp make clear.

Dukes' niece). Penelope trades sex for material rewards, as her early scenes with Winthorp make clear. Like Ophelia, she has a "literary" name, and in both cases the allusion highlights the differences between the literary character and her *Trading Places* namesake. Ophelia is perhaps the most sane, least deluded of the film's characters. As she acknowledges herself, reminding Winthorp that this is not a play, she is not going to be deranged by love. Nor is Penelope going to display patience and fidelity to her beloved. As soon as Winthorp falls from grace, she immediately shifts her allegiance to one of the other preppy suitors. The names of these women thus underscore the tenuous quality of nominal distinctions in the world of *Trading Places*. The "good" woman and the "bad" woman have allegiance to the same thing, money. And money comes in all instances here, as power does in the death-rehearsal films, from white men. Thus when Penelope discards Winthorp as a bad investment, Ophelia picks him up as a potentially good one. Like everyone in the film, Ophelia is investing in futures, and she succeeds because she, like Valentine, is a better trader than Penelope or the Dukes. She understands which man to back, and no matter what level of affection she may develop for Winthorp, their relationship is foremost a business venture.

In this context, the comparisons of *Trading Places* with *My Man Godfrey* take on additional significance. In *Godfrey*, too, the man turns out to be a good investment, one that returns immense benefits—financial, emotional, and psychological—for the upper-class Bullocks. Irene's man, however, doesn't give to her anything that she doesn't already have. This is a basic principle of pastoral. (Consider, for example, *The Wizard of Oz*.) Godfrey merely returns the investment that Irene put in him by simplifying and focusing her energy. Ophelia, however, serves no commensurate role, despite the paral lels that can be drawn between her and Irene as the women who rescue their "man" when he is down and out. Whereas Irene discovers herself in her man, Ophelia discovers nothing; she merely turns a profit in the same way she turns a trick. The market system functions independently of her investment, so her relationship to it is purely parasitical and speculative. She exists completely apart from the source of power, the market itself, which is personified by the president of the Exchange (Alfred Drake), who calls in all the accounts on the commodities exchange at the end of the day. He breaks the Dukes with the same neutrality that he makes Ophelia, and it is his agency that empowers trading in futures. As the illegal information makes clear, the fair market is a myth. Nevertheless, faith in that fair market and the rules that it ostensibly follows must be maintained at all costs. Thus, like the women in the death-rehearsal films, Ophelia must trust a power that exists elsewhere, in the absence of empirical evidence.

In many ways this defines the terms of upward mobility for women in President Reagan's America. As Susan Faludi has extensively documented, most aspects of American life during the 1980s manifested a shrinking of women's power, authority, and real income. At the same time, Faludi makes clear, a popular rhetoric emerged that suggested women were more successful and less happy *because* of their alleged advances. "Just as Reaganism shifted political discourse far to the right and demonized liberalism, so the backlash convinced the public that women's 'liberation' was the true contemporary American scourge—the source of an endless laundry list of personal, social, and economic problems."[1]

"Part of the ideological project of the right in the eighties," Marsha Kinder notes, "is the restoration of the family to its former status as a strong Ideological State Apparatus and the reinstatement of the father within this patriarchal stronghold. Hence the focus on fathers and sons and the further marginalization of the female."[2]

The successful woman, in this context, must be like the girls and women of the death-rehearsal films, someone who will revive patriarchal authority rather than challenge it. And like Ophelia, no matter what service they are ostensibly selling or giving away, they remain in a largely parasitical relationship to the patriarchal source of power. More significant, they are parasites whose body is controlled by the patriarchal host. As Ophelia explains, her body is her capital, something also explicitly true of Vivian Ward (Julia Roberts), the prostitute in *Pretty Woman*, and, I will argue, implicitly the case for the principals in *Working Girl* and *The Little Mermaid*. Subordination of sexual—and by implication reproductive—freedom in these films becomes the necessary condition for changing classes.

In 1988, the Academy Award–winning song was "Let the River Run," from the movie *Working Girl*. This song, with its upbeat rhythm and uplifting tones, heralds the New Jerusalem and lauds material success by creating a musical site that combines gospel and rock in a way that purges the ethnic roots of both to give us what could best be called a disco hymn. Like the music, the lyrics endow Tess McGill's (Melanie Griffith) success—a successfully manipulated corporate acquisition, one that will preempt an "unfriendly" Japanese takeover—with moral as well as financial virtue. Her reward, an executive office in a Manhattan skyscraper, thus becomes a holy site, through the beneficence of the corporate god, Mr. Trask (Philip Bosco), capable not only of rewarding the good girl but also of destroying the bad one, Katherine Parker (Sigourney Weaver), by firing her summarily from a corporation he does not even own. In the New Jerusalem, the corporate Jerusalem, the tycoon is God, and no rules apply save those that please or trouble him. His power is limitless, and, as one of his employees says after receiving uncanny phone instructions from him in the middle of a business meeting, "he knows everything." And thus he knows enough to bend the rules of corporate ethics in order to reward a working girl who has helped the New Jerusalem merge, and acquire, and fend off the Japanese. This is a success story, on moral terms as well as material, and as the ringing tones of Carly Simon affirm, this is a "feel good" movie.

The following year, the Academy Award winner was also a feel-good song that creates a mythical kingdom, the Little Mermaid's world "Under the Sea." Like *Working Girl*, *The Little Mermaid* is a young woman's success story, but in this case, the song describes the world she leaves behind to acquire her castle and prince. And it is not surprising, therefore, that the upbeat rhythms come not from a disco sound but from a calypso. In juxtaposing these two films about mergers and acquisitions—films that reveal a great many similarities—we can start by noting the way in which their lauded songs exist in an economy affirmed by the academy of Motion Picture Arts and Sciences, one that marks the kingdom lost for the kingdom gained, the under (the sea) class for the skyscraping class, the steel drum tonalities of ethnicity for the bleached-flour white bread of disco.

The argument for the moral and practical value of such an economy could be identified as a thematic of the Reagan presidency. And at the time that these two films were being made, that thematic was being reiterated with a vengeance, in the form of the Bush election campaign. George Bush inherited the feel-good aura of Reaganomics, and as he himself urged, concluding his first debate with Michael Dukakis, "If you want a change, vote for me. I am the change!" Whether President Bush was the change or merely the loose change is of less importance than the way that he and the Republican party, in the preparation for and in the aftermath of the 1988 election, codified the national narratives of the Reagan presidency. Although there were an array of such narratives, the ones that are germane to this discussion embody a series of false economies, ones that substitute credit for exchange, a form of single-entry bookkeeping, with only a credit column and never a debit, in which there is only profit and never loss. What keeps this ledger balanced, furthermore, is the image of the patriarch, one who can wipe the moral ledger clean, along with the financial, and distribute goods, so long as his authority is not challenged, his position not critiqued, his assertions not refuted.

In the Walt Disney version of *The Little Mermaid*, the Hans Christian Andersen story is altered not only to allow the mermaid an escape clause on the trade she makes (her voice for her legs) but also to permit a happy ending effected by her having both voice and legs (with a bonus of the prince as husband). This "voodoo" economy, in which exchange becomes pure acquisition, constitutes the only possible means by which Ariel, the princess of mermaids under the sea, can become princess of the world to which she aspires, up there on land. That world is one she has fetishized by collecting human implements—which in her ignorance she misunderstands and misuses—that have trickled down to the bottom. "I just can't see," she reasons, "how a world that makes such wonderful things could be bad." She is seduced, in other words, by the products of the "human" world, to which she

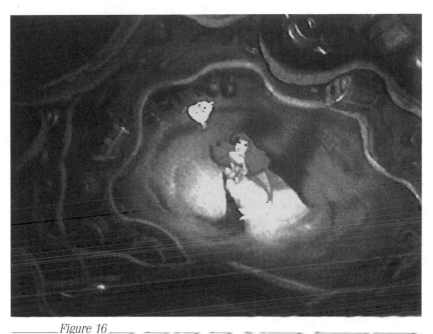

———— *Figure 16* ————

In her grotto, Ariel, the little mermaid, has fetishized human implements that have trickled down to the bottom.

ascribes the highest moral value. Amid her plentiful collection of material possessions, she plaintively sings in the song "Part of That World," "I've got gadgets and gizmos a plenty. I've got whozits and whatzits galore. . . . But who cares. No big deal. I want *more*." Wanting more for Ariel equates to moving up: "*Up* where they walk," she sings. "*Up* where they run, *up* where they spend all day in the sun. . . . Wish I could be part of that world" (emphasis added). As in "Let the River Run," the upward mobility in this song is represented as leaving the water for land: "Out of the sea, wish I could be, part of that world."

The chief distinction—emphasized repeatedly—between the two worlds is that one world is composed of fishes and the other is where they are eaten. The segment that opens the film shows the hero, Prince Eric, along with his crew hauling a huge catch of fish; only when one escapes overboard is our gaze led to King Triton's world of mermen and mermaids. Triton furthermore explicitly forbids Ariel to go near the surface and associate with humans because they are fish eaters. "Do you think," he asks, "I want to see my youngest daughter snared by some fish-eater's hook?" This theme, reiterated in several ways throughout the film, is the central theme of the song "Under the Sea," in which the crab Sebastian sings to Ariel about fish on land, "One day when the boss get hungry, guess who goin' on the plate." Under the sea, he stresses, "Nobody beat us, fry us and eat us in fricassee. We want the land-folks not to cook. Under the sea we hide the hook." Sebastian's song is very nearly prophetic, as he later narrowly escapes being cooked for lunch by the prince's chef.

Ariel's desire for upward mobility, in other words, is explicitly represented as a desire to join the class of fish eaters, despite the fact that her closest friends are fish. Nor should we ignore the predatory quality of that desire. A mad scramble in the kitchen precedes Ariel's eating scene, which is one of her basic initiations into the human world of the prince's castle. In that kitchen scene, Sebastian, the court composer and her father's adviser—a member of the Under the Sea aristocracy—is pursued by the working-class chef, who has explained in graphic detail his delight in preparing fish meals. "First I cut off their heads, then I pull out their spines," he says while per-forming these tasks on screen. Escaping from the chef, however, moves Se-bastian from the frying pan to the platter, as he finds himself served for lunch along with the dead crabs. Although Ariel helps him hide, we can assume that she eats some of the dead crabs, although the scene ends before we are allowed to see this act. Instead of being appalled by Ariel's near cannibalism, therefore, we are gratified by her rescue of the single, privileged crab. The privilege of this crab, of course, is the privilege of assisting Ariel to a posi-tion where she can eat crab everyday, legitimately.

Ariel desires this legitimately predatory position for romantic as well as material reasons, having glimpsed and fallen in love with Prince Eric. But it is important to note that she has fallen in love with the world first, and part of her attraction to Eric is that he has all the things she loves. For Ariel, in other words, humans are fetishized objects, attractive *because* of their mate-rial possessions and attractive *like* them.

Exactly the same fetishizing of the accoutrement of affluence occurs in *Working Girl*, when Tess rummages through the residence of her affluent boss, Katherine. The chandelier, the exercise equipment, the evening gowns, the makeup are all things Tess has studied from afar, things that make

_____ *Figure 17*_____ _____

Escaping from the chef, however, moves Sebastian from the frying pan to the platter, as he finds himself served for lunch along with the dead crabs.

Katherine's role so attractive, before Tess has met Katherine. In *Pretty Woman*, too, the objects of affluence—initially the *very* expensive car Edward (Richard Gere) drives—single him out to Vivian. From there, each article of clothing, accessory, convenience identifies the penthouse world from which Vivian finds herself unable to return to the street. As she emphasizes to Edward, she wants the full fairy tale. She wants, in other words, to be exactly like the little mermaid in Disney's version of story. Like Ariel and every human being in President Reagan's America, Vivian wants *more*. Wanting more, worshiping accessories, craving acquisitions—these not only define humanity in *The Little Mermaid* but also justify all other actions.

When Ariel saves Prince Eric after a shipwreck, she flees the shore before he can see her clearly. Nevertheless, Eric has fallen in love with Ariel, retaining instead of her glass slipper the sound of her voice. But when King Triton learns of Ariel's love for a human, he denies her any hope of ascent, so she enlists the aid of Ursula, the powerful sea witch, who gives her legs in exchange for her voice, with the understanding that if the prince kisses

Ariel within three days, the voice will be returned, and if not, Ariel becomes the property of the witch.

Although Ariel articulates the price of humanity as permanent separation from her origins—"If I become human, I'll never see my father or sisters again"—the rejection of her own kind for humankind is not a very difficult choice. As Sebastian clearly realizes, "You could go home with all the normal fish and just be . . . just be . . . just be miserable for the rest of your life!" To be human is to be involved with and loved by the source of the immense material overflow of goods and services. If Triton is the god of the land under the sea, where, as the film represents it, predatory relationships are rare and the inhabitants make music rather than cook food, then Eric is the prince of the gross national product, where predatory behavior is a necessary human trait.

Ariel's ascent to "humanity" is endangered, however, not by her reluctance to forsake her friends and family, that is, by her scruples, but by the sea witch, who only wants Ariel to think she can become human. Ursula's deception is part of a plot to destroy Triton's patriarchy. In this way Ursula typifies the "feminists" of the backlash culture Faludi describes. These feminists (or Femi-Nazis, as they are called by Rush Limbaugh and Camille Paglia, among others) aim, according to the mythology of backlash, not to advance women so much as to destroy male-dominated institutions. Women, in this scenario, are their innocent victims, not their beneficiaries. In adhering to this description, Ursula attempts to undermine the advances she has facilitated so that Ariel and, more important, Triton will be in her complete control. Ursula thus disguises herself as a maiden and uses Ariel's voice to lure the prince to her. By using Ariel's voice, she is able to take credit for Ariel's deed, for hearing the voice, the prince mistakes the disguised Ursula for his savior and sets an immediate wedding date. Although Ariel discovers the ruse in time to thwart the wedding, she nevertheless loses her wager and surrenders herself to the sea witch. But since the sea witch's real goal was not to capture Ariel but to destroy patriarchy by capturing Ariel's father, she trades Ariel for Triton's full surrender and acquiescence, thus changing the terms of Ariel's choice. It is no longer between the benign musical ethnic world under the sea and the predatory one above but rather between the beautiful, bountiful predators on the surface and the ugly, parsimonious one beneath, between the good prince and the evil queen.[3] This horrible condition, moreover, was made possible by Ariel's naïveté; her error was not in loving Eric or wanting to be a fish eater but in trusting Ursula to help her. When Ariel and her prince unite to kill the sea witch, they not only effect Ariel's ascent to reign in the world of fish eaters but also restore the patriarchal authority of Ariel's father. Thus her actions produce a kinder and gentler patriarch by confirming the fact that she desires not to diminish his authority but to preserve it by destroying his true enemy, the overly ambitious, powerful woman.

The sea witch's representation, furthermore, is a perversion of the goddess in matristic religions, religions suppressed under the name of witchery, by Western patriarchy. In the last two decades there has been extensive research on the role of the goddess or goddesses in prepatriarchal cultures that antedate by as much as thirty thousand years the last three millennia in which patriarchal religions and belief systems have come to dominate.

Although there seems to be little evidence of a period dominated by matriarchal societies—societies in which women *ruled* largely or completely to the exclusion of men—there is much evidence of a period when matristic religions proliferated. Those religions figured the highest deities in female form, making the mother figure, not the father figure, the center of myth and worship, the imagined source of power. According to Merlin Stone's groundbreaking study, "the archeological artifacts suggest that in all the Neolithic and early Chalcolithic societies the Divine Ancestress, generally referred to by most writers as the Mother Goddess, was revered as the supreme deity."[4]

The 1970s witnessed a reemergence of interest in the goddess—or more commonly in the issues of female power and independence that she symbolizes— that, as many critics have noted, threatened the traditional assumptions of Western patriarchal dominance. As Gloria Feman Orenstein has pointed out, "Patriarchal tale telling and myth making have described reality in ways that disempower women, and these tales and myths have constituted the fund of knowledge and the consensus of the versions of myth and literature that have reigned in the West and fueled our educational systems for hundreds of years."[5] The question is not whether women actually ruled society (in general they did not) but rather to what extent a legacy of myth and belief vesting supreme power in the father—of worshiping the patriarchal—have affected attitudes toward women. The versions of myth, literature, and religion to which Orenstein refers have been agents in the disempowerment of women, and with the origin of power in God the father, the goddess becomes the rival associated, as in the idea of witchery, with Satan—in other words, with that which seeks to undermine God.

This clearly describes the representation of Ursula, who, as the sea *witch*, not the sea *goddess*, represents an evil counterforce, not an originary power. Someone who, like Satan, had been expelled from the patriarchal realm, she is driven by revenge and thus defined in terms of her aberration from the patriarchal norm. "She competes," James Livingston points out, "directly with the king for control of Ariel's future, as if she were, in fact, the mermaid's mother."[6] "What makes [Ursula's] rebellion so awful?" Livingston asks. "And why is Ariel's rebellion acceptable in the end? Both stand up to father, remember. But one is killed by Ariel's husband-to-be, the other is rewarded with entry into the civilized world of men on earth. One is driven out of the king's castle, the other chooses to leave. One tries to change the relation between father and mother, the other wants to recreate this relation in a new family. One breaks the law of the father, the other upholds it."[7] Ursula thus embodies woman feared and hated by the Religious Right to which Reagan owed so much of his political power, for she threatens not only the hierarchies upon which the Religious Right models its social order but also the mythological origins upon which it bases its cosmological authority.

Preservation of the American way, in this construction, demanded a halt to equal power or representation by women in the political process. The leaders of the Religious Right are quite explicit on this issue. Jerry Falwell, leader of the Moral Majority, accused feminism of launching a "satanic attack on the home," Faludi points out in her discussion of this extensive vilification of the women's movement. "The depiction of feminists as malevolent spirits capable of great evil and national destruction," she explains,

> was also a refrain. The opening of the American Christian Cause's fundraising newsletter warned, "Satan has taken the reigns of the 'women's liberation' movement and will stop at nothing." The Christian Voice held that "America's rapid decline as a world power is a direct result" of the feminist campaign for equal rights and reproductive freedom. . . . Feminists are already a deadly force, as the commentators on the evangelical 700 Club explained it, precisely because they threatened a transfer of gender power; they "would turn the country over to women."[8]

In light of these sentiments, we can see why Ursula would seem most dangerous when she towers over the ocean wearing Triton's crown and looking exactly like a grotesquely evil Statue of Liberty. Her height of menace is linked visually with her aspiring to represent the national interests, her agenda merging with the iconography of the American nation. Although her rise from under the sea fulfills Ariel's desire, Ursula, the film makes clear, is not the kind of woman who should be upwardly mobile, even though she shares with humans the carnivorous, predatory practices. Not her values but her refusal to subordinate them to the political realities of patriarchal culture make her incompatible with above-the-sea behavior. Ariel, on the other hand, understands her place as a woman, is glad to have saved the prince, grateful to be chosen by him, delighted to assume her subservient role in the world where they devour her kind.

The same hatred of one's own class—and almost exactly the same plot—informs *Working Girl*. There again, having fetishized the upper-class life as it has trickled down through its representation in the print media that she compulsively reads, Tess desires upward mobility into the world where people know how to use makeup and clothing correctly. The world that she desires to join is represented not by the land as seen from under the sea but by the skyscrapers as seen from the Staten Island ferry.

In the opening shot sequence of *The Little Mermaid*, we follow a seagull as it circles down from the clouds until we are at water level, tracking with dolphins along the side of a ship. From this water-level view we enter the ship. As the credits appear in *Working Girl*, the camera starts with the same gull's-eye view of the water. While the soundtrack features in booming tones Carly Simon's paean to a new world, the camera slowly circles the Statue of Liberty—that icon of upward mobility for which Ursula represented the evil Other—starting with a close-up of the head and circling back and away and down to include the Manhattan skyline and the Staten Island ferry cruising toward it. As the ferry approaches the city, the camera zooms in on the ferry, tracking alongside the lower deck, just as it does in *The Little Mermaid*, then through a dissolve tracking along the aisle inside. The shot gives the crowded lower deck the look of steerage, encouraging an association between the rush-hour commuters and immigrants heading for Ellis Island. But it is, of course, the financial district rather than Ellis Island that is being imbued with all the theological and nationalist overtones of Simon's lyrics.

_____ *Figure 18* _____
The Staten Island ferry's crowded lower deck has the look of steerage, encouraging an association between the rush-hour commuters in *Working Girl* and immigrants heading for Ellis Island.

Although Tess is a citizen, in President Reagan's America, she still has immigrant status, accentuated by her thick New York accent. Tess has gotten her college degree at night, and having achieved honors in the lower-class world, she wants an entry-level position in an executive training program. She further proves her worth by giving her bosses astute analyses of stock investments, lodged like Valentine's analyses in *Trading Places* in anecdotal understanding. As the sleazy men who are her superiors imply, however, she is not suitable for that class. Indeed, she looks, talks, and dresses like her equally unsuitable friends from the secretarial pool. As made clear by her thickly accented banter on the Staten Island ferry with her friend Cyn (Joan Cusack) and the shots that present them, with little depth of field, as equal faces in the crowd, neither is suited for an executive position. They do not, in fact, wear suits, and they are as poorly suited as they are made up for the roles. The difference in Tess's and Cyn's education serves to differentiate them far less than the similarities in their clothing, hairstyle, makeup, accent, and demeanor unite them. As in *Little Mermaid*, their inadequacy comes not from their inability to recognize the trappings of the other class but from their inability to use them properly. Like Ariel, whose table manners are hampered by the belief that a fork is used to comb one's hair, Tess and her friends can acquire the best makeup but they don't know how to put it on.

Vivian Ward (Julia Roberts), the prostitute in *Pretty Woman*, has all of the above problems. Her accent is poor, her clothing vulgar, and her manners crude. Like Ariel, she needs help from an adviser, in this case the hotel manager, Barnard Thompson (Hector Elizondo), on the use of forks. In Vivian's case, the crucial mealtime test comes when, instead of crab, she has to eat caviar (fish roe) and escargot. In the world of posh restaurants and the Beverly Hills penthouse hotel suites, Vivian is simply a fish out of water. Even chairs present problems, as she seems to have no clear idea of where to sit or, particularly, what to do with her legs when she does. Whatever she does, her legs seem to jut out inappropriately or dangle conspicuously. While bathing with Edward in the penthouse's huge sunken bathtub, she calls attention to her legs, telling him that since each one is forty-four inches long, he has eighty-eight inches of therapy wrapped around him.

Legs are equally fetishized in *Working Girl*. When Tess first comes to work, the camera tracks with her as she crosses the crowded office and rounds her desk, centering on her legs as she changes from running shoes to work shoes. Later in a limousine, with a sleazy executive, Tess's legs crossed in the foreground become the point of visual attention for both the camera and the executive. When Tess helps Katherine try on her ski boots, the scene is shot at nearly floor level to foreground a contrast between Tess's legs and Katherine's, and later, when Tess has passed out in a taxi, all we see of her through the open door is her legs.

In this way, both Vivian and Tess are versions of Ariel, for whom legs are the most prized possession. Legs, in other words, are the means for being like the people up there, for having more. They are also the privileged body part that makes them attractive and hence useful to men. As the case of Ariel makes clear, the acquisition of legs is the deformation of fins and the alteration of the reproductive half of Ariel's body. In addition to her appearance, in other words, she also changes her mode of reproduction. Since the repressed history of the goddess mythology is grounded in the idea of the

_____ *Figures 19 & 20*_____
In the posh world of Beverly Hills, Vivian is simply a fish out of water with no clear idea of what to do with her legs.

female as the source of creation, the evocation of the goddess as witch makes clear in all of these tales of upward mobility the ways in which President Reagan's America connects that mobility to control over the woman's body.

The alacrity with which Vivian and Tess let men control their legs rivals the ease with which Ariel will alter the shape of her body—and with it her entire reproductive system—to suit the prince. This echo of the surrender of reproductive freedom, never articulated as such, suggests the added costs of the commodification of women's bodies endemic to these films.

But just as Ariel discovers that legs are necessary, but not sufficient, Tess, too, learns that there is a gap between the world she desires and her ability to attain it, a gap signified by her clothing, makeup, and speech. It is this gap that Katherine mediates by owning and using the proper clothing and makeup, by living in Manhattan, and by intimating that she will be Tess's bridge to a trainee position. Because Katherine has a skiing accident that keeps her out of town, Tess has to go to Katherine's home and in the process discovers that Katherine has stolen her idea that Trask Industries should acquire a radio network. She discovers this accidentally when she is playing Katherine's tape recorder, which she is using to practice her diction and change her accent. In trying to acquire Katherine's voice, in other words, she discovers that Katherine has usurped hers.

In this context, Tess's idea is given material value. And although this may be a stretch of even the most generous interpretation of intellectual property laws—how would one copyright an idea for a business acquisition?—it suggests the way in which finance acquires cinematic values and wealth merges with stardom. What Katherine has actually stolen is a story idea that can be worked into a successful narrative, wherein Trask Industries can remain a patriarchal enterprise by virtue of its ability to resist unfriendly Japanese intrusions. This story of America's victory over the Japanese is a fanciful pastiche constructed by Tess from her assiduous gleaning of popular magazines and newspapers, society pages, and gossip columns.

Hearing her idea on Katherine's tape recorder, Tess has the shock of discovering that Katherine has taken Tess's fantasy, at the moment when Tess was trying to acquire Katherine's, for in Tess's mind lifestyle has completely merged with the work of mergers and acquisitions, such that she cannot acquire the job she dreams of without also acquiring the style she attributed to it in her fantasies. She wants the kind of executive role illustrated in films, not taught to her in her classrooms.

Figure 21

In a limousine, with a sleazy executive, Tess's legs crossed in the foreground become the point of visual attention; . . .

Figure 22

. . . when Tess helps Katherine try on her ski boots, the scene is shot at nearly floor level to foreground a contrast between Tess's legs and Katherine's; . . .

Figure 23

. . . later, when Tess has passed out in a taxi, all we see of her through the open door is her legs; . . .

Figure 24

. . . and when Jack carries Tess to his apartment, her legs remain prominent.

Her understanding of the role, in other words, is synonymous with Reagan's understanding of holding high political office. One must create credible narratives and play roles credibly. Although she is at the center of our cinematic experience, in the story of her own life Tess has remained in the supporting cast. Even her surprise birthday party is set up such that she has to alter her plans and act surprised to please her friends. Her birthday gift from her live-in boyfriend (Alec Baldwin) is gaudy underwear that will enhance his pleasure in her sexual performance. In attempting to suggest that she wants a different role, she expresses desire for some other form of gift— "something I could wear out, like a sweater." She wants to move from a supporting role in a private performance to a public role in which she might be a star. Because Katherine represents such a role to Tess, Tess can see Katherine as preying on Tess's fantasy of leaving the supporting cast for stardom. Therefore Tess decides to take advantage of circumstances. While Katherine's broken leg places her in a supporting cast, Tess will assume the lead. This means, of course, not only assuming Katherine's business role but also borrowing her home and clothing, because these all go together.

Assuming the leading role also means, in the classical Hollywood tradition, acquiring the love interest. In uncannily parallel sequences, Tess first glimpses her future beloved much as Ariel discovers Eric. Ariel first sees Eric when fireworks draw her one night to the ship, where a party of the sort she had never imagined is taking place. "I've never seen a human this close before," she says. "Isn't he the most beautiful thing you've ever seen?" The party is disrupted by a violent storm in which Eric is thrown overboard and, unconscious, brought to shore by Ariel. In *Working Girl*, Tess, too, crashes a posh evening party on a ship, putting her closer, in the class-stratified taxonomy of the film, to real "humans" than she has ever been before, a perspective reinforced by increasing visual disparity in scenes of Tess on Staten Island, wherein her friends seem to be members of a grotesque, almost subhuman world. When Tess first sees Jack Trainor (Harrison Ford), moreover, the film emphasizes the idea that he is a human being—refusing to tell her his name, he says, "Let's just meet like human beings for once." Their meeting is abruptly terminated, not in this case by a sudden storm of the sort that disrupts Prince Eric's party, but by Tess, who, like Ariel and Vivian, misunderstands how to use the materials of the class to which she aspires. In Tess's case, the misused item is Valium appropriated from Katherine's medicine chest, which she mixes with the tequila Jack offers. This causes her to become very spacey and, in the process, to articulate the dilemma of her split circumstances, a split that Ariel's physique literalizes: "I have a head for business and a bod' for sin." Avoiding disastrous recognition by one of the other executive women in her firm, Tess staggers to a cab, where she passes out.

Although Tess, rather than Jack, escapes disaster and passes out, the "meet cute" of this encounter, in which Jack ends up carrying Tess to safety and then admiring her beauty while she remains unconscious, resembles strongly the rescue in *The Little Mermaid*. But just as Prince Eric is attractive to Ariel before she meets him, by virtue of the world in which he lives, Jack Trainor is someone Tess wants to meet professionally prior to their romantic meeting. And as much as she would like to keep business separate from romance, she cannot because, as the film represents it, high finance is erotic. As they come closer to closing the deal, they become more aroused by each other's presence, building toward the verboten kiss that is the privileged event, as well, in *The Little Mermaid* (and also in *Pretty Woman*). The successful merger and acquisition, moreover, will help keep Jack from sinking in the precarious seas of the financial world. As he admits, he has had a bad run and will drown if one more deal goes down the drain.

Unbeknownst to Tess, her relationship with Jack also puts her in a rivalry with Katherine, just as unbeknownst to Ariel, she is in competition with Ursula for Eric's love. As in the case of Ariel and the sea witch, Tess becomes the powerful woman's rival for the same man, and, like Ariel, with that man's help she destroys the powerful woman. This act earns Tess, as it did Ariel, her position in the upper-class world.

Of particular significance during the course of this ascent, as I have noted, are the scenes that show Tess's returns to her lower-middle-class Staten Island world. They all involve interactions with her boyfriend, first when she finds him in bed with one of her friends, then at Cyn's engagement party, when he asks for her forgiveness and publicly asks her to marry him, and finally at Cyn's wedding, where he is dressed in an exceptionally gaudy and tasteless light blue tuxedo with a shirt full of garish ruffles. There he has clearly formed a couple with the other girl. Like Tess, he is ambitious, and during the course of the film he gets a loan approved to buy a charter boat, purchases the boat, and has it booked up for several weeks. And like Tess's, his ethics are questionable.

_____ *Figure 25*_____

At Cyn's wedding, Tess sees her former boyfriend dressed in an exceptionally gaudy and tasteless light blue tuxedo with a shirt full of garish ruffles, and he has clearly formed a couple with the other girl.

What differentiates them is the nature of their transgressions and, more significant, of their ambitions. He is willing to cheat on her sexually, and she is willing to cheat her boss and her corporation, to deceive three other corporations, and to cause a man (with whom she eventually falls in love) to jeopardize his own career because he took her at her word and presumed she was acting in good faith. Nevertheless, the film valorizes her deceits while showing nothing but disdain for the former boyfriend, who appears sleazy or pathetic. As Tess says to Trask, "You can bend the rules plenty once you get upstairs, but not while you're trying to get there. And if you're someone like me, you can't get there without bending the rules." Trask endorses this ethic not only by hiring Tess but by turning her exception into the rule: "You've go a real fire in your belly. Or was this just a one time stunt you pulled? . . . I mean, are you willing to go out on a limb every day working for me? Legitimately?"

Trask articulates the essence of Reaganomic deregulation. As the financial markets and the savings and loan institutions demonstrated, in an unregulated atmosphere, anything is possible. Legal relationships are replaced by predatory ones, and Trask's appropriation of the rules is justified by his vulnerability in a predatory financial environment. This indeed reflects the sensibility in a business climate marked by a frenzy of "unfriendly" takeovers. When Tess explains to Cyn, therefore, "I'm not going to spend the rest of my life working my ass off and getting nowhere just because I followed rules I had nothing to do with setting up," she is demonstrating that she understands Trask's ethical code. Tess is like Trask, just as Ophelia and Valentine resemble the Dukes. Drawing again on the social Darwinist model, the question is survival, with those who opt for following the regulations seen as least fit. Since following the rules is the fatal sin, the case for doing so is fittingly made, therefore, by Cyn.

In the value system of *Working Girl*, the rules applying to ethics are subordinate to the rules for applying makeup. In this regard, *Working Girl* is strikingly similar to *Pretty Woman*, the following year's hit film about an upwardly mobile working girl. Also set in the world of mergers and acquisitions, *Pretty Woman*, like *Working Girl*, structures its love story around the acquisition of a paternalistic firm. In this case, however, the hero, Edward Lewis, is the predator, and the patriarchal industrial leader, Mr. Morse (Ralph Bellamy), is the prey. What remains the same is the pervasive commodification of all relationships. "No matter what they say, it's all about money," a magician tells people at a party, as the opening credits appear. "So let's imagine, ladies, that you're a Savings and Loan officer. See, you've got it all and we've got nothing," he states as he makes coins appear and disappear from his hands and from theirs. "But I wouldn't trust you with real gold," he explains as he converts their coins into a large penny.

By the time that *Pretty Woman* opened, the prestidigitation of savings and loan officers was well known, as was the way in which many had converted gold into pennies, but in this version, the wealthy ladies are mock savings and loan officers. Their hands are in the hands of other manipulators who control as if by magic the ladies' power and wealth. In this way the women at the party are placed in exactly the same position as the prostitute, Vivian Ward, through the course of the movie, in which she receives gold as if magically. The fairy tale of savings and loans told by the magician, in other words, anticipates the fairy tale of Vivian's ascent from streetwalker to society lady.

The parallels between *Pretty Woman* and *My Fair Lady* are clear and probably intentional, as suggested by the moment near the end of the film when Edward buys flowers for Vivian from a flower woman who says, "Thank you, love," in a thick cockney accent, thus alluding to Shaw's (and Lerner and Loewe's) Eliza Doolittle. Instead of a flower girl, Vivian is a prostitute, and Edward does not adopt her because of a wager. Rather, he hires her on a lark. Nevertheless, he effects a makeover of her that renders impossible her return to the streets. In both cases, the makeover includes teaching the woman a new set of manners and giving her a new appearance. But in *My Fair Lady* these changes are secondary to the difficult education of Eliza, focusing on her speech. When Henry Higgins, as the Pygmalion figure, falls in love with his own creation, therefore, he is falling in love with the fruits of his own labor. Like the pastoral figure, Eliza is giving Higgins back to himself. In Shaw's revision of the myth—slightly undermined by the musical adaptation of the play and the subsequent film—Eliza's own efforts create a surplus of value, more than Higgins can expect to accrue to himself. *Pretty Woman*, in exchanging fairness for prettiness and converting a "lady" into a "woman," removes all questions of the woman's labor, reducing the whole relationship to appearance, which, as the magician said at the outset, is "all about money."

In this way, *Pretty Woman* glosses both *Working Girl* and *The Little Mermaid*. "*Pretty Woman* reprises many of *Working Girl*'s strategies," Harvey Roy Greenberg points out, "albeit in much cruder fashion. Whereas Tess only appears naive, Vivian is manifestly stupid . . . [and] Edward's character conflates Trainor's 'new man' vulnerability with Trask's omnipotent patriarch power."[9] Vivian is the working girl who longs to be like the people up there, where mergers and acquisitions are completed as the commodified metamorphosis of all relationships. Although Edward is a workaholic, none of his energy is devoted to personal relationships, but rather than redirect his energy, Vivian teaches him to forgo it, advocating leisure activities, such as taking a day off, vegging out in front of the television, and shopping. Shopping is the particularly privileged activity in the film because it is a leisure activity that equates metamorphosis with acquisition. Greeting Vivian with glee one morning, Edward says, "Wake up, it's time to shop," and when he learns that the exclusive stores on Rodeo Drive have been hostile to Vivian, he escorts her personally and tells one store manager, "We're going to be spending an obscene amount of money in here, so we're going to need a lot more help sucking up to us." This is the fairy tale ending to the story of President Reagan's America: that anyone can be upper class, that is, be woken to a call to shop and spend enough money to demand "sucking up."

By endorsing the manager's delight in this subservient relationship, and ridiculing the shop attendants who refused to accommodate Vivian, the film foregrounds the predatory relationships that unite all of these films. In these relationships, the members of the subservient class accept their roles in full complicity with the relationship. So strong is their identification with the people up there—so strong in Fussell's terms is the desire to be in the *upper* general group—that those who are not prefer to worship those who are. Just as the fishes at the end of *The Little Mermaid* cheer Ariel's new status as fish eater, those in the secretarial pool that Tess has left cheer her ability to be not-like them. The general applause in both cases is the class self-hatred that Fussell uncannily identified as being at the crux of Reaganism. Fussell discomforted his readers by reminding them of the class to which they appear to belong, just as Reagan conversely comforted them by providing a narrative by which they could escape the implications of their own appearances and, as well, their own education, history, or family in the same way as they do when watching a movie.

The informing fairy tale in *The Little Mermaid*, therefore, is not one derived from Hans Christian Andersen or the Brothers Grimm, but from movieland. This point, too, is underscored by *Pretty Woman*. Near the opening, the camera dwells on the large hillside letters that spell "HOLLYWOOD" as Edward drives past on his way, as it turns out, to finding Vivian. At the corner where they meet, we hear a street hustler say, "Everybody comes to Hollywood got a dream. What's your dream?" and in the final scene, when Edward climbs Vivian's fire escape to become her Prince Charming, the street hustler's voice is heard in refrain at the film's conclusion: "This is Hollywood. Always time to dream. So keep on dreamin'." The hustler who concludes the film by linking Hollywood to the fulfillment of dreams suggests the ways in which the American Dream has in President Reagan's America become purely cinematic. Whereas Hollywood has more commonly been regarded as the producer of fantasies, of escapes from reality, in this construction, it is a place where dreams may really come true, where dreaming can be rewarded.

Thus Vivian fulfills the dream of Ophelia, Tess, and Ariel, made all the more fantastic by its total abandonment of any form of labor or sacrifice. The key to this miraculous conversion from dream to reality can be found in juxtaposing the hustler's closing pronouncement with the magician's opening one: "It's all about money." Whereas Eric is rich because he is the prince, Edward is Vivian's Prince Charming because he is rich. His wealth creates the conditions under which she may enact the ritual of many fairy tales by waking Edward with a kiss, just as it allows him to be her fairy tale Prince Charming. After experiencing a week of the affluent life, Vivian refuses Edward's offer to be his kept mistress, not on moral grounds, but because, like Ariel, she wants more: "The whole fairy tale," as she puts it.

Considering these films in juxtaposition, we can see the ways in which they both manifest the hatred of one's own class and origins, that the myth of "trickle-down" both promoted and masked in the same way that the Reagan style did. We can further see the ways in which upward mobility has been transformed from the universal right it represented in the post–World War II era to the competitive one it represents in the Reagan era, despite the fact that the potential for wealth and material acquisition is represented as even more limitless than in the 1950s. Finally, we can see in this economy one more reinscription of the centuries-old suppression of matristic power by representing it as the witchery that must be destroyed for patriarchy to function benignly.

The way *The Little Mermaid* and, by extension, *Working Girl* validate the predatory food chain connects control of the body to control of the natural environment, which like the woman's body can be constructed as serving the predatory designs of national, commercial, or consumer interests. In the figure of the sea witch/goddess—vilified in *The Little Mermaid* as Ariel's subversive antagonist—the issues of reproductive freedom and commitment to the earth as a fertile environment merge. She can also serve as a reminder that provides an antidote to what Orenstein calls a "culturally induced amnesia"[10] and focuses issues of appropriative power that have in some ways relegated women and the environment to similar status.

The chief claim of eco-feminists, in this regard, is that ecology is a feminist concern because of a thirty-thousand-year-old tradition that associates fertility with the feminine. Whether this is an essential or historical connection is not important, because as Annette Kolodny's groundbreaking study, *The Lay of the Land*, demonstrated, the tendency of American settlers to regard the land as female opened it to appropriation, pillaging, rape.[11] The point, therefore, is not whether the goddess provides a "natural" bond between women and fertile land but whether the association of the land with the feminine has opened both to the same form of subordination, appropriation, and exploitation.

The two clearest ways in which these issues are manifest in President Reagan's America are in Reaganism's deregulation of environmental protections and its attempted regulation of women's reproductive freedom. Both of these policies participate in narratives that privilege those who appropriate over those who produce. Perhaps the most vivid example of this appropriational attitude can be found in the policies and pronouncements of Reagan's appointee, James Watt. A born-again Christian, Watt grounded his environmental policy in Christian theology, explaining that as secretary of the interior he would be guided by the Scriptures, "which call upon us to occupy the land until Jesus returns."[12] By "occupy the land," of course, Watt meant sell it off for private development. A person who divided the country into two types of people, "liberals and Americans," he saw his appointment as being called to a mission by God —Reagan's "'crusade for America'—in which he must 'emotionally, spiritually and intellectually . . . withstand the onslaught' of liberals."[13] Watt, antagonistic to even the most respected and mainstream environmental groups, such as the Audubon Society and the National Wildlife Federation, acted with what Cannon called "imperious disregard for federal law" in his efforts to convert public lands to private use and to expedite the exploitation of natural resources. "The best thing that can be said about Watt's hostility to the environment," in Cannon's judgment, "is that he never disguised it. 'We will mine more, drill more, cut more timber,' he said, and he meant it."[14] And Watt, Cannon further points out, "was doing what Reagan wanted done."[15]

At the same time, the administration was paying another debt to the Religious Right by attempting to overturn the Supreme Court decision *Roe v. Wade*, which asserted the constitutional right of a woman to an abortion. Although Reagan announced support for a constitutional amendment outlawing abortion, the issue was pursued chiefly through two other avenues, Supreme Court appointments and the Justice Department.

Left out of the Supreme Court rulings, however, Ellen Willis argues, are the implications of forcing a woman to bear a child, which would be the consequence of outlawing abortions, despite the claim that "pregnancy doesn't happen by itself," which, as Willis explains, implies ultimately that sex should be restricted to procreation. It amounts to saying that

> if women want to lead heterosexual lives they must give up any claim to self-determination, and that they have no right to sexual pleasure without fear.
>
> Opposition to abortion, then, means accepting that women must suffer sexual disempowerment and a radical loss of autonomy relative to men: if fetal life is sacred, the self-denial basic to women's oppression is also basic to the moral order. Opposing abortion means embracing a conservative sexual morality, one that subordinates pleasure to reproduction. . . . Opposing abortion means tolerating the inevitable double standard by which men may accept or reject restriction in accordance with their beliefs, while women must bow to them out of fear—or defy them at great risk.[16]

Willis is foregrounding the control of a woman's body that has been taken for granted by many on both sides of the abortion debate. Even the majority opinion in *Roe v. Wade* takes for granted the woman as environmental site for "viable" fetuses, and much of the abortion argument has been waged between "life" and "viable life." The woman's body, like the public land in James Watt's view, lay at the tacit disposal of a fundamentalist religious agenda, derived from the religions, moreover, that originally supplanted matristic beliefs in the privileges of the female body.

Ursula is thus the trace of female self-empowerment, suppressed beneath the surface for thirty to fifty centuries, now resurfacing, but in this narrative of President Reagan's America as an evil that must be destroyed, so that Ariel can cooperate in the pillaging of the environment from which she was born and of which she was an integral part. The destruction of the sea witch/goddess is not just the co-optation of Ariel but the reassertion of cultural amnesia. It symbolizes the forgetting of one's natural origins—the earth and/as womb—for a form of class distinction that subordinates the welfare of all other species to human needs and desires. The same process is replicated in *Working Girl* and *Pretty Woman* as a forgetting of social instead of natural origins. Like Ariel, in acquiring the aerial view of society from the skyscraper executive office or the penthouse suite, these pretty women get more by forgetting the place from which they have risen, substituting economy for ecology.

In this economy, however, what ultimately trickles down is not wealth but ill will disguised as good will in the form of a promise that regardless of your class you can identify with someone who has learned to be not-like-you. The rite of passage from under the sea to the New Jerusalem or to the Beverly Hills penthouse, then, is not a coming of age or a getting of wisdom; it does not entail putting one's dreams into perspective or acquiring a sense of human limits. The rite of passage is the valorization of self-hatred that turns the naturalist narrative—itself, as June Howard has shown, an issue of class[17]—up one notch by defining success not as the transcending of one's environment but as the destruction of it, with the ultimate environment being the womb, and the image of earth as womb linked to the matristic powers of the mythic goddess who must be destroyed to preserve the patriarchal hierarchy upon which success depends in these narratives.

What I am suggesting finally, then, is that the cultural narrative in which these three films participate connects the pervasive classism of the Reaganomical myth of success to Reaganism's exploitation of the environment on the one hand and Reaganism's control of the womb on the other. Read in juxtaposition, the films suggest that these are not separate, disparate traits of President Reagan's America but rather integral parts of a coherent patriarchal narrative— underscoring the debt of the Reagan presidency to the Religious Right—that valorizes dominance, acquisition, exploitation and, ultimately, self-destruction.

Four

"I'm Not Really Bad. I'm Just Drawn That Way": The Compulsive-Attraction Film

Alex Barnes (Debra Winger) in *Black Widow* has much in common with the working girl Tess McGill. Like Tess, she is stuck in an office job too limiting for her ambitions. Working as a statistical analyst in the criminal division of the federal government, she longs to get qualified for field assignments. "I've been in this office for six years, this goddamn government office with green windows!" she screams to her boss about a crowded workplace with bland decor and a lack of private space. Although Alex has a more sophisticated (and no doubt higher-paying) job than Tess, she is still lost in a sea of crammed desks, in an office that resembles the secretarial pool of *Working Girl*. Her way out, as she sees it, is to pore over statistical information to find connections that reveal hidden narratives, acts of organized crime. With the aid of computers, information banks, highly honed research skills, and a compulsive personality, she replicates at a more sophisticated level Tess's practice of constructing narratives about corporate mergers by clipping newspaper and magazine items.

Doing this work, Alex uncovers the mirror opposite of a potential merger that will save a rich patriarch—a pattern of "mergers" that lead to the murder of the rich patriarchal figure. Theresa Russell[1] is systematically marrying wealthy older men, killing them in ways that make the deaths look natural, liquidating the estates, and then disappearing. Because the film starts by following Russell's actions (as she returns to New York for the funeral of a husband), we know before we have even met Alex that Russell is a murderer, and the crosscutting between Russell's actions and Alex's create a set of parallels and differences long before they meet. After they meet, the parallels are accentuated, as they form a quasi-sexual relationship in which men, money, and each other's real identities are the signs that circulate in the economy of their relationship.[2]

Like Alex, Russell is obsessive and compulsive about her work. She is a bright, careful researcher and a good student, who prepares extensively and thoroughly for her next victim. Like Russell, Alex has less-than-perfect relationships with men. She has not gone on a date in six years, and although she has many male cohorts with whom she has a good working relationship, she finds herself standoffish and uncomfortable when any of these men tries to become more intimate. Russell, surprisingly, is also somewhat standoffish with men, parceling her sexual favors frugally, as leverage for marriage proposals. Neither, in any case, is capable of forming a sustained heterosexual relationship.

In some ways, moreover, Russell represents a fulfillment of Alex's desires. Whereas Alex complains about the confinement in her life, Russell demonstrates the ability to uproot herself completely, changing not only her venue but her identity, tastes, style, retaining only her compulsive pursuit of her prey as the central thread—the informing narrative—of her life. The compulsive pursuit of her prey drives Alex so strongly that rather than subordinating it to her job, she quits her job so that she may pursue Russell. Her focus on Russell, in other words, enables her to emulate Russell's lifestyle. In pursuit of Russell, she liquidates all her assets, moves to the city where the object of her obsession lives, and changes her name, even burning the identification tags on her luggage.

Nor is this symmetry wholly accidental. As she says to her boss, "You want to catch her you got to think like she does." Underscoring the parallels, her boss responds: "All I know is she's obsessed with killing and you're obsessed with her. What worries me is that you may be as wacky as she is." This discussion strongly resembles the one between Tess and Cyn, about the efficacy of Tess's charade, especially in light of the fact that Tess, too, has abandoned her identity, her home, her lifestyle, and, in a manner of speaking, her job in order to pursue a dream of advancement, facilitated by a narrative she has constructed out of the unlikely confluence of details in her research. Especially important, however, is the way in which lifestyle is foregrounded, such that in some ways Theresa Russell is to Alex what Katherine Parker is to Tess—the person whose life she wants to absorb, the embodiment of the lifestyle she wants to acquire.

The crosscutting of scenes involving Russell with those involving Alex make this graphic. We first see Russell on an airplane, from which she goes to a limousine. The sequence ends with her return as a new widow to the very spacious, rich, and tasteful apartment she shared with her husband, where she disposes of the poisoned brandy that caused his fatal heart attack. Her clothing, like the interior she inhabits, has all the elegance Alex lacks. If Tess was too garish, Alex is too frumpy. Always carrying more than she can hold comfortably, her slightly hunched posture vaguely suggests a rushed and bundled refugee. Like her clothing or her office, her desk and her apartment do not provide as much space as she seems to need.

In contrast, Russell's interiors display *inordinate* space. More even than the proliferation of valuables, the vastness of the rooms typifies Russell's worlds. Regardless of the style, all the homes of her husbands were equally spacious, and the difference between Alex's lifestyle and Russell's is signified visually by the way they inhabit space. If the crosscutting implies parallel obsessive personalities, the mise-en-scène indicates that the subjects differ in class, not in kind. Like the framing in *Trading Places*, the mise-en-scène here becomes a class signifier, one that constructs class cinematically. Mise-en-scène is a basic element of cinematic representation, of which framing is a part. In addition to the visual boundaries of the gaze, mise-en-scène determines how the cinematic space is filled. Costumes, sets, lighting, actors—their motions, expressions, auras—provide valuable information, independent of the plot.

The mise-en-scène in this film constructs a world—an alternative universe, a lifestyles-of-the-rich-and-famous place—identified with Russell, prohibited to Alex (and most of the audience, that is, most Americans). To acquire Russell's life, in the code of the film, is to enter her mise-en-scène. Thus the last scene of Alex in her old environment is set in her virtually barren apartment, where she anticipates a change in scene through the alteration of the mise-en-scène. Her final promise to her boss underscores the change by saying that she'll return with a tan, that is, with a new look signifying the leisure class, not the working class.

The reference to the tan is particularly resonant in this regard, moreover, because of an earlier interchange Alex had with Etta (Diane Ladd), the sister of one of Russell's victims. Etta had accepted a large settlement in exchange for not contesting the will, despite her suspicions about Russell. She acknowledged to Alex that the possibility of Russell's foul play had crossed her mind, in an interview that took place while Etta was lying under a tanning lamp. When Alex bluntly attributes her refusal to pursue the suspicions to the payoff she received, Etta ends the interview by saying, "Can I buy you a tan?" Linking her tan to her buying power, Etta makes Alex's pallid face a class signifier, as complexion always is in film.

Alex believes, like the working girl or the pretty woman, that she can change her life if she can insert herself into the proper setting. This helps explain why Alex's pursuit of Russell also becomes a friendship. They become partners in a scuba diving class, practice mouth-to-mouth resuscitation, and go out for drinks. Russell loans Alex a dress so that they can go to a party together. Alex, in other words, is not only investigating Russell but also becoming her. As Russell's boyfriend says when he meets Alex, "I know the dress, but who is the woman?"

In the same way that Russell claims to love her prey, Alex clearly has affection for Russell and, equally, for the world Russell inhabits. At Russell's encouragement, Alex even sleeps with Russell's boyfriend (i.e., her latest prey), before Russell reclaims and marries him. Indicating that she knows who Russell is, Alex gives her a black-widow-spider brooch as a wedding gift. To this Russell responds, "Black widow—she mates and she kills. The question is, does she love? It's impossible to answer that—unless you live in her world." She follows this with an intense kiss on Alex's lips.

The film thus acknowledges not only the love/hate relationship between Russell and Alex that replicates the relationship between Russell and her victims, but also the way in which they are framed by a specific setting. Alex knows what Russell is because she has been trying to live in her world. Russell has lured her further into that world, moreover, because she is planning to frame Alex for the next murder. That framing will, temporarily, place Alex behind bars and drape her in a prison smock, that is, remove her from Russell's setting and place her in its antithesis. In a final jail visit, the tables are turned on Russell, and the role reversal becomes complete when Russell is arrested and forced to enter the world that Alex is currently occupying.

This contest between two compulsive personalities typifies obsessive-compulsive films of the late 1980s. This period produced an extraordinary number of films—only some of which I discuss here—that, although ostensibly representing myriad traditional genres, tend when examined together to suggest, like the death-rehearsal films, a common cultural narrative, one based on compulsive attraction; they depend not only thematically but structurally on obsessive-compulsive behavior.

Barfly, for example, was about alcoholism, and *Clean and Sober* about drug and alcohol addiction. In *Fatal Attraction, Siesta, 9 ½ Weeks*, and, in part, *No Way Out*, sexual addiction replaced substance abuse. The latter film also focused on addiction to power and to revenge, as did *The Untouchables, Mississippi Burning*, and *Batman*. In *Wall Street* a business tycoon illegally manipulated the marketplace with a compulsiveness that transcended any financial motivation, just as in *Black Widow* Russell continued compulsively to marry and murder wealthy men, long after she had amassed great affluence, and the equally compulsive Alex became obsessed with her murders. *Gorillas in the Mist, Broadcast News*, and *House of Games* all focused on compulsive professional women; the woman in *House of Games*, in fact, was a psychologist who had written a best-selling book, entitled *Driven*, on managing obsessions. Even the "toons" in *Who Framed Roger Rabbit* were characterized by their compulsive personalities. As Jessica Rabbit says, punning on the word "drawn" to merge her marked desire with her unalterable design, "I'm not really bad. I'm just drawn that way."

These films redefine the concept of dramatic motive. No longer need events cause action; rather, compulsive behavior generates an array of acts greatly in excess of their motivation. This pattern sharply revises Aristotelian poetics, which demands that action have appropriate motive. Hamlet, as author and director of the revenge tragedy in which he is to act the leading role, ponders exactly this problem when he asks what the player would do, "had he the cue and motive for passion that I have." The question of cue and motive is disdained by the alcoholic poet in *Barfly* whose life is framed, as is the film, by a random series of pointedly pointless fistfights, most of which he loses. If, for Aristotle, character is Fate, in *Barfly* character is also plot, and the film is thus a pure character study, the study of the character of a "poet" whose poetics dictates that his life be indistinguishable from his essentialist view of himself. The narrative poetics of the film thus manifests the lyrical poetics of its central character by suggesting that the character's indifference to circumstances signifies his ability to transcend them.

Although this quality certainly has its antecedents, in film noir, for example, or in the compulsive behavior of social deviants such as gangsters, in the late 1980s compulsive behavior functions often unhinged from any ethical mandates or value judgments, any of the elements, that is, that necessarily portend tragedy. As a donee, they function outside any dramatic or moral connection to outcomes. If this structure obviates specific dramatic responsibilities in a film, it also obviates the moral responsibilities of the film's characters. Not answerable to their conscience, social protocol, or legal code, they are simply driven.

Their unregulated behaviors thus become parables of deregulation that mirrored far too closely the activities in the Reagan administration and in the commercial and industrial world it was charged with governing. Haynes Johnson identifies two principal areas of ethical misconduct that typified the Reagan years: ideology and deregulation run amok, and large-scale corruption.[3] Kickbacks, "consulting fees," use of agency employees for personal work, and the billing of the government for personal expenses typified practices in numerous agencies, including the Environmental Protection Agency, the Federal Aviation Administration, the Department of Agriculture, the Department of Health and Human Services, the Federal Home Loan Bank, the Veterans Administration, the Legal Services Corporation, the Federal Emergency Management Agency, the U.S. Commission on Civil Rights, the Transportation Department, the Occupational Safety and Health Administration, the Consumer Product Safety Commission, the Economic Development Administration, the Social Security Agency, the Bureau of Land Management, the Postal Service, and the Pentagon. "At their heart," Johnson explains,

> were insensitivity to appearances of conflicts of interest and desire to take advantage of the very federal offices and programs that the officials said they sought to diminish. "If they're going to shower all this money around, we're going to get some of it," Reagan's former Secretary of Agriculture John Block told the *Wall Street Journal* when questioned about why he had applied for federal aid for his own farm in Illinois. As secretary Block had been a strong advocate of slashing farm subsidies.[4]

This is one example of many in President Reagan's America where deregulation meant not only changing rules but abandoning principles. As exemplified by Block, often those who abused the system and those who objected to the abuses became one and the same. The invisible lines that differentiated the legitimate from the illegal, the ethical from the questionable, public service from personal gain, were repeatedly crossed with the ease and alacrity of walking onto a movie set. Members of the administration, such as Meese, Deaver, and Nofziger, placed themselves apart from the public interest; because they had won, they were entitled to the spoils. In cinematic terms, they had reframed the scene, such that holding public office was not the reward for victory but rather personal profit—emanating from the very "mismanagement and waste" they were elected to eliminate—was the reward for holding high public office. Like any actor who doesn't deviate from his script, Reagan was silent in the unscripted area of professional ethics or standards of conduct. "The standard that he set and that was followed by many whom he appointed to serve him," Johnson points out, "was not to police or regulate the system; rather it was to disband and deregulate it. The idea was to let private market forces work in the public sector. They did."[5]

The scene as conceived by the makers of President Reagan's America was one in which government was a marketplace and they were free traders. Influence thus acquired the status of a commodity, a status validated by those in the administration's trading places. In this regard, *Black Widow* is the dark side of *Trading Places*. Like Valentine, Alex manages to understand the affluent world all too well, because she has already adopted the characteristics of that world. If in Valentine's case they are the values of a hustler, in Alex's they are the compulsion to win. Having the right traits, all Valentine and Alex need are the opportunity to trade places with the people like them.

Which is all Reagan and his administration needed, as well. Entering the scene of the White House, they could cross the ethical line, because in this narrative of President Reagan's America, winning vindicates all other actions. This motif appears widely in the compulsive-attraction films. In *Wall Street*, the characters repeatedly cross the line between using legitimate information and getting illegal information, from tactics like passing on insider information to those of gathering it from spying or breaking and entering. In *Gorillas in the Mist*, when Dian Fossey (Sigourney Weaver) tortures a gorilla poacher by allowing him to think he is going to be hanged from a tree, to the point of even kicking a chair out from under him before she lets the rope fall free, her assistants point out that she has crossed an unacceptable line. *Clean and Sober* starts with a testimonial in which a recovering addict talks about the minute when he, like all addicts, crossed a line into the world of unregulated behavior: "You always remember the time you knew . . . your life is no longer manageable," which describes as well the situation of the sexual addiction in *9 ½ Weeks*, when Elizabeth (Kim Basinger) says to John (Mickey Rourke), "You knew it would be over if one of us said stop; you wouldn't say it, and I almost waited too long." Jane Craig (Holly Hunter) in *Broadcast News*, discovering that TV journalist Tom Grunig (William Hurt) had fabricated his teary-eyed response to an interview with a victim of date rape, breaks off her personal relationship with him. "You totally crossed the line," she says. And in *Mississippi Burning*, FBI Agent Ward (Willem Dafoe) makes a pledge to Agent Anderson (Gene Hackman) to "nail [the people who have killed the civil rights workers] any way we can." He agrees to do it Anderson's way, "whatever it takes" (which means extralegally). In *The Untouchables*, Elliot Ness (Kevin Costner), having participated in a similar pact with Malone (Sean Connery), says, "I have foresworn myself. I have broken every law I swore to defend. I have become what I beheld, and I am content that I have done right." In becoming what he *beheld*, Ness is articulating the act of spectral identification on which cinematic reality depends. Having seen, he is capable of being put in the scene (literally, mise-en-scène). For him, to become what he beholds is made synonymous with crossing the line of ethics and law by participating in the construction of a subjectivity consistent with the cinematic gaze.

As an obsessive student and imitator of Hitchcock, *Untouchables* director Brian de Palma would no doubt be keenly aware of the implications of framing and the power of film to manipulate the audience through control of what it sees. De Palma, perhaps even more than Hitchcock, knows that films not only construct a point of view but also form a frame of reference derived from other films. He makes this point through repeated references to Hitchcock films. At the beginning of *The Untouchables*, for example, a little girl is blown up, not knowing there is a bomb in the briefcase, as she attempts to return it to someone who left it in her father's store. This horrible scene derives not from the records of mob activities in Chicago during prohibition but from the horrifying scene in Hitchcock's *Sabotage* that takes place on a bus. The final scene in which Ness has captured one of Capone's men on the roof of the courthouse similarly echoes scenes from *Vertigo* and *Saboteur* rather than any historical event. And in perhaps the most self-conscious allusion, a shoot-out at the Chicago train station contains an extended—almost comic—re-creation of Eisenstein's famous baby-carriage-on-the-steps montage sequence.

The point I am making here is that the self-consciousness with which de Palma constructs his version of "history" differs little from the way Reagan's handlers used media to the same ends. The relationship between Reaganomics and economics was purely stipulative, a media convention, supported not by facts about the economy but by election results. By convention, if Reagan won, then he must be right. And when, as the nation's highest elected official, he says that government *is* the problem, he is creating a media space exactly like the one occupied by de Palma's Elliot Ness when he constructs his role as its own antithesis. When Ness first agrees to this route, Malone asks him if he knows what a blood oath is. Ness says yes, and Malone responds, "Good, because you've just taken one." The blood oath to win at all costs, to become what he has beheld, translates in President Reagan's America into the oath of office. In taking that oath and thus assuming the role of president, Reagan has indeed become what he has beheld, that is, the lead in a movie loosely based on America. In this film, like de Palma's Elliot Ness, or Alan Parker's Agent Ward, he can swear to uphold the Constitution while also maintaining that government is the problem.

The equation between winning and legitimacy makes the games model a paradigm of which compulsive-attraction films are symptoms by substituting the structure of games for the structure of stories, in that the players are, theoretically, equal and interchangeable. Each act responds to the immediate situation, with the only objective being to win. Since a game has no justification beyond its own arbitrary existence as the source of equally arbitrary roles, efficacy is the only ethic, and anyone who invokes other restraints, either internal or external, is simply a bad player. The films further emulate professional sports by suggesting that the rules of play include not only the official rules but also any and all possible violations that escape detection. The problem for the "Black Widow," for example, is not her run of successfully executed marriage/murders but rather her inability to stop in the face of scrutiny.

We can see clearly the traits of these films and understand, as well, their role as a cultural product of Ronald Reagan's America if we examine closely *House of Games* and compare it with *The Sting*, which is a product of the Watergate era. In the latter, the scam is worked as a form of revenge against the mobster, legitimized as a successful businessman connected with all the bankers. The benign con men pit their cleverness against the brute force of organized crime. At all times they are more threatened than they are threatening. They are also altruistic, working as much for the pleasure of righting an injustice as for that of making money, and their respect for each other offsets their cynicism about legitimate authority. They are artists—in fact, thinly disguised filmmakers—who use their craft subversively to correct social injustice when the legitimate authorities have failed to function. In seeing their production through, from initial financing, to script approval, casting, costuming, set design, rehearsal, and shooting, they present a narrative of filmmaking as a socially responsible act in a world of privilege and inequality.

In many ways, then, we can see this as a Watergate era film, marking the failure of the Establishment. The filmmakers have created con men as surrogates who create a narrative that provides justice and closure. They succeed, in other words, by constructing a coherent narrative in exactly the way that Richard Nixon, all the president's men, all the newspapers, media, congressional hearings, and Gerald Ford failed to.

In *House of Games*, on the other hand, the game is not motivated by the desire for justice or the need for revenge. The target, Margaret Ford (Lindsay Crouse), is picked because of her psychological attraction to the game. An addictive personality obsessed with winning, Margaret is in many ways interchangeable with those conning her, and she is drawn to the competitive male world of gambling and conning out of a compulsive desire to play and to win. Unlike the men, however, she lacks the capacity to lose. Her obsession with control—which explains her fascination with rigged games rather than gambles—drives her to force the outcome she desires and allows her to commit murder. It is important to note, therefore, that whereas revenge is the motive for *The Sting*, it is the result of the con game in *House of Games*. The motivation on both sides in *House of Games* is purely personal and appeals to no external value system.

Nor is it possible, as it is in *The Sting*, to tell the good side from the bad. We have entered a world where efficacy is the only ethic and, as it turns out, all the players are bad players, even if the woman is the most dangerous bad player, the most out-of-control player. As such, moreover, Margaret is also the biggest con artist in that she has acquired wealth by writing a book that cons people into believing she knows how to control obsession. Her adventure with con men only leads her and us to discover what she was at the outset. The plot is, therefore—albeit more subtly so—like the plot of *Batman*, because it forms a tableau for her compulsion, one that continues to reduce possibilities until she can confront her enemy and rival so as to acknowledge their symbiotic relationship.

In this regard, the movie differs significantly from *The Sting* in that it has no subplots or red herrings. Whereas *The Sting* has a number of different plot lines working simultaneously in ways that may interfere with one another and thus create an array of possible endings, *House of Games* treats alternative possibilities as though they are irrelevant. And in compulsive-attraction films they are, for in these films action is not motivational but compulsive. The characters in *House of Games*, moreover, are not surrogate filmmakers but surrogate actors, working out improvisational scenes based on a few character details, a briefly sketched situation, and a cue. These exercises in characterization function independently of one another, connected only by the deftness with which they are performed, only by the actor's desire to act convincingly. The extent to which this one desire constitutes the life of the characters is underscored when Mike is called on to play the role of a man begging for his life. When he cannot improvise that role effectively, he loses the game and his life.

Since professional sports still remain largely a male bastion, furthermore, we can see the ways in which the large number of compulsive women presented by this genre suggests the threat of female competitiveness without the sports arena to channel it. The films, in other words, can be seen as reflecting anxiety in the political unconscious of President Reagan's America about the increasing entrance of women into male domains. *Barfly*, *Siesta*, *No Way Out*, *Clean and Sober*, *Gorillas in the Mist*, *Broadcast News*, *Black Widow*, *Fatal Attraction*, and *House of Games* all present women—for the most part successful career women, accomplished professionals—out of control. In general suffering for their compulsions far more greatly than do the men, none of these women achieve their goals, and in five of the nine films they die. In one of the other films, a women is arrested for her murders and

_____ *Figure 26*_____
In the final confrontation in *House of Games*, Mike is called upon to play the role of a man begging for his life.

in another the woman becomes a murderess. Only the already marginal, pathetically alcoholic barfly is allowed to maintain the status quo in her life.

Even as a child in 1968, Jane, the hero of *Broadcast News*, is portrayed as being compulsive. When her father, telling her to go to sleep, interrupts her writing by telling her, "I don't want you getting obsessed about these things," she compulsively lectures him in order to prove that she is not obsessed: "Obsession is practically a psychiatric term concerning people who don't have anything else but the object of their own obsession, who can't stop and do anything else." Since she *is* interrupting her activities to correct her father, she feels that she has proved she is not obsessed, rather than that, as is evident, she has demonstrated her compulsive personality. This compulsion that renders her incapable of letting any detail slide makes her a top-flight television news producer in the Washington bureau of a major network. It also makes her miserable. As she says, early in the film, "I have passed some line someplace—I'm beginning to repel people I'm trying to seduce." She punctuates her depression with moments of controlled hysterical sobbing; periodically throughout the film, she methodically unplugs her telephone, cries, replugs, and returns to work.

A creation of James L. Brooks, one of the producers of *The Mary Tyler Moore Show*, Jane is the dark side of Mary Richards, the compulsively pleasing associate producer of the nightly news on a local Minneapolis station. Whereas Mary was compulsive about her interpersonal relationships, always afraid of criticizing or offending, Jane is compulsive about her job, no matter whom she may offend or alienate. In the midst of a disagreement with the station manager, he says to her, "It must be nice to always believe you know better; to always think you're the smartest person in the room." "No— it's awful," she replies. Indeed, for Jane has crossed the line of good social behavior; for her, professional success is completely divorced from, is in fact paid for with, personal success and self-satisfaction.[6]

At stake in *Broadcast News* is the production of a contained screen, a visual image of reality, disseminated as "news," that poses the ethical problem of being a news producer without producing news. The question is what to put in the scene. While Jane has strict guidelines—adhered to compulsively— the network rewards those who blur the lines in several ways, those who stage events, manipulate the people whom they are covering, or allow the reporter to become the story. This last form of indiscretion relies on an imaginary line between the reporter and the event: To what extent is the reporter part of the mise-en-scène, and to the extent that he or she is—that he or she shares the frame with the news—to what extent does this turn the reporter into an actor? Because Jane is attracted to Tom (William Hurt), an anchor man who allows himself to focus the news, who is willing to act before the camera, these questions have personal implications. If Tom can act the role of Tom in reporting the news, then does he stop acting that role when interacting with Jane? If he can enter the frame of the news genre, then does a script of the romance genre frame his love interests?

The myth of news coverage, after all, is that it provides a window on events, not a mise-en-scène, but at the same time without the conventions of mise-en-scène, news coverage becomes incomprehensible, something Jane herself understands when she has a feature on a returning veteran dissolve into a Norman Rockwell picture that frames the homecoming event very differently and thus frames the news feature with the appropriate contrast and irony. Although this is not, by Jane's high ethical standards, crossing the line, it nevertheless validates the conventions that make that cross possible. These are the conventions, as we have already seen, that sustained the Reagan presidency. As Leslie Stahl learned from Richard Darmon, "the picture always overrides what you say."

Thus Jane's compulsive border maintenance becomes a personal judgment, a basis for personal decisions and personal relationships, rather than a professional victory. Her professional success—keeping her job during a budget crisis, receiving a promotion—has nothing to do with either personal success on the one hand or professional ethics on the other. No doubt there were members of the Reagan administration who did not abuse their offices for personal gain, misuse their agencies to benefit vested interests, or simply in the name of deregulation abandon their legal charge and the mandates of their posts. (Secretary of Education Terrel Bell was one such person.)[7] But these instances of personal ethics did not affect the nature of the Reagan presidency or of President Reagan's America. Like broadcast news, President Reagan's America demonstrated the power of mise-en-scène over the ethics of it. The compulsive personality, grafted here to the image of the ambitious woman, becomes an aberration, one who has a small effect on video reportage at a very high personal price.

Gorillas in the Mist represents the ecology movement in much the same way that *Broadcast News* represents television news coverage. Again a compulsive woman, Dian Fossey (Sigourney Weaver), attempts to establish borders between ethical treatment and unethical treatment of the gorilla population. Her compulsiveness is established very early, when she relentlessly pursues Dr. Leakey to get an assignment. Hearing that a previous field worker nearly died because of appendicitis, she even arranges to have her own, healthy appendix removed prior to her trip. Although she is sent to count the gorillas, she extends the limits of assignment by actually interacting with the population and then organizing a small armed force to patrol the area and protect the gorillas from poachers. At one point she is called "the only woman in the world with her own private army."

During her years in Africa, Fossey, with the help of *National Geographic* magazine, does call attention to the possible extinction of the gorillas and with the help of local officials does decrease the poaching. But if she is somewhat more successful at stabilizing the gorilla population than Jane is at stabilizing the integrity of newscasts, Fossey pays a much higher price. Refusing to leave what she eventually calls "my mountain," she breaks her engagement to her fiancé and eventually destroys her romantic relationship with photographer Bob Campbell. Her obsession with protecting the gorillas makes her a thorn in the side of the local officials and also alienates her from student interns. Eventually she is murdered in her bed, in an unsolved crime. The inference, of course, is that the murder was committed by one of the many groups—poachers, the tribes they hire, the zoo collectors, or the government officials who do business with them—Fossey alienated with her threats and assaults. The film thus becomes simultaneously a tribute to her results and a cautionary tale about her methods. Even when her objectives are uniquely laudable, the film suggests, the obsessive-compulsive woman is a danger to others and, ultimately, to herself.

The natives, moreover, think she is a witch, a role she assumes with alacrity and supports with her actions, such as making witch designs on trees and wearing Halloween masks. In *Working Girl*, released the same year, Weaver had played the role of the female villain who, as we have seen, bore

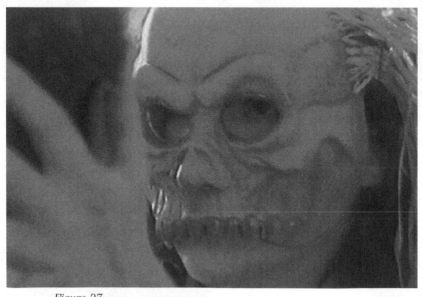

Figure 27

To scare the natives, Dian Fossey uses a Halloween mask to assume the role of witch.

a strong resemblance to Ursula the sea witch of *The Little Mermaid*. At one point in *Working Girl*, moreover, Weaver exits a helicopter holding a huge stuffed gorilla. In a complicated play of intertextual references, she thus helps propagate the image of the unscrupulously ambitious woman as witch. At one point, practicing psychological torture on a captured poacher, she assumes the persona of the witch to play the role of castrating woman. "Tell him," she instructs her native assistant, "he no longer has his courage or his manhood." When even her loyal assistant tells her she has crossed a line, we see that she has indeed entered into the same blood oath as Elliot Ness. But in her case, the ends do not justify the means. Whereas Ness is allowed, after destroying Al Capone, to return to the family life he values, Fossey is buried on the mountain, next to her favorite gorilla, Digit, earlier murdered by poachers while defending his family. As the credits appear, Fossey's native assistant, Sembegare, is making a bridge of stones between her grave and Digit's, indicating a bond in the afterworld of the sort between husband and

_____ *Figure 28*_____

As the closing credits appear, Fossey's assistant, Sembegare, makes a bridge of stones between her grave and Digit's, indicating a bond in the afterworld of the sort between husband and wife.

wife. Thus, Diane Sippi argues, the "transubstantiation of Digit from ape flesh to transcendent African to God-like savior, mystifies Fossey's relation with him as 'Immaculate Miscegenation.'"[8]

This image's Darwinian implications are significant. Fossey was originally inspired to this calling by the anthropologist Richard Leakey, who was responsible for many discoveries important to the understanding of human evolution. The film begins with her attending one of Leakey's lectures in which he explains that gorillas provide clues about the "missing link." Since Fossey made direct contact with the gorillas by her slowly learning to imitate them, we see a woman learning to act like a gorilla, that is, taking a step backward in the evolutionary process at the same time as the gorillas befriending her look as though they are taking a step forward. The stone link between Fossey's grave and Digit's thus frames the site of the missing link, the quest for which initiates Leakey's interests and the film's action. The missing link, by definition, must no longer exist, having been left behind by the evolutionary process that enabled us to get from there to here. In framing her as the missing link, the obsessive-compulsive female—the witch—represents both a necessary stage and one that must ultimately be rejected. The process of natural selection must cast her aside, moreover, not because of her animal characteristics but because of human ones—her use of force, her assertion of authority, her desire for control.[9] Whereas these tactics represent progress for Ness or the FBI agents in *Mississippi Burning*, in Fossey they ultimately represent an unacceptable threat.

In *Clean and Sober*, a Darwinian principle operates along class as well as gender lines. Daryl Poynter (Michael Keaton) is a high-earning commercial real estate salesman with serious cocaine and alcohol problems who wakes up in bed after a one-night stand to discover that the woman beside him has had a cocaine-induced heart attack. With his credit (illegally) overextended by fifty thousand dollars, he seeks refuge in a drug treatment facility where he detoxes, goes through some therapy sessions, goes to an AA meeting, and upon release tries to live a clean and sober life. Only two women figure prominently in the rehab group, Iris (Claudia Christian), who is expelled from the group for returning to drugs, and Charlie (Kathy Baker), a forklift operator in a steel mill who uses drugs with her degenerate live-in boyfriend, Lenny.

Daryl has become friendly with Charlie, and after their release from the center he stays in touch with her until the relationship becomes a love affair

and Charlie leaves Lenny to move in with him. When Charlie decides to return to Lenny and to the drug use that eventually results in her death, her
parting speech marks the decision distinctly in terms of class: "You don't need
me, Daryl. Look around you. Look at all you've got. Your placemats, your . . .
you don't drink out of jelly jars. You want to say something you sit down and
figure out how to say it. You cut your goddamn grass. What the hell do you
need me for?"

Charlie uses the mise-en-scène to describe the difference in their class,
which turns out in the film to be the difference in their fitness for survival.
The props, the decor, the living space thus signify the characters' places on
the evolutionary spectrum. In the new drug-inundated environment, only specific people are capable of survival, and as with any evolutionary process,
there is nothing an individual can do to alter the general course of things.
Daryl, in fact, is chastised by his AA sponsor, Richard, for thinking otherwise.
"You're thinking you could have done something for her, right? It's your fault,
right?" he asks Daryl, and he then tells Daryl that "a guy who thinks he can
control somebody else's addiction needs to know how overblown his thinking is. Could anybody make you stop, Daryl?" The emphasis on class distinctions is all the more stark, moreover, because the film allows Daryl
virtually no insight into his own behavior. In the rehab center, he does not
participate in the group therapy sessions, and his intimate discussions are
markedly unselfreflexive. Not his insight, sensitivity, or character suggests
reasons why he endures. Only his class singles him out.

Even the fact that he is a criminal, having embezzled an escrow account
of eighty thousand dollars, doesn't differentiate him from those fit for survival. In fact, as is generally the case, this kind of unregulated behavior identifies him with the successful rather than the failed. When the executives of
his firm tell him he could go to jail, he stresses the ways in which the rule of
law is irrelevant. "Go to jail?—Hey, we could go to jail—all of us could go to
jail on a lot of stuff. Did you ever get a look at this guy's appraisals?" When
the executive replies that they are not that bad, Daryl spells out in detail the
ways in which the firm's unregulated behavior is synonymous with his, that
is, the ways in which they both replicate the practices of most agencies in
the Reagan administration: "Oh fuck you—Not that bad, man, this guy, this
Vietnam vet, this all-state athlete, he gets 90 percent financing on a three-
hundred-thousand-dollar building that's only worth two, right? Then he takes

the extra cash and he buys an apartment complex, sells it for double, gives the bank their money, and then takes what's left and puts it in a company boat. Get the fuck outta here—a company boat??? How's the fishing Ron, Hank, Bob?" In this speech, Daryl not only points out the interchangeability of the "reputable" and the disreputable, the successful and the criminal, but also in truncated fashion touches on areas that accounted for the biggest waste and fraud under the Reagan administration's deregulation: housing, banking, and taxes. The failure to regulate bank investments, especially in dubious real estate, led to the collapse of numerous savings and loan institutions, while billions of dollars were funneled into the hands of Republican campaign supporters through the offices of the Department of Housing and Urban Development, and the changes in the tax code rewarded the wealthy while tripling the national debt.

The executives decide not to prosecute Daryl for playing fast and loose with the law, but they do fire him. Clearly, his fault was not breaking the law but losing money. As they point out, when asked how the fishing is on the "company boat": "better than the stock market." Winning validates everything, and success delimits the frame. In many of these films, therefore, it is not surprising that the "good" and "bad" characters become mirror images of each other, neither of them governed by external values but rather by internal compulsions to achieve their ends.

These films define success as the product of the compulsion to win at all costs, which is the driving force in *The Untouchables* and *Mississippi Burning*. Nor is it coincidental that the films are both "historical" dramas, based on specific events in American history, which they then distort with the same ruthlessness with which their heroes violate the law, so that the films set historical narrative in competition, both structurally and thematically, with the premise that all events are ahistorical, generated by inexplicable personal compulsions. This converts the past into a site colonized by obsession. It is as if history has become one more enemy to be defeated in the interest of making a point, so that the compulsive obsession of the theme becomes the authority to which the past must submit.

Both *The Untouchables* and *Mississippi Burning* are films about young idealistic law enforcers who, coaxed by veteran subordinates, realize that in order to combat criminals they have to embrace lawlessness. So long as he tries to bust Capone's operation using standard procedures, Ness remains ineffectual. One reason is that he is fighting a world, as the film represents it, not of quotidian crime but of mythic evil. As the text that opens the film announces—as if to locate Chicago of the Prohibition era as outside the space-time continuum—"It is the time of the gang lords. It is the time of Al Capone." We are not in historical America but a place more like the "Old West," the galaxy far far away of *Star Wars'* Evil Empire, or, as we shall see, *Batman's* Gotham City.

In this ruthless place, bombs, hand grenades, machine guns, and shot-guns make murders a feature of daily life. On the scale of violence portrayed in this film, it is hard to imagine that an event so small as the St. Valentine's Day Massacre was even reported in the press. In particular jeopardy in this mythic Chicago are policemen, so much so that Malone as regular procedure answers his door by pointing a sawed-off shotgun at his visitors. The first rule of law enforcement, Malone tells Ness, is: "Make sure when your shift is over you go home alive." Although there was a fair degree of graft in the Chicago police force of the 1920s, there was little physical danger to law enforcement officials from organized crime, and the general level of danger suggested by Malone's advice and everyone else's behavior is absurd.

Mississippi Burning creates a 1964 Mississippi analogous to *The Un-touchables'* Chicago. The disappearance of three civil rights workers is only one of numerous acts of violence perpetrated by the white southern racists in the short time span of the film. Others include beating up a black boy be-cause the FBI agents sat down next to him at a lunch counter, bombing the motel where the agents are staying, bombing blacks' houses, bombing a church, kidnapping a black man off the street and beating him, beating up a cameraman, firebombing a house, firebombing a barn and lynching the black man who owns it, and beating the wife of the deputy police chief for giving information to the FBI. These acts of violence continue to be perpetrated by the "bad guys" in this *very* small Mississippi town, almost on a daily basis, despite the presence in the film of more than a hundred FBI agents, all of whom seem to disappear when the sun goes down, leaving the blacks at the mercy of a dozen or so racists. The unregulated power of the villains depends, in other words, on their villainy having mythic proportions of the sort found in comic books or in *The Untouchables*.

In both cases, however, these mythic/comic-book sites resemble President Reagan's America in that, for both, government is the problem. Following bureau procedure renders the FBI agents thoroughly helpless in Mississippi. They cannot find the missing bodies, protect the blacks from violent retaliation, successfully prosecute the retaliators, or even—in the most ludicrous moment of the film—prevent a riot in the black section of town in which the blacks burn down one another's houses after some whites receive a suspended sentence for terrorizing blacks. The only thing accomplished by following procedure is, as Anderson warns, to start a war.

Malone, *The Untouchables'* counterpart to Anderson, also refers to law enforcement as a war and warns Ness that if he goes through the door on his first raid, he's "walking into a world of trouble and there's no turning back." But Ness has already taken his blood oath:

"Do you really want to get him? What are you prepared to do?"
"Everything within the law."
"And *then* what are you prepared to do? If you open the ball on these people, you must be prepared to go all the way, because they won't give up the fight until one of you is dead. You want to get Capone, here's how you get him. He pulls a knife, you pull a gun. He sends one of yours to the hospital, you send one of his to the morgue. That's the Chicago way, and that's how you get Capone."

Ward takes a similar oath. "We'll go after them together," he promises Anderson:

"You don't know how."
"You're gonna teach me."
"You wouldn't have the guts."
"Not only do I have the guts, I have the authority."
"What is that supposed to mean?"
"New rules—We nail them any way we can, even your way."
    . . .
"We do it *my* way?"
"Your way."
"With *my* people?"
"Whatever it takes!"

Ward is driven to accept "Anderson's way" by circumstances that reveal vividly the narrative's implicit racism, a point made concisely by Sundiata K. Cha-Jua:

After scores of people are beaten and their churches burned, Ward and Anderson are finally driven to rage only when Deputy Pell beats his wife. It seems odd, in a movie which the director alleges is about racism, that the pivotal event dramatizing the movie's main proposition—that "the rule of law needs to be the rule of force"—is the beating of a white woman by her husband. The message conveyed is: it is acceptable to terrorize Afro-Americans (including Afro-American women), but it is not acceptable to assault one white woman.[10]

Anderson's way includes kidnapping the town's mayor and taking him to a secluded shack, where, gagged and tied to a chair, he faces a self-assured northern black man who threatens to cut off his testicles with a razor blade. When they send off the black, flown in and out on a small prop plane for the sole purpose of torturing the mayor, Ward asks Anderson if he works for the FBI, to which Anderson replies, yes, "he's a kind of specialist." It would be hard to imagine the exact title on this specialist's job description: "Image-of-the-Dangerous-Black-Man-Who-Wants-to-Cut-Your-Balls-Off Senior FBI Agent," in the "Psychological and Physical Torture Division"? Or perhaps his title is simply Black Terrorist. One could speculate on the range and frequency of his activities. Clearly there must be enough work to keep this specialist employed full-time, even prior to the late 1960s, when, no doubt, he was one of the infamous FBI agents who penetrated groups like the Black Panthers in order to instigate terrorist activities. This anonymous black man, of course, is not really an FBI specialist, especially since there were only five blacks in FBI employ at that time, and their specialties were the driving of J. Edgar Hoover's car, the cleaning of J. Edgar Hoover's house, and the delivering of J. Edgar Hoover's messages. The anonymous black man in this film is actually the projection of white America's racist anxiety about nonsubservient black men. He is the FBI's counterpart to the Ku Klux Klan, or to Al Capone in *The Untouchables.*

Capone is also represented as a psychopathic terrorist. At one point, during a private dinner gathering of perhaps a dozen of his associates in a very elegant restaurant, Capone, while giving a speech on teamwork, calmly uses a baseball bat to crush the skull of one of the cohorts, while the others, aghast, watch speechlessly. *Batman* presents a similar scene, in which the Joker (Jack Nicholson) hosts a meeting of gang lords. In front of the group,

_____ *Figure 29*_____

The kidnapped mayor of the southern town in *Mississippi Burning* faces a self-assured northern black man who threatens to cut off his testicles with a razor blade.

also seated around a table, using an electrified ring, he literally fries a dissenting underworld boss.

This is just one of the striking similarities between Capone and the Joker. More generally they are both dynamic, grotesque personifications of evil, made all the more prominently so by virtue of their being played by major stars, De Niro and Nicholson, known for excessive characterizations. Clearly more dynamic than their adversaries, their characters emphasize the plot as a game infused with intense personal rivalry. "I want to hurt the man!" Capone screams about Ness at one point, and at another, "You got an all-out price [*sic*] fight, you wait till the fight's over. One guy's left standin' and that's how you know who won." The latter statement is made to a press corps that seems constantly to be following and interviewing Capone. Being a gang lord, in other words, means being a media celebrity. Since little else in the film has any historical accuracy, there is no reason to detail the discrepancies in the portrayal of Capone. More significant is the kind of representation that de

Palma substitutes for the historical Al Capone. This Capone is a genuine celebrity—a cross between Donald Trump and Joe Namath, or perhaps Mike Tyson and Hulk Hogan—who could have his admirers and supporters. He has humor, charisma, a strong following, and, to some degree, an adulating press.

Capone is, in other words, just like the Joker. The Joker, too, is both hero and hoodlum, followed attentively in the press, and intent not only on terrorizing a whole city but also on winning a public relations victory over Batman. As the Joker's rival, Batman also resides outside the law and is suspected of being a villain. Like a presidential election campaign, the battle between Batman and the Joker is over image. Vicki Vale (Kim Basinger) makes this point to Batman:

> "A lot of people think you're as dangerous as the Joker."
> "He's psychotic."
> "Some people say the same thing about you."
> "What people?"
> "Well, I mean let's face it—you're not exactly normal, are you?"
> "It's not a normal world."

More even than in the abnormal worlds of "Chicago" and "Mississippi," in Gotham, mise en-scène determines all. Batman and the Joker both function by inserting themselves in the scene, converting a normal situation into an abnormal one. The Joker creates these scenes in front of City Hall, on the main street, or in the public museum, so that, as "the world's first fully functioning homicidal artist," he can practice mass murder. The issue of framing is thus crucial to the Joker's activity. Rhetorically and visually, he frames his activities as a form of art. In the museum, his spray-painting of the framed paintings reframes the individual canvases, making them motifs in his staged event. Poisoning the news anchor and taking control of television channels, the Joker in effect reframes the whole realm of broadcast news, turning it into an advertisement for himself. He replicates, in other words, the dominant procedure of electoral politics in President Reagan's America, the mastery of which earned Ronald Reagan the title the "great communicator."

Batman thwarts the Joker by putting himself in the scenes the Joker creates. Little else matters in the film, and much of what we might identify as the plot resembles more closely the preliminary matches and verbal bouts in a showdown between two wrestling stars. The costumes, the threats, the insults, the gimmicks seem to come from the World Wrestling Association. In that it accentuates its resemblance to professional wrestling, *Batman* merely makes more visible the simplistic, violent merger of sports and morality drama at work in films like *Mississippi Burning* and *The Untouchables*.

Since in compulsive-attraction films the plot need not provide motive, the plot itself becomes dispensable, replaced structurally by a repetition of thematic tableaux. *Batman* systematically removes characters and situations and, therefore, complications. By the end of the film, Bruce Wayne's rival suitors, like the Joker's rival criminals, are either dead or forgotten. The police and the politicians similarly fail to figure prominently in events so that the premise for the climax is solely the confrontation of irrationally compelled egos who can then confess their chicken-and-egg interrelationship. In their final fight, the Joker tells Batman, "You made me," referring to their early confrontation when Batman threw Jack Napier into a bubbling chemical vat. Batman responds, "You made me first," referring to the fact that Napier had murdered Bruce Wayne's parents in front of him. The Joker then reverses the response one more time by making a joke of this irony: "I said you made me, so you had to say I made you." This confrontation of compulsive personalities—like the confrontation between Alex and Russell in *Black Widow*, between Daryl and his bosses in *Clean and Sober*, Fossey and the poachers in *Gorillas in the Mist*, John and Elizabeth in *9 ½ Weeks*, or Ness and Capone in *The Untouchables*—implies some profound understanding about the relationship between good and evil.

It is, however, significantly superficial in ways that exemplify some prominent narratives of President Reagan's America: that we play roles, that the roles are equal and interchangeable, that the roles are the function of games, rather than values, and therefore that they are defined exclusively by the outcomes. We are thus given a picture of a world in which roles are arbitrary and everyone is out to win, a world in which injustice is a given and not the result of specific prior events, in which the losers become winners by resorting to violence, and in which the only difference between the powerful elite and the marginal underclass is whom they are conning and whether they get caught.

It is the world, in other words, of President Reagan's America, the world that fails to distinguish, as in the case of Attorney General Edwin Meese, unethical behavior from criminal indictment or, as in the case of Oliver North, fails to recognize as criminal crimes confessed under immunity from prosecution. It is the world of "deregulation"—the code name for legalizing violations by removing the rules that could be violated or the inspection process that would determine the violations, or both. It is the world—marked by bank failures, public housing fraud, unsafe airlines, acid rain, global warming, and an eroding ozone layer—in which success sanctions all behavior such that sanctions are unworkable and unsanctioned behavior is limited to that which does not work. It is a world of purely situational ethics—as typified not only by the covert diversion or overt mismanagement of funds or trust but also by the news bite or photo opportunity as the paradigmatic unit of organization. Like the con artists in *House of Games*, public figures delimit discourse within the parameters of improvisational scenes acted out so convincingly that they undermine narrative coherence. The scenes share neither facts nor causes but merely our knowledge that they contain the same actors manifesting the compulsive— and thus compulsively amoral—need to act, to perform, to win.

If the idea that "winning is the only thing" derives from a current sports cliché, we should remember that that cliché has more or less replaced an earlier cliché: "It's not whether you win or lose, but how you play the game." The decline of the latter motto in favor of the former correlates, we should also note, with the growing cognizance in public perception that sports is a business. In business, of course, it does matter whether you win or lose (although, some would contend, *not* how you play the game). The play of frames in these films about gamesmanship and the compulsion to win thus correlates with the reframing of sports as a business further reframed within the more general category of a game—like running for public office—the sole business of which is to win.

Exactly this relationship between business and sports is foregrounded in another compulsive-attraction film, *Wall Street*. In many ways, *Wall Street* glosses several of the compulsive-attraction films and, as well, many other films, by foregrounding the ways in which the compulsive behavior is a form of business ethics in President Reagan's America. The villain of *Wall Street* is Gordon Gecko (Michael Douglas), a business tycoon who articulates the virtues of unregulated behavior: "Greed works! Greed clarifies, cuts through. Greed will save that malfunctioning corporation, the United States." Greed in the film's lexicon makes people want to be "players," that is, involved in the play of investments and the flow of money that creates wealth. Gecko also describes it as a form of mise-en-scène—"If you're not inside, you're outside"—when trying to lure Bud Fox (Charlie Sheen), an equally compulsive neophyte, an outsider who wants to be an insider. In order to get inside, he crosses the ethical line by sharing insider information with Gecko. Bud comes from a working-class background—his father is an airplane mechanic—and his desire to become a player is represented by the mise-en-scène that fetishizes interior space as the commodification of aspirations. The decor of Gecko's home is explicated in terms of its commodity value by Darien (Daryl Hannah), an interior decorator whose personal relationship with Bud is made visually synonymous with her decorating his new high-rise apartment. The apartment in which they live together, financed by Bud's (illegal) work for Gecko, frames Darien's relationship with Bud. When Bud defies Gecko, therefore, Darien leaves.

In many ways, Bud also resembles Tess McGill, whose unethical actions in the area of mergers and acquisitions earn her, as they do Bud, upward mobility. Both films, in fact, use the Statue of Liberty and the water surrounding lower Manhattan as important images to represent the compulsion to escape one's class. We never discover whether Tess learns when to stop, what constitutes enough, but Bud eventually learns when he inadvertently contributes to the possible dismantling of the airline for which his father works and serves as a union leader. In order to right this error, Bud engages in equally illegal insider practices to assist a rival tycoon in ruining Gecko's takeover plans and punishing him financially as well. The strategy is very similar to the one employed in *Trading Places*, wherein the Dukes are defeated by Valentine and Winthorp.

When Bud confronts Gecko by asking the question endemic to all compulsive-attraction films—"How much is enough?"—Gecko's response articulates the ethics of deregulation in President Reagan's America by evoking the connection of money to the sleight of hand that, from the outset, frames *Pretty Woman*: "It's a zero-sum game. Somebody wins; somebody loses. Money itself isn't lost or made, it's simply transferred—one perception to another, like magic."

If money and image are thus synonymous, the blood oath implicitly or explicitly taken in so many of these films is one that crosses the line between matter and image, between the material and the imaginary; it is the oath to conform to popularly deployed images. In *Broadcast News*, Aaron Altman (Albert Brooks) underscores this point by explaining the significance of the interchangeability of good and evil characters, in a speech that describes all too accurately the Reagan Presidency: "[The Devil] will be attractive. He'll be nice and helpful. He'll get a job where he influences a great God-fearing nation. He'll never do an evil thing. He'll never deliberately hurt a living thing. He'll just bit by bit lower our standards where they're important. Just a tiny little bit, just coast along, flash over substance."

Five

Home and Homelessness Alone in John Hughes's America, or Dennis the Menace II Society

As we noted earlier, the *Back to the Future* series makes clear that the Hill Valley marked by graft, corruption, vice, urban blight, drive-by shootings, and black neighbors, shown briefly in *II*, is an aberration from the "correct" space-time continuum. Doc stresses to Marty that their revision of Biff's revisions to their revised history will restore the "real" 1985.

That artificially constructed "real 1985" preserved by the cinematic manipulations of time travel is the site of John Hughes's America. Hughes is one of the most successful filmmakers of the 1980s, having written since 1980 screenplays for more than fifteen films, many of which he also produced and/or directed. As a composite, these films (including *Mr. Mom, Weird Science, Sixteen Candles, The Breakfast Club, Pretty in Pink, Some Kind of Wonderful, National Lampoon's Vacation, National Lampoon's European Vacation, National Lampoon's Christmas Vacation, Home Alone, Home Alone II, Uncle Buck, Planes, Trains, and Automobiles, Dennis the Menace, Curly Sue*, and *Ferris Bueller's Day Off*) outline the parameters, as perhaps no other film opus does, of the world inherited from the ghost patriarchs whom I discussed in Chapter 2, one in which dysfunctional families save themselves through the successful fending off of the invasive strangers who bring the social problems of another time and place to the site of President Reagan's America, which is otherwise fundamentally safe, suburban, and white.

To establish this American scene as the definitive world against which deviations in class and external threats can be measured, Hughes makes extensive use of the cinematic convention of the establishing shot. A shot—usually a long shot—that tells us where we are, the establishing shot is the vital cue to stabilize the continuity disrupted by the manipulation of time and space endemic to filmmaking. Typically the shot of a building, an institution, a town, or a human or natural environment, the establishing shot locates the place and often the time of the action. Without establishing shots, the discontinuity, disorientation, and arbitrariness of cinematic representation—in short everything that Marty and Doc labor to disguise about Hill Valley, in the same way that Reagan's handlers worked at disguising President Reagan's America—would become a little more apparent. In many ways, in other words, the establishing shot is the representation of the Establishment, in that it presents the unchallenged assumptions necessary to allow the scene to unfold. It frames the framing of the subsequent shots by delimiting the imaginary space in which they are situated; it allows the inference of a scene that is the necessary condition for the mise en scène.

Think, for example, of the way in which the evening news establishes its credibility through shots of the White House. A newscaster at 11:00 P.M. reporting on a veto that took place at noon will give his or her report "live," with the White House directly behind, framing the report. That great house establishes the legitimacy of the reportage, despite the temporal disparity between the event and the report. The White House, still there at 11:00 P.M., establishes a *scene* that substitutes for the *seen*; the inanimate White House is the requirement for the "live" shot, not the completely interchangeable reporter, who simply connects the live shot to the now dead event.

Just as the White House does in the evening news, any establishing shot, of course, operates merely by convention. In film, it does not tell us where we are but rather where we are supposed to be. The establishing shot of an office building followed by the shot of the interior of an office tells us that the office is *supposed* to be in the building we have seen, even though, in all likelihood, it is in a completely different space; it may not even be an office at all but rather a set, meant to look like part of an office so long as the shot is framed narrowly enough to hide the absence of a ceiling or a fourth wall. Because the audience is so extensively acclimated to the codes of cinematic representation, these juxtapositions can function safely, so long as nothing

_____ *Figure 30*_____
The privileged sites in John Hughes's films are usually center-door colonials on well-landscaped lots in comfortable, northern, suburban neighborhoods. Andie, in *Pretty in Pink*, admires such a home; . . .

_____ *Figure 31*_____
. . . Ferris Bueller lives in one; . . .

_____Figure 32_____
. . . so does the Griswald family, here adorned with Christmas lights; . . .

_____Figure 33_____
. . . it is the home which Neil Page uses planes, trains, and automobiles to reach; . . .

_____Figure 34_____
. . . and the house that Kevin McCallister defends when he is left home alone.

breaks the frame to reveal the elements of the cinematic apparatus that have created the illusion of a continuous space.

The establishing shot thus frames the difference between realms. It is not surprising, then, that Hughes uses as a virtual signature the establishing shot of a house. In film after film, he returns to shots of an upper-middle-class (in Fussell's sense of that classification) home. It is usually a center-door colonial on a substantial, well-landscaped lot, in a comfortable, northern, suburban neighborhood. Ferris Bueller lives in such a home, as does the family for which Uncle Buck babysits. It is the home of the Baker family in *Sixteen Candles*, and the home to which marketing executive Neil Page keeps trying to return via planes, trains, and automobiles. It is the home of the vacationing Griswald family, and the site of their Christmas vacation. It is the house that Kevin McCallister defends from vandalizing burglars when he is left home alone.

This domestic site is the common denominator connecting Hughes's films to the death-rehearsal films with which this book began and the invidious-stranger films I discuss in the next chapter. Here, too, we have the child at risk and a patriarch who is tantamount to dead. As the teenaged daughter, Tia, says in *Uncle Buck*, "We need boys so that they can grow up, get married and turn into shadows." Hughes's version of this narrative, however, relegates the beneficent black to a superficial role—the good cop—and depends on the child himself to save the home. Although intruders into the neighborhood pose a physical threat, the vulgarity of the lower class and the elitism of the upper are equally problematic. In many ways, like Marty at the beginning of the *Back to the Future* series and all the satiric subjects of Fussell's *Class*, Hughes's characters find their ethos in the angst that separates "middle" from "upper middle" class. No matter how many times Hughes reconfigures the principals and their conflicts, they are all established within the frame of white, suburban America, where virtually all internal conflicts arise from the friction caused by combining traditional Republican types with Reagan Democrat types, in other words by the class frictions *within* the electoral coalition that facilitated President Reagan's America.

National Lampoon's Christmas Vacation provides a virtual topography of this social landscape through vignettes chronicling the attempts of Clark Griswald (Chevy Chase) to celebrate a "traditional" Christmas holiday at his home. Although it is very hard to fix with any clarity the "tradition" that provides this ideal, a number of traits remain clear. The Griswald traditional Christmas requires a natural Christmas tree, much quaint paraphernalia and nonreligious decorations inside the house, and numerous lights and prominent lawn decorations outside. It includes a prolonged family visit and a large Christmas dinner, followed by the reading of "The Night before Christmas." In pre-Christmas socializing, eggnog is the drink of preference, served in glass mugs with antler handles that reveal immediately the exact rung of Fussell's class ladder ("middle" or perhaps "high prole[tarian]") on which the Griswald family has come to rest.

In this regard, class figures far more prominently than does tradition. Like the ethnic background of Clark Griswald, his wife, Ellen (Beverly D'Angelo), and all of their parents, the number of years the traditions span remains obscure. At one point, accidentally trapped in the attic, Clark discovers home movies from his childhood Christmases, which he watches with evident nostalgia. These home movies, set in 1955, implicitly constitute the paradigmatic Christmas Clark struggles to re-create in President Reagan's America. Like the death-rehearsal films, the home movies make the 1950s the route back to the future, so that, as in Dickens's *A Christmas Carol*, Christmas present and future are forever haunted by the ghost of Christmas past, against which everything is normed. Clark thus resembles Marty and Doc in that he can succeed only to the extent that he manages to retain, against all odds, *his* version of the 1950s.

The viewing of the home movies, situated near the middle of the film, thus become an important reminder for both Clark and the audience of the ideal toward which he strives and struggles. Like the model house and town stored in the Maitlands' attic in *Beetlejuice*, these home movies in Clark's attic constitute the anecdotal version of the past upon which the credit for his contemporary excesses relies. As in *Beetlejuice*, moreover, Clark must struggle to preserve his version of reality from assaults by both vulgarians and elitists.

Elitism is represented in this film by the yuppie couple next door, Tod (Nicholas Guest) and Margo (Julia Louis-Dreyfus), who wear, exclusively, expensive designer sportswear. They live their impeccably coiffed lives on lush carpets, surrounded by trendy furnishing and state-of-the-art audio equipment. Given that stains, body odors—or, by implication, mismatched dinnerware and last season's color combinations—are an anathema to them, they evince nothing but contempt for the Griswalds in the same way that *Beetlejuice's* Dietzes reviled small-town Connecticut. Because Tod and Margo are childless and, so far as we can tell, friendless, their expensively furnished house is a personal cul-de-sac organized to indulge their self-centered pleasures and self-serving attitudes. They are out of place in this bedroom-community bastion of the nuclear family. Although they live in the community, their periodic insults and condescensions have, like the Dietzes', a clearly invasive quality that threatens to reject the "family values" that have defined these communities since the end of World War II.

At the vulgar end of the spectrum, we have Clark's sister-in-law, Catherine (Miriam Flynn), and her husband, Eddie (Randy Quaid). These in-laws pay a surprise visit in their claptrap recreation vehicle, which they have traded for their home. Unemployed, virtually penniless, and, for all intents and purposes, homeless, they cannot even give Christmas presents to their waiflike children. The most endearing traits of their large dog—named Snots because of its sinus condition—include rummaging through garbage, chasing things through the house, and masturbating on people's legs. Although

_____ *Figure 35*_____

Tod and Margo, the neighbors in *Christmas Vacation*, live their impeccably coiffed lives on lush carpets, surrounded by trendy furnishings and state-of-the-art audio equipment.

Clark shows (slightly) more tolerance for Eddie than Tod and Margo show for Clark, it is clear that Eddie is as much a threat to the community as are Tod and Margo, just as it is clear that Beetlejuice in exorcising the Dietzes will provide a cure that is worse than the disease.

One sign of the problem with Eddie's family is the drain they make on the already overtaxed household. With both sets of in-laws staying at the house, the Griswald children, Russ and Audrey, are forced to share a bed, and Clark's parents must share children's bunk beds. The breakfast scene is messy and chaotic. Saying he hates to impose, Eddie asks if his children can stay in the house (not for their sake but so that he can be alone with his wife in the RV), and he asks Clark to buy the Christmas gifts for his children. Clark assents despite that fact that his own checking account is overdrawn. Although he makes a very good living in the products development division of a large Chicago firm, he has in anticipation of his annual Christmas bonus placed a down payment of seventy-five hundred dollars on an in-ground swimming pool. A reasonable calculation would thus situate Clark's bonus as somewhere between fifteen and twenty-five thousand dollars, and his ability to spend all of it on the pool indicates that he earns enough without it to meet his normal expenses. The pool is a luxury that the film's plot turns into a necessity because of the debt Clark has accrued to obtain it.

The film, in other words, evokes greater concern over Clark's swimming pool than over Eddie's homelessness. Although Eddie's situation is bleak, his problems are represented as the product of his own stupidity and concomitant crudity, so that, once classified as lower class, Eddie and his problems invade, burden, and threaten the ideal Christmas that Clark had planned. To put it most simply, Eddie's problems make us feel sorry for Clark, who is already beleaguered enough by the fact that he may lose his down payment on the swimming pool.

The bigger problem, therefore, the real Scrooge of this Christmas vacation, is Clark's boss, who economized by substituting an annual membership in the "Jelly of the Month" club for a five-figure bonus. When Clark learns in the midst of the Christmas Eve celebration of this policy change, he goes mildly berserk, and his manic behavior—including the sawing down of a pine tree on his lawn to make a new impromptu Christmas tree—prompts his in-laws to attempt to leave before things get worse. He prevents them, shouting, "Worse? How could anything be worse? Take a look around you. We're on the threshold of Hell!" Pushed to the threshold of Hell by the loss of an in-ground swimming pool, Clark differs from Tod and Margo not in his materialism but in its family orientation. Being oriented toward the model of family life alluded to by his 1950s home movies makes Clark forgivable.

The model of a traditional family Christmas is also suggested by the Victorian Christmas Advent calendar in the form of a model house, each door of which opens to count the days until Christmas. Like everything in the film this house is no doubt ersatz, a replica adapted for contemporary American use. As the Victorians bowdlerized pagan and mid-winter celebrations in their own consumer culture, so the Griswolds mimic Victorian traditions—at everfurther remove from authenticity. This American version substitutes for the period of Advent, the week during which Clark awaits his bonus. Hughes periodically uses close-ups of this house calendar to mark the progress of time, so that the establishing shot of a house is doubly instanti-

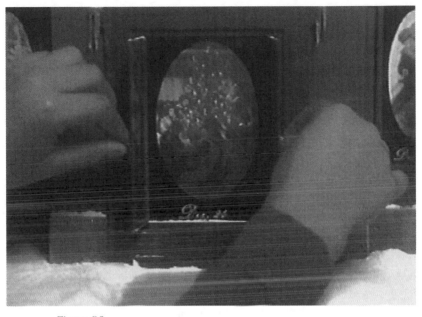

_____ *Figure 36*
The Victorian Christmas Advent calendar, in the form of a model house, each door of
which opens to count the days until Christmas.

ated in the film as the constant against which time and space unfold. The Victorian house thus becomes the model of itself, suggesting a lost ideal in the same way that the home movies do.

But Clark harbors a model that exceeds the home movies. It is a model for which the home movies ostensibly constitute a cogent reminder, but as his father reminds him, the actual holidays that these movies capture were every bit as unbearable as Clark's attempt to replicate them. The Christmas that Clark wants would re-create neither the home movies nor the life those movies document. Nor are the Griswalds connected to a historically or ethnically rooted Christmas, with traditions that have evolved over centuries. Rather, they are connected via the power of (home) movies to an originary site in the 1950s caused, as it is in *Back to the Future*, by a fork in the space-time continuum. That site, I think, is the cinematic space created by film and television. Clark is trying to create the sort of American family Christmas represented in countless 1950s television shows. Those shows—special dramatic and variety shows, episodes of soap operas, sitcoms, even westerns—deployed in an unprecedented manner cinematic versions of American life that created oxymoronically instant traditions, traditions, in other words, of the sort that the Reagan presidency substituted for historical traditions.

The break in the space-time continuum signified by the home movies occurs in the same period in which Marty reinvents the McFlys' history, that is, at roughly the moment when the majority of American households acquired televisions. The home movies thus indicate the cinematic origins of Clark's traditions and also locate those origins at the moment of television's ascendancy. Clark does not want the Christmas that his family filmed but the one that the people in the films saw on television. He wants for the Griswalds, in other words, exactly the same cinematic/televisual reality President Reagan wanted for all Americans, a connection implied by the fact that Clark's senile great-aunt, when asked to say grace over the dinner, recites the Pledge of Allegiance, and at the end, when an explosion sends the lawn ornaments of sled and reindeer rocketing into the sky, starts singing the Star-Spangled Banner. Upholding the traditions based on cinematic representations of Christmas thus becomes a patriotic mandate, for Christmas occupies in Clark's sensibility exactly the same place that America does in Reagan's—as an ideal that we know about only through movies, the viewing of which, especially on television, is the only real American experience, the only experience that makes possible the fortuitous fork in the space-time continuum.

The childlike naïveté that invests itself so completely in crediting the reality of cinematic narratives associates Clark equally with Reagan and with numerous other John Hughes characters. Like the teenagers in *Uncle Buck*, *Sixteen Candles*, *Pretty in Pink*, and *Some Kind of Wonderful*, Clark is in love with an image. In *Sixteen Candles*, sixteen-year-old Samantha Baker (Molly Ringwald) is in "love" with Jake (Michael Schoeffling), an affluent senior with whom she has never had a conversation. Her affection and his reciprocal feelings (of which she remains unaware until the end of the film) are legitimated by establishing shots of Jake's big house, which punctuate the middle of the film, and by the many cars (including a Rolls Royce convertible) that his family owns.

The limitless resources of the house allow Jake, like many of Hughes's characters, to let it be trashed when he is left home alone. Andie (also played by Molly Ringwald), the heroine of *Pretty in Pink*, articulates the fetishizing of great houses that pervades Hughes's world when she ritualistically drives up at night to her favorite wealthy house and says, "I wonder what it's like inside. I bet the people who live there don't think it's half as nice as I do." The problem with the rich, thus, is that they do not share adequately in Hughes's fetishizing of wealth. In *Pretty in Pink*, when Steph (James Spader), a teenager who has the kind of "fuck you" money that Donald Regan bragged about to Reagan, tries to convince his equally affluent friend Blaine (Andrew McCarthy) not to date the middle-class Andie, Blaine accuses Steph of only caring about money, to which Steph responds, "Would I treat my parents' house like this if money was any kind of an issue?" For Hughes, indifference to money is the luxury of the same class that sees it as definitive. For this reason Keith (Eric Stoltz), the middle-class hero of *Some Kind of Wonderful*, spends all the money he saved for college, earned by pumping gas, to buy diamond earrings and rent a limo for his first date with Amanda (Lea Thompson), a popular former girlfriend of the one of the rich boys in his high school. To justify this, he tells his father, "Believe me, there's a good reason behind all this. You've just got to trust me." When his father says that he does but that there are limits, Keith, in effect echoing many indicted savings and loan officers, replies, "How can you put limits on trust?"

Limitless trust is what most of Hughes's teenagers ask, no matter how untrustworthy they prove to be. Like Samantha in *Sixteen Candles*, Keith insists he is in love with someone he barely knows, and the diamond earrings are his way of being worthy of that love because being able to give them will change his image. He is, he explains to his father, a misfit: "I like art. I work in a gas station. My best friend is a tomboy. These things don't fly too well in the American high school." In this way, Hughes uses the resources of the narrative to redeem the misfit, who is typically characterized as being resourceful, self-centered (as a virtue), and romantic.[1]

Hughes's quintessential teen hero is Ferris Bueller (Matthew Broderick), who combines the traits of the misfits to create an unfathomable center of popularity. Living in a nice suburban house, having affluent friends, a plethora of electronic devices, and a pocketful of cash, he also has a limitless cache of time. In one school day, he gets his girlfriend released, picks her up at school, drives from the suburbs to downtown Chicago, visits the top of the Sears building and the Chicago Commodities Exchange, has lunch in a fancy restaurant, goes to a Cubs game, visits a museum, participates in a parade, returns to the suburbs, goes for a swim, puts his friend's car up on a jack in an attempt to reduce the odometer by running the wheels in reverse, and runs home in order to return to his alleged sickbed before his parents return from work. It is equally important to Ferris that he have a good time and that he manage to retain his angelic image with his parents. The ability to exploit the financial and physical resources of the home derive from the credit given to his character, credit that has been earned, he makes clear, through unrelenting faith in himself. Thus the film stands, as Vicky Lebeau makes clear, "as a key example of a cinema that colludes with a representation of youth rebellion as nothing more than a series of tricks and revels in parental and personal wealth and status. The film then takes on the imaginative poverty, the materialism and the reactionary politics of which not only this cinema but its consumers stand accused—that is 'Thatcher's children,' or rather, the children of a political and cultural exchange between Margaret Thatcher and Ronald Reagan."[2]

Under these circumstances, Ferris qualifies as an unmistakable leader. He has the ability to coerce anyone from snobby restaurant captains to the operators of parade floats to submit to his will, although virtually everything he says is untrue. To call Ferris in this regard a miniature Reagan is oversimplifying. More precisely, I think, he encapsulates the manipulation of narrative and image that the film medium employs and that the Reagan presidency legitimated as the source and site of workable credit; he puts into personal practice the unregulated behavior implicitly legitimated as public policy with Reaganism's motto, "Government is the problem."

He thus articulates the formation of ad hoc policy based exclusively on legitimating self-interest: "I do have a test today," he explains to the audience,

> that wasn't bullshit. It's on European socialism. I mean, really, what's the point? I'm not European, I don't plan on being European, so who gives a crap if they're socialists. They could be fascist anarchists—it still doesn't change the fact that I don't own a car. It's not that I condone fascism, or any ism, for that matter. "Isms," in my opinion, are not good. A person should not believe in an ism; a person should believe in himself. I quote John Lennon: "I don't believe in Beatles. I believe in me." A good point there. He was the walrus. I could be the walrus. I still have to bum rides off of people.

As this speech makes clear, Ferris operates in pure supply-side mode, seeing economic systems as completely independent of his experience as a consumer. Not part of a global economy, Ferris frames his consumption strictly in terms of his home. Like most of Hughes's principals, he is home alone, fending for himself. At the same time, *Ferris Bueller's Day Off* is the story of someone who is not home at all, but just seems to be. His bedroom and home are as vacant as his identity, which is also a mechanical contraption, like the dummy in his bed, the answering machine at his door, or the computerized sound effects on his audio equipment, one that enables him to substitute image for labor.

His influence in this regard is profound, in that he manages to encourage his friend Cameron to rebel against his oppressive father. Because parking attendants have run up the mileage on his father's vintage Ferrari, Cameron realizes that his father will discover his adventures and after a period of depression concludes: "I sort of watched myself from inside. I realized it was ridiculous, being afraid, worrying about everything, wishing I was dead. All that shit. I'm tired of it. It was the best day of my life." Extending Ferris's belief in self-confidence to its absurd limits, he espouses taking a stand, regardless of its content: "I gotta take a stand. I gotta take a stand against him. I am not going to sit on my ass as the events that affect me unfold to determine the course of my life. I'm gonna take a stand. I'm gonna defend it. Right or wrong I'm gonna defend it." While the cynical might suggest that Cameron sounds like someone on the verge of invading Grenada, he has, in any case, come to the same position as many of the compulsive-attraction films, that there is no difference between taking a stand that is right and one that is wrong.

In the process of issuing his tirade, Cameron inadvertently kicks his father's Ferrari off the jack, and because the engine is still running in reverse, the car speeds through the rear wall of the garage, into a ravine, to which Cameron responds, "I don't care. I really don't. I'm just tired of being afraid." Cameron is taking his stand, in other words, on his right to wreck his father's vintage Ferrari, an event that follows from his taking a stand, not the one on which it is based. As in the pervasive attack on regulations that characterized Reaganism, the question of who or what is destroyed becomes ancillary to the principle that self-assertiveness takes precedence over regulations.

The childishness of this (lack of) perspective is completely consistent with the perspective in all of Hughes's films, for in all of them childishness triumphs. This is true for the teen heroes of *Pretty in Pink, Sixteen Candles, The Breakfast Club, Ferris Bueller's Day Off, Some Kind of Wonderful*, and *Weird Science* or the child heroes of *Home Alone* (I and II), *Curly Sue*, and *Dennis the Menace*. Even Hughes's adult heroes, Uncle Buck, Clark Griswald, and Del Griffith (of *Planes, Trains, and Automobiles*), are most notable for their extreme immaturity.

In the end, however, immaturity proves to be their saving grace. Only Clark Griswald's childlike faith in the traditional family Christmas—in other words, his ability to believe in what he saw on television—makes a successful Christmas possible, just as his infantile tirade provokes Eddie to kidnap Clark's boss and thereby creates the circumstances under which the bonuses are restored for the whole corporation. Bound and surrounded by the extended Griswald family, Clark's boss realizes the error of his ways: "I guess a healthy bottom line doesn't mean much if to get it you have to hurt the people you depend on. It's people that make the difference, little people like you."

In the cosmology of John Hughes's America, those who can't afford swimming pools on their regular salary are at the bottom rung. They are the "little people" who constitute the base reality with which the boss had fortuitously been put in touch as a result of Clark's persistently childish activities. Clark does not lapse into a childish mode but rather persists in adhering to one when circumstances urge otherwise. That becomes his triumphant virtue, as it does Uncle Buck's.

An unemployed, overweight bachelor who smokes, drinks, and gambles, Buck (John Candy) is reluctantly called by his upper-middle-class brother to babysit while he and his wife go to Indianapolis to attend to her father, who has had a severe heart attack. The family that Buck takes over is particularly problematic because of the pervasive hostility of the eldest daughter, Tia (Jean Louisa Kelly), a teenager who resents her parents for moving away from Indianapolis and her younger siblings for no particular reason. She is generally abusive to and about her mother and, when he arrives, to her uncle as well. Although Buck brings a strictness to the household that it had formerly lacked, he enforces his regulations with childish tactics. When Tia refuses to let Buck pick her up after school, he threatens to drive her to school the next morning wearing his bathrobe and to escort her personally to her first class. Later he threatens her boyfriend using a hatchet, an electric drill, and a golf club. At one point he literally drives the boy away by driving golf balls at his head. By the end of the film, however, these tactics not only make him Tia's hero rather than her adversary, but they also facilitate a reconciliation between Tia and her mother, in a scene anticipating the reconciliation between Kevin and his mother at the end of *Home Alone*, as does Buck's ingenious use of common household implements. He saves the home and family, in other words, by indulging his childhood fantasies rather than by outgrowing them.[3]

The idea of empowering the child is taken to its logical limits in *Home Alone*, one of the most successful films of all time. In *Home Alone*, we once again have the affluent, but barely functional, family thrown into chaos during the Christmas holiday season. This indeed could have been named "Christmas Vacation II," as it chronicles the attempts of the McCallister family and that of Frank McCallister's brother to spend Christmas in Paris. Because a temporary power outage during the night disrupts the alarm clocks, they find themselves asleep when the airport shuttles arrive at their home. In the process of trying to catch the flight and funnel two sets of adults and eleven children into vans and cabs, the McCallisters (John Heard and Catherine O'Hara) accidentally forget their eight-year-old son, Kevin (Macaulay Culkin), who is asleep in the attic. Kevin, who felt both neglected and unfairly harassed by his parents and siblings, had gone to bed wishing they would all disappear. Awaking to find his wish come true, he feels responsible for their disappearance and therefore is loath to tell anyone about his predicament. Kevin thus falls victim to his childish fantasies both of power and of guilt. The plot first invests Kevin with the fantasy of power, which then enables him to turn the fantasy into a reality by fending off the onslaught of burglars for several days and finally assaulting and (with the aid of a neighbor) capturing them.

Succeeding where his neighbors and the police have failed, Kevin demonstrates the virtue of maintaining a constant state of delusion. He is deluded about what he has done, about his ability to call the police, about his responsibilities to his home. In the long run, however, the film makes clear, the home is safer when Kevin's fantasies are indulged, just as the spirit of Christmas is best realized by indulging Clark Griswald, and the children are better cared for when adhering to Uncle Buck's ideas of appropriate behavior. The reason is that these children of all ages are endowed with special powers in John Hughes's world, as is the tenacious naïf—who will grow up to be Forrest Gump—in President Reagan's America. Like Reagan, these children assume a cinematic understanding of their identity and of the powers of good and evil that surround them.

In many ways, Kevin is another version of Dorothy in *The Wizard of Oz*. Like Dorothy, he finds himself misunderstood by the indifferent and tyrannical world of adults; he then makes a wish to separate from them (although in his version *they* go over the rainbow, in a jet plane), then finds the wish has come true and that as a result he is in even greater danger. Like Dorothy, he finally destroys the villains and then discovers that there's no place like home.

The reversal of venues for their adventures, however, is significant. The makers of *The Wizard of Oz* carefully distinguished the fantasy world of Oz from the "real" world of Kansas. The juxtaposition of black-and-white and color sequences, the double-exposure and spinning images when Dorothy is struck on the head, and the return to Kansas as a return to consciousness all locate Dorothy's adventures firmly in her imagination. In going and then returning, she thus learns the ways in which her imagination provides an inadequate venue for a satisfactory life, and the film thereby turns the imaginary adventures into a form of self-instruction.

Kevin McCallister learns just the opposite—to prefer his imaginary appropriation of the world to circumscription by adult limitations—and so do the adults. When Kevin says the rest of his family are jerks, so far as we can tell he is right. In addition to ignoring Kevin, his parents have unwittingly played into the hands of the burglar, Harry (Joe Pesci), who, disguised as a policeman, acquires a full rundown of their travel plans and security measures while he casually cases the house. Subsequently, he explains to his partner, Marv (Daniel Stern), that the McCallister house is "loaded. . . . It's a gem."

In his fetishistic desire for the contents of the big house, Harry shares the perceptions of Andie in *Pretty in Pink*. Like typical television viewers, both Harry and Andie equate desire with a laying-on of eyes, which becomes as well a form of identification with the homes, lifestyles, and class from which they are barred. If Andie manifests this desire through her proprietary interest in her rich boyfriend, Harry manifests it through a proprietary interest in the block on which the McCallisters live. Having studied the block carefully, Harry knows who is away, where they have gone, how long they will stay, and even the exact moment when their automatic lights come on. He is indeed a kind of inverse Santa Claus (who knows when they are sleeping and knows when they're awake, and knows when they've been good or bad . . .), one who will slip into their homes at Christmas to *take* valuables instead of *delivering* them.

Harry's omniscience about the lifestyles of the upper middle class, however, reflects not his superiority but his inferiority, his class difference mediated by common appreciation of the goods they have and he lacks. Those goods—the trappings of their class—become the common denominator between Harry and the McCallister block, as is evident by the care and attention he gives to the goods he steals. Pillaging the house across the street from the McCallisters', he examines the gifts under the Christmas trees almost as if they were presents rather than booty. Particularly taken with an antique-style kaleidoscope, he stops to play with it, like a child on Christmas morning. While he plays with this kaleidoscope, the message Marv hears on the

_____ *Figure 37* _____
Pillaging the house across the street from the McCallisters', Harry examines the gifts under the Christmas tree as if they were presents rather than booty.

phone answering machine confirms Harry's belief that the McCallisters are in Paris, despite the appearance to the contrary caused by Kevin's tricks. Contemplating his designs on the McCallister house, Harry looks at the beautiful designs in the kaleidoscope that fill the screen. The scene thus ends merging the attractive optical illusions of the appropriated Christmas gift with Harry's delusion that he can acquire that which his gaze has appropriated, the contents of the McCallister home. In his cinematic relationship to the McCallister home, Harry has mistaken the world he sees, in its kaleidoscopic display of material wealth, for the one he can have.

In this way, Harry typifies many Reagan supporters. Like the "Reagan Democrats" (and like Marty in *Back to the Future*), he has traded his origins for an opportunity to identify with the images he has seen on movie and TV screens, and, like many Reagan appointees, he is a crook. But Harry has more in common with the Reagan administration than a collision path with criminal prosecution. This is merely the by-product of deregulation. More fundamentally, Harry believes he can have what he sees and wants: the white house that he enters, however illegitimately.

This belief puts Harry in sharp contrast with his stupid partner, Marv, who prefers against Harry's wishes to destroy the houses they burglarize (by flooding them with water). Because Marv vandalizes what Harry fetishizes, he has no vested interest in gaining access specifically to the McCallister house, whereas for Harry, it becomes a raison d'être. Later, when they know Kevin is home and Marv wants to pass up the house, Harry reiterates his determination to break in: "Ever since I laid eyes on this house I wanted it."

But Kevin must not allow Harry to share the abundance of the McCallister house; he must stay home alone until the people who are naturally entitled to its resources return. Those resources, the very ones that attract Harry to the house, are his undoing, because Kevin's unlimited resourcefulness at every point is indebted to his unlimited resources. When Harry tells Marv that the house is "loaded" full of "top-flight goods: stereos, VCRs," to which Marv adds "toys," they are listing the very things that Kevin will use to exclude and punish him. It is not surprising, therefore, that until his final role as a guerrilla warrior, Kevin assumes the role of consumer more than anything else. Whether eating junk food, watching trashy movies, emulating men's toiletry commercials, buying a toothbrush, shopping in the supermarket, or even talking to a local Santa Claus, Kevin pervasively identifies himself as the subject of a consumer culture. When he buys a toothbrush, for example, he asks the drugstore clerk, "Is this toothbrush approved by the American Dental Association?"—clearly not a concern taught by his family but learned from television commercials.

Hughes spent seven years in advertising before he started writing screenplays, and his sensibility is acutely attuned to the kind of sound bite that characterized Reagan's communicative skills. Like Reagan's rhetoric, Hughes's scripts blend catchy one-liners and self-contained anecdotes, and they operate on the same marketing principles that produced the Reagan presidency. As we have already seen, Reagan was not the formulator of a policy but the professional who acted as its most prestigious spokesperson, as he was at General Electric. Candidate Reagan and President Reagan were the agents of a marketing strategy that packaged a right-wing agenda in images and expressions meant to appeal to the broadest possible audience. For such a goal, the details of a complex defense budget or the highly technical safeguards of SEC regulations are irrelevant, and the rules of good government—sound laws, fair enforcement, concern for public interest—are subordinated to the rules of good advertising. These include: poll continuously to find out what people want to hear and then tell it to them; never try to convey a concept and an image at the same time; if you opt for a concept ad, stress one or at the most two concepts; be succinct; be memorable.

Having learned the advertising trade well, Hughes could apply to films the same concepts that Reagan's handlers applied to campaigning and governing. Hughes has asserted careful control over the marketing of his films, and he has been emphatic about the audience orientation of his work: "I have no interest, none whatsoever, in doing something for myself instead of the audience. My movies are popular because they do what they're supposed to do."[4] Hughes is, of course, merely parroting the guidelines for good advertising, implicit in the motto of one major advertising firm: "It isn't creative unless it sells."

The corollary to these principles is the unspoken converse: don't tell people anything they don't want to hear. In a world where the upper-middle-class house constitutes the most pervasive establishing shot, people don't want to hear about homelessness. For Reagan, as for Hughes, homelessness visibly cracks the facade of his imaginary America. Perhaps this is why Reagan took even less interest in housing than he did in most areas. Beyond the incident in which Reagan greeted Secretary of Housing and Urban Development Samuel Pierce as Mr. Mayor was Reagan's general inability to see housing as a government concern, which his faux pas too aptly symbolized. More substantive and profound problems riddled HUD, as Cannon succinctly points out:

> What was probably the biggest domestic scandal of the Reagan administration occurred in the Department of Housing and Urban Development. . . . "During much of the 1980s, HUD was enveloped by influence peddling, favoritism, abuse, greed, fraud, embezzlement and theft," the House Government Operations Committee concluded unanimously after a protracted investigation. "In many housing programs, objective criteria gave way to political preference and cronyism, and favoritism supplanted fairness."[5] Two years after the end of the Reagan presidency, Pierce and other former HUD officials remain under investigation by independent counsel Arlin Adams. *Reagan never once during his presidency visited the Department of Housing and Urban Development, an agency he considered a notorious example of unneeded government.*[6] (emphasis added)

At the same time, of course, the number of homeless in America climbed to epidemic proportions. Most of the research on the subject of homelessness points out that its causes are complex and inextricable from the social fabric and public policy of American society. Thus rises in the level of substance abuse and the number of deinstitutionalized people with mental instabilities contribute to the number of homeless. Peter Marcuse, however, identifies with cogent clarity two factors that contributed to the sharp increase in homelessness in President Reagan's America: increasing poverty, and not enough affordable housing. "Appropriations," he notes, "for new public housing—the housing of last resort for many of the poor—were virtually eliminated under the Reagan administration."[7] "The long-term trend," he concludes, "will be that the number of homeless will rise as both the number of the poor and housing costs rise. That is the current situation in the United States."[8]

Reaganomics' promotion of a bipolar economy that accelerated the gap between rich and poor also contributed greatly to the homelessness epidemic. Among the chief causes of the problem, therefore, were increasing poverty and decreasing assistance, according to Mary Ellen Hombs, who points out that in 1987 the "most wealthy 20 percent of the population received the highest percentage of income ever recorded (43.7 percent), while the poorest 40 percent received 15.4 percent, the lowest ever recorded."[9] Moreover, because a high percentage of new jobs created during the 1980s were lower—often minimum—wage jobs, affordable housing moved out of reach for the working poor. At the same time, the policies of Reaganism created a sharp cut in "safety-net" social programs. "Under President Reagan . . . the budget for federal low-income housing programs plummeted drastically from 1981-1988," even though the cuts were smaller "than originally requested by the Reagan administration."[10]

Since 1980, according to Roberta Youmans, "not only has the number of families assisted been reduced but the method of financing them has also been altered. Instead of subsidizing the actual construction of low-income housing, the Reagan administrations and then the Bush administration have fostered a shift to housing allowances. . . . The voucher concept assumes that an adequate supply of housing exists. But in many markets, the only housing that exists is beyond the means of most poor families, even with the help of this subsidy."[11] "The link between private housing supply and homelessness is constantly ignored or directly denied. For instance Reagan's Secretary for HUD once asserted, 'The problems of the homeless rarely relate to lack of available shelter.'"[12]

Another way to look at this problem is to consider the "fair-market rent" (the cost of a two-bedroom apartment in the lowest-cost metropolitan community in each state) in relation to monthly income at minimum wage. In 1979 fair-market rent was under 40 percent of income at minimum wage in nine states, and under 60 percent in forty-five states; in only three, including Alaska and Hawaii, was it over 80 percent of minimum-wage income. In other words, in almost all the states, the least-expensive two-bedroom apartment in the least-expensive community required roughly half the annual income of the lowest wage earners. By 1990, however, in the majority of the states, the same apartment required between two-thirds and all of a minimum-wage income: the fair-market rent was under 60 percent in less than one-third of all the states, and over 80 percent in ten.[13]

For people living on government assistance, the problem is even worse. In 1979, the fair-market rent was less than 100 percent of the maximum Aid for Families with Dependent Children (AFDC) grant for a family of three in thirty-one of the fifty states, and under 150 percent of the maximum grant in all but four. By 1990, in only eleven states was fair-market rent less than 100 percent of the maximum AFDC grant, while in Washington, D.C., and in fourteen states, it exceeded 150 percent of the maximum grant.[14] In almost four out of every five states, by the end of the 1980s, AFDC grants were inadequate to pay for suitable shelter, even if not one penny of the money were spent on food, clothing, transportation, or utilities.

These statistics indicate graphically the ways in which the yuppie gentrification of urban communities and tax sheltering through second homes in exurban communities combined with the easy credit available from underregulated savings and loans to create a real estate boom that, in light of the social policies of President Reagan's America, threw hundreds of thousands of children into the gutter. These children are the exact inverse of Kevin McCallister, who knows that in his class, even when his family disappears, he still has his home and all the creature comforts it affords him. Kevin protects that home and, implicitly, his right to it at a time when the right of American children to a permanent residence was in practical terms becoming more and more visibly a point of dispute.

Homelessness, therefore, clearly signals the failure of Reaganomics, providing vivid evidence that the supply side is balanced by scarcity, not abundance. Because the social policies that attend to those who cannot attend to themselves and the economic policies that inflect the distribution of goods and services constitute the woof and warp from which the fabric of homelessness is woven, the problem tugs on all the threads of Reaganism. For the homeless we could say, ironically, that by the time he was done, Reagan was correct: government *was* the problem.

Despite the overwhelming evidence to the contrary, however, even despite the fact that the most rapidly growing segment of the homeless population is children, Reagan minimized the issue, saying in a nationally televised "interview a month before he left office . . . that 'a large percentage' of them were 'retarded' people who had voluntarily left institutions that would have cared for them."[15]

Hughes manifests the same denial of homelessness, treating it not as retardation but as a lifestyle decision. In *Home Alone II*, which shifts the site of the action from Kevin's suburban home to a New York hotel, the old man next door, who eventually saves Kevin, is replaced by a homeless woman who lives with her pigeons in Central Park. The sentimental shot of her at the close of the film shows her in the park, smiling, surrounded by her pigeons as the snow is falling on her. She is obviously happy, and her happiness allows us to enjoy the holidays by denying the misery of homelessness and our knowledge of the people who must face it even after we are safely home. *Curly Sue* also presents a con man and his unofficially adopted daughter as a pair of homeless hustlers who again are homeless as a matter of choice.

So is Del Griffith, the shower curtain ring salesman with whom marketing executive Neil Page is thrown together, in *Planes, Trains, and Automobiles,* for two excruciating days as they try to get from New York to Chicago at Thanksgiving time. After the snowbound O'Hare Airport closes, on the Tuesday before Thanksgiving, Neil eventually ends up flying to Wichita, where he is stranded for the night. With no other place to stay, he accepts Del's offer to share a motel room. During the night, a burglar empties the cash from both of their wallets, and in the absence of flights they end up getting a lift on the back of a pickup truck to a city where they can catch a train to Chicago. When the train breaks down, they have to take a bus to St. Louis, where Neil, after a car rental mishap, accepts a lift from Griffith, who was more successful at renting a car (although he used Neil's credit card to do so). Unfortunately, as they are driving to Chicago, Griffith accidentally starts a fire in the car, which turns it into a scorched, albeit drivable, topless frame. After they again share a motel room and set off for Chicago, a highway patrolman prevents them from driving the unsafe vehicle any farther, and they travel the rest of the way in the back of a truck. Arriving in Chicago on the afternoon of Thanksgiving Day, they part at a Chicago rapid transit station, but Neil, on the verge of reaching home, realizes that the large trunk Del lugs through these adventures contains all his possessions, and Del has no home. Returning to the transit station, he finds Del and brings him to the Page suburban home for Thanksgiving dinner.

Although technically homeless, Del fits neither a demographically accurate profile nor the one harbored by Reagan. Del is employed and reasonably successful at his occupation. Clearly, he has an extensive network of clients with whom he has a good rapport and, as the desperate hustling of shower curtain rings in the Wichita train station illustrates, he is a very effective salesman. He thus has no reason to be homeless. All of his acquaintances, however, lie outside Neil's range of experience. Neil travels first class and, as numerous establishing shots of a "Home Alone"–style house indicate, lives

_____ *Figure 38*_____

Griffith accidentally starts a fire in the car, which turns it into a scorched, albeit drivable, topless frame.

in a very comfortable Chicago suburb. The shots of Neil's house allow the film to crosscut between the family activities of Neil's wife and two children and Neil's mishaps in trying to return to them. Instead of, and in contrast to, his family, Neil has Del, who is crude, overbearing, and catastrophe-prone, albeit well intentioned.

So distinctly marked are the class differences between Neil and Del that Hughes could just as well have been using Fussell's book as his informing text, and these differences virtually define the anecdotal plot. This contrast is established early and overtly when Neil first must sit next to Del because there is no room in the first-class section of the plane. Neil does not want to leave his class to ride where he must rub shoulders with people in another class, a point illustrated by the literal impingement on his shoulders by the head of a sleeping man on one side and the heft of the overweight Del on the other. We could sum up the plot, in fact, by saying that it recounts the misfortunes of a traveler when he is bounced from his designated class. His middle seat among a spectrum of middle-class (in Fussell's sense of the term) people leads him on an unpleasant journey through a world filled with class signifiers he doesn't understand.

The pattern of crosscutting, which frequently makes Neil's home a point of reference, never includes an alternative site for Del—a home or normative life to which he is returning. Since crosscutting, as we have seen, allows cinematic narrative to draw on an infinite credit bank of space and time, certainly there must be reserves enough to give Del a home. Yet the reality constructed by the use of cinematic codes in this film omits such a possibility, and what should be a symmetrical relationship instead becomes unequally triangulated. Regardless of the sympathy that Del may evoke, therefore, he may never become the equal opposite of Neil in the narrative of two different people trying to get to two different homes. Instead he becomes the alternative to Neil's home. Neil is situated between the two lives: suburban affluence signified by his wife, family, and home, and homelessness, signified by Del. Del does not live outside Neil's world; he *is* the outside. In this way the establishing shots that orient the crosscuts indicate that Neil belongs to the Establishment but that Del does not.

Whereas Neil is used to being part of the Establishment, his being outside becomes a motif in the film, starting with his being kept out of a taxi cab. Stranded in Wichita, he finds no vacancy in hotels of the sort he is used to. To travel the forty or more miles to the nearest passenger train station, he has to ride outside in a pickup truck, and when the train breaks down, he has to trek more than a mile outdoors to the highway where the bus awaits. When he is dropped off in the car rental lot by the airport shuttle bus and discovers no car in the designated slot, he is left outside in the parking lot and must walk miles back to the terminal, and when the fire burns the top off the car, he again finds himself driving in the open air.

Neil's exposure to the environment only underscores the numerous other ways in which he is on the outside, incapable of carrying on conversations with Del or the others he meets. On the bus to St. Louis, the riders start singing, but Neil's offering, "Three Coins in the Fountain," meets with silence and stares, while Del gets the whole group to sing "Meet the Flintstones." Neil is not only outside the world of the affluent house—to which he wishes to return—but he is also outside the world into which he has fallen. A lost soul in an alien place, Neil is in Hell, and he makes his anger about his undeserved torture repeatedly evident.

Given Neil's consistent hostility, which takes the form of loud tirades, snide remarks, and condescending silences, why does he focus so acutely Del's desire for friendship? Del obviously has many friends of his own class, people who treat him warmly, do him favors, and appear to like him. Nevertheless, Del measures his success as a person by his ability to become Neil's friend, although virtually nothing in Neil's behavior indicates that Neil is desirable as a friend.

When they first share the motel room, Neil, already disgusted with Del, tells him off in a tirade that concludes by telling Del how boring he is: "Everything is not an anecdote. You have to discriminate. You choose things that are mildly amusing, or interesting. You're a miracle. Your stories have none of that; they're not even amusing accidentally. When you're telling these little stories, here's a good idea: have a point—it makes it so much easier for the listener."

For Neil, Del's biggest fault is that he is not a good subject for cinematic framing; he would bomb as a guest on the *Tonight Show*. Living outside the powers of representation codified by President Reagan's America, he doesn't understand that most favored of Reagan devices, the anecdote, and doesn't know how to use the sound bite or control his image. Del admits as much in his response: "I'm an easy target. Yeah you're right. I talk too much. I could be a cold-hearted cynic like you, but I don't like to hurt people's feelings. Well you think what you want about me. I . . . I'm not changing. My wife likes me. My customers like me, because I'm the real article. What you see is what you get."

This response not only accepts Neil's characterization but counters it in part with a fiction. Because Del's wife has been dead for eight years, his self-esteem depends on harboring an image of himself based on validation that no longer exists. In this way, again, he resembles the Reagan Democrats who have found their prestige and economic power base greatly diminished, their prospects limited, and their values challenged. In a world in which the media highlight the yuppified minority, and the celebrity cornucopia spills into public consciousness entertainers, businessmen, athletes, politicians, ministers, felons of all sorts, as well as their respective friends and lovers, the Del Griffiths are suitable only for the condescending limelight of freakish display on a show with Oprah, or Montel, or Geraldo: "The topic today is working widowers who choose to be homeless." Where is the potential site of identification in contemporary media for the group that demographically constitutes the Reagan Democrat? Certainly not on *Dallas* or *Dynasty*, or *L.A. Law*, a show in which even the mentally retarded man who works in the mailroom, when he dines out, eats in restaurants that have linen table cloths and crystal drinking glasses. Only by clinging to fictions derived from an earlier period in which the possibilities of American upward mobility seemed more universal can people like Del create sites of identification.

When Del says that he is "the real article," moreover, he is implying that Neil is not, although Neil's tirade suggests just the opposite—that he is being completely sincere in his dislike for Del. But Del has a vested interest in assuming that Neil's anger is artificial, for otherwise rapprochement with Neil would be impossible. The tirade must be based on something cynical, on Neil's proclivity to present himself as other than he is, because Del desires that Neil like him. And Del so desires because he is taken with Neil's image, in almost exactly the same way that Tess McGill in *Working Girl* is taken with Katherine Parker's image. In saying he is "the real article," therefore, Del treats himself like a commodity, one that he wants Neil to acquire, so that he may acquire the ability to identify with Neil.

In the visual lexicon of the film, Neil is particularly desirable because of his home and the life it signifies. The asymmetrical triangulation of shots makes the house the site of common desire, establishing for Neil as a presence what they establish for Del as a lack. The distinct class differences between Del and Neil thus present a success/failure relationship, with the lavish house being the default factor, and the ability to establish intimate familial relationships thus a class indicator. Failing to establish a close relationship with Neil indicates Del's unsuitability as a partner and housemate, a defect that Del acknowledges himself, in a dialogue with his deceased wife that explicitly identifies Neil as someone special to him, someone whom he really likes. Neil's rejection thus focuses Del's self-loathing, and Neil's final acceptance of Del as a Thanksgiving guest becomes a display in every detail of the life that Del normally cannot have. The shots of Del suggesting both his gratitude and envy punctuate the final scene in Neil's house, so that *Planes, Trains, and Automobiles* resolves its conflicts in the same way that Reagan maintained his coalition, galvanizing the middle class who suffered greatly under Reaganism's deregulation by validating their envy. Translating self-loathing into a form of cinematic identification, the film, like Reaganism, forges a bond based solely on image, between Del and everything he will never be.

Through the power of cinema, Del and Neil have come to occupy the same space, just as the pre- and postrevisionist McFlys do in *Back to the Future*.

And in many ways, Neil's adventures echo Marty's in that he, too, has taken a fork in the space-time continuum. He leaves a New York office at 5:00 P.M. Manhattan time with the intention of being home for dinner around 7:00 P.M. Chicago time but instead finds himself in a virtual time warp wherein a three-hour trip of under one thousand miles spans more than two thousand miles over nearly forty-eight hours. In order to effect this lengthening, the film must overcome the relationship between time and distance. When Del and Neil arrive in St. Louis on Wednesday afternoon, they are only a five-hour drive from Chicago. They drive through the late afternoon into the evening and still manage to be about a hundred miles from Chicago (according to a road sign) when their car burns. Even at fifty miles an hour, they are no more than two hours from home. They drive in the car for some distance the next morning before the patrolman forces them to abandon it. Still they remain several hours by truck away from the city. The ellipses by which cinematic representation condenses elapsed time make it impossible to measure precisely these disparities. This device is thus significant in that it is used simultaneously to expand and condense. Once we concede by convention that the film may edit time, we have no way of regaining the referents by which to test the tenets of the experience we are taking on credit.

That is why the delays place Neil in an alternative reality, as alien as the McFlys at the beginning of *Back to the Future* would be to the McFlys at the end of the film. Neil experiences the nightmare from which the McFlys are preserved: living in a class significantly below his own. The converse, of course—living in a class above one's own—is not a nightmare. It is the so-called American Dream, which Marty fulfills cinematically. The impossible continuity of McFly families is made possible, I am suggesting, by exactly the same devices that force the bond between Del and Neil and as well between the elements of the Reagan coalition.

The dark side of that forged coalition is the scapegoating that exempts from Del's blame those who exclude and reject him. Some of that scapegoating, as I have already noted, manifests itself as self-loathing. And some, as we have seen at various points in this study, manifests itself as racism, through the evocation of a siege mentality. As Edsall and Edsall succinctly point out about the 1984 election campaign:

> For disaffected white voters, Reagan drew the connection between taxes and "groups" and "special interests"—adding to Republican rhetoric phrases

and words that now bore a new meaning—signifying for many working and middle-class voters the reliable opposition of Reagan and the Republican party to benefits targeted at Blacks, feminists, homosexuals, and others seeking new rights, protections or preferences from government.[16]

Whom should people like Del blame for their inability to have a home, family, or life comparable to Neil Page's? Reaganism's answer was the Democratic party, because it gave to the poor and to racial minorities benefits rightfully earned by those in Fussell's "low prole[tarian]," "high prole[tarian]," and "middle-class." The Bush election campaign well codified this perception:

> By 1988, the perception of a link between the Democratic party and controversial government policies on race, rights, and taxes had become imbedded in the conscious and unconscious memory of American politics—a perception still close enough to the surface to be accessible to political manipulation. This perception often exerted influence on an unarticulated level, a level at which the national Democratic party was still tied, in the minds of many voters, to the problems of crime, welfare, school failure, family dissolution, spreading urban squalor, an eroding work ethic, and global retreat.
>
> In 1988, the Bush campaign assembled and deployed a range of symbols and images designed to tap into these submerged concerns—concerns often clustering around the nexus of racial, ethnic, cultural, and "values" anxieties that had helped to fuel the conservative politics of the post–civil rights era. The symbols of the Bush campaign—Willie Horton, the ACLU, the death penalty, the Pledge of Allegiance, the American flag, "no new taxes," the "L-word," and "Harvard boutique liberal"—conjured up the criminal defendants' and prisoners' rights movements, black crime, progressive liberal elites, a revenue-hungry state, eroding traditional values, tattered patriotism, and declining American prestige. Themes and symbols tapping these issues became for the Republican party the means of restoring the salience of associations damaging to Democrats, and the means of maintaining the vitality of the majority conservative coalition.[17]

Although the racial dimensions of this scenario are extensive and profound, Hughes, of course, never uses blacks to represent the Others who threaten white suburbia. The blacks in his films rarely have speaking roles, and when they do, they most frequently portray benevolent policemen, that is, public servants. These black servants lead the raid on Clark Griswald's house to rescue his kidnapped boss and assist in the arrest of Marv and Harry at the end of *Home Alone* and *Home Alone II*. In *Dennis the Menace*, the chief of police of Dennis's idyllic small town is played by the respected black actor Paul Winfield, who gets a somewhat prominent credit in the opening titles, although he has less than a handful of lines that demand only token acting ability in a role thoroughly trivial. He might just as well have been cast as the metal lawn jockey repeatedly knocked over by the cab driver and the pizza delivery boy in *Home Alone*.

As Hughes himself admits, he has little knowledge of or experience with blacks, and he simply doesn't know how to integrate them into his world. Just like his characters and his intended audience, in other words, he has difficulty imagining an integrated world, for the models are not to be found in his life experience or in the cinematic versions of small-town America on which Hughes's idealism is based. Tim Burton's *Batman* is set in the inner city but acknowledges the existence of only one black (again a prominent actor, Billy Dee Williams) in the meaningless role of a public servant—this time a district attorney—whose activities are peripheral to the plot. Nor does the suburbia of Burton's *Edward Scissorhands* admit blacks. Like the Joker in *Batman*—who, as Andrew Ross has demonstrated, substitutes through an array of semiotic codes for blacks[18]—the (potential) menace, Scissorhands, appears overly pallid, whiter than white. In *Dennis the Menace*, as in the simplistic white world Burton creates for *Beetlejuice*, the threat comes from a white vulgarian, in this case named Switchblade Sam (Christopher Lloyd). A homeless vagabond, Sam universalizes the threat posed by Harry and Marv. Whereas they have staked out one block, Sam seems to be the ubiquitous—and sole—cause of crime in Dennis's town. Immediately upon arriving, Sam assesses the whole town by saying, "I'll bet they don't even lock their doors."

The homeless Sam personifies evil in a town where there are no robbers, and heretofore the only menace has been Dennis. In the end, Dennis, who has run away and been taken hostage by Sam, turns Sam's life into a living hell, in which he is nearly hanged, nearly drowned, partially immolated, beaten, battered, and brained. Since most of these tortures result from Dennis's attempts to help rather than harm, Dennis becomes a virtual satire of the social programs meant to help the homeless, the criminal, or the disadvantaged, at the same time that Sam associates homelessness with threats to the quaint imaginary towns that essentialize President Reagan's America.

If Hughes will not use blacks as perpetrators of crimes, moreover, nor will he let them be seen as the victims of crime—which they are in disproportionate numbers—or suggest the ways that white America (with the active and passive encouragement of Reaganism) has been asked to see blackness as the quintessential threat to everything from personal safety to upward mobility. The menace Hughes creates is a childishness that is also the community's salvation, in the form of Clark Griswald, or Uncle Buck, or Kevin McCallister, or Dennis Mitchell. Dennis succeeds by banishing the single homeless man and only criminal in his town after treating him to brutalities of the sort that often befall homeless people. The partial immolation, for example, echoes all too uncomfortably the systematic murder of sleeping homeless people in that fashion that occurred in one city in the mid-1980s. But Dennis is a hero because he proves that in the end—in the right communities—there are no menaces, only youthful enthusiasm, uncontrollable curiosity, and misguided benevolence.

This is the world to which Del Griffith wishes admission and the one from which Neil Page has fallen, which is why his money is stolen. The dilemma of this world that focuses both Del's envy and his self-loathing can be seen in two dialogues at the end of *Some Kind of Wonderful*. In the first Amanda confesses to Keith her anxiety about dating a rich boy and hanging out with a rich crowd: "I hate feeling ashamed; I hate where I'm from. I hate watching my friends get their hearts' desire; I gave in to that hatred and I turned on what I believed in. I didn't have to. You didn't." Articulating a sentiment that could be shared by Del Griffith and Tess McGill, Amanda is bemoaning the plight of spectatorship in President Reagan's America. The process of *watching* her friends makes her ashamed of the subjectivity constructed by virtue of her gaze. But her shame about her own situation becomes hatred of those fortunate others who, like movie stars, occupy a space from which the gaze is nonreciprocal. Her hatred of them is thus asymmetrical and as such allows her to convert the loathing into envy. Keith, however, offers her what he thinks will free her permanently from this cycle of envy and self-loathing: a pair of diamond earrings purchased with his college money. "So you won't do it again," Keith responds. "You won't have to, ever." The solution to Amanda's problem is to have the things she envies, the valuable accessories of an affluent life. With them she (like Vivian, and Tess, and Ariel) can stop being ashamed of herself in the same way that Marty can stop being ashamed of being a McFly.

The second conversation takes place a little while later when Keith's "tomboy" friend gets the same earrings after Amanda realizes, even before Keith does, that she is his true love. When Keith gives her the earrings, she says, "Well how do I look?" and the film ends when he responds, "You look good wearing my future," meaning that he has traded his college education for the right to have a girlfriend who, now having genuine diamonds in her lobes, doesn't have to be ashamed.

Obliterating the distinction between present and future, "you look good wearing my future" is a catchy sound bite, perfect for cinema or any other medium that subordinates time to image, such as news broadcasting or political press releases. Once again we have come back to the future, and this time it's a gem, purely decorative and unequaled in its adamancy.

Six

Seas of Love and Murderous Doubles: AIDS Narratives and the Dangers of the Other

Because we live in a time when love and fear have become completely and inextricably connected by the presence/absence of incurable disease, it is not possible to talk about AIDS films as a genre or category. Like the disease itself, its signifiers fail to remain within a definable discursive family, within a stable risk group. Rather than circumscribe the risk *groups*, AIDS narratives more typically resemble the "Risk" board game, which distributes the known world along polar axes—monopolar, bipolar, tripolar, quadripolar, depending on the number of players at "Risk" around the family dinner table—of Other and Same, only to demonstrate that the playing of the game renders its given boundaries meaningless. Destroyed by the ebb of random probabilities, these borders become sites not of containment but of seepage, flow, invasion. In the "Risk" game, the contingent nature of defined populations renders virtually every site vulnerable, every border a myth. So too with AIDS films, as with AIDS itself. If the ideology represented by the term *family values* requires a safely defined family group, then AIDS is a threat to family values not because it signifies the abandoning of the values but because it challenges the stability of naming and grouping on which the concept of the family depends. In fact, even the films I discuss comprise only one branch of what could be called a family of AIDS films, akin to branches I only mention, like the "What's-come-over-you?-You-don't-look-anything-like-the-person-I-fell-in-love-with" films, such as *The Fly*, *Darkman*, and *Prelude to a*

Kiss, or the "Death-as-a-loss-of-innocence" AIDS pastoral films of the early 1990s, such as *My Girl*, *Man in the Moon*, *Fried Green Tomatoes*, *Rambling Rose*, and *Paradise*.

Primarily, I want to focus on films that deal with AIDS specifically as an invasive threat—the other menace to John Hughes's and President Reagan's America—and identify modes of AIDS representation that have infected much of Hollywood's output, blending with films and categories I don't identify and also seeping into a world of just-plain-old films—"innocent" films—whose only fault is that they were conceived in the same way that the tainted films were, in a fifteen-minute pitch on some producer's couch, which brought into play all the history that informs the typical experience of Hollywood professionals. The reproductive nature of Hollywood plots and formulas, as with the cultural narratives they proliferate, have spread AIDS themes through copious productions, and, just as the threat to which these films respond remains unabated, so too do the narratives that emerged during the period of President Reagan's America. I am issuing a warning, therefore, that this chapter could contaminate future filmic experience; because AIDS could be found anywhere, decoding can be contagious, and although this chapter is just a speculative diversion, no one has yet determined conclusively exactly what can or cannot be transmitted through casual interactions.

Two films about compulsive behavior, *Fatal Attraction* and *Who Framed Roger Rabbit*, mentioned in Chapter 4 but not discussed at length, reflect narratives that, I believe, construct the poles of a dilemma over AIDS with which the narratives of President Reagan's America never successfully dealt, although the attempts to do so proliferated exponentially. In this chapter, therefore, the narratives of President Reagan's America are examined as motifs evoked in futile attempts to contain the implications of the uneasy and uncontrolled linkage of love and death in the current epidemiology of American culture.

In *Who Framed Roger Rabbit*, when Jessica Rabbit says she is just "drawn that way," she is, as noted earlier, admitting that she is compelled to behave as she does. The pun on "drawn," however, invokes the idea of a predetermined nature. Jessica is also compelled by some internal force, some sexuality, that draws or attracts her to, in the murder story, a potentially fatal situation. Her problem, like those in the other compulsive-attraction films, is thus psychological. She can't help her overt sexuality, shouldn't be blamed for her fatal attraction, because it is a form of compulsive behavior. At the same time, as a toon and thus the product of her maker, she participates in the essential qualities of someone else's design. Her sexuality, to which Eddie finds himself attracted and of which he is censorious, can be read as an essential aberration or a psychological deviance. In any case, Jessica is *not* a woman, we are constantly reminded, but merely a toon who looks like one; she is, in other words, by design or inclination, a female impersonator. "You don't know how hard it is being a woman," she explains, "looking the way I do."

She and her partner, the lisping Roger Rabbit, who is always trying to kiss the tough private eye, Eddie, are the film's chief representatives of a community at risk, one associated with the entertainment industry. This community is threatened on several fronts, endangered as much from the legal sanctions against it as from the invidious liquid—the dip—that is capable of destroying the otherwise immune physical constitutions of the toons. But equally the toons are threatened by the indifference, resentment, and even toonaphobia of the general post–World War II American dominant culture. The cult of domesticity, instituted with a vengeance with the rise of the Cold War, constructed a particularly strong need for closeted behavior in what was tantamount to a surveillance state that branded any form of nonconformity a threat to domestic security.[1]

The response of the toons to their marginal status is a compulsive parodying of the dominant culture, and, as Roger makes clear, sometimes laughter is their only defense. "If you don't have a good sense of humor," he asserts at one point, "you're better off dead." "A laugh," he later explains, "can be a very powerful thing. Why sometimes it's the only weapon we have." This defense system, represented as a genetic trait of toons, is connected with their genetic incapacity to do harm.

It is particularly significant, therefore, that Judge Doom (Christopher Lloyd), the agent of their potential extinction and the manufacturer of the deadly liquid dip, is a toon in disguise. More than in his appearance, effected by the disguise, Judge Doom is aberrant genetically—unlike other toons, he cannot tolerate laughter and fixates on harm. He is, in other words, a toon whose immune system has broken down and become perversely destructive, but because he represents a doom targeted exclusively at the marginal toons, the community at risk has trouble getting help or protection from the general population.

Eddie Valiant (Bob Hoskins) had once been a champion of the toons. He and his brother ran a detective agency, and as Roger points out, "Everyone knows when a toon's in trouble there's only one place to go—Valiant & Valiant." His brother's death at the hands of a toon, however, has changed Eddie. The murderous toon, distinguished by his red eyes, dispelled for Eddie the idea that toons are genetically benign and made him hostile to all toons. Although we never see Eddie's brother, we do see photos of him in which he lacks any female companion, whereas Eddie is paired with his girlfriend, Dolores (Joanna Cassidy).

In the context of these photos and Eddie's toonaphobia, we can understand some of the reasons that Eddie's involvement with Roger is so upsetting to him. In following Jessica, Eddie is made uncomfortable by his attraction to Ms. Rabbit's sexuality and finds "her" affection for the effeminate Roger a quandary. He is censorious of Jessica's "playing pattycake" with Marvin Acme, and when Roger is charged with Acme's murder, Eddie is irked to find Roger hiding out in Eddie's bed. He is even more irritated by Roger's kissing him. At one point, when Roger says, "You saved my life—How can I ever repay you?" Eddie responds, "For starters, don't ever kiss me again." If Eddie starts to believe in Roger's innocence, he remains suspicious of Jessica. This is, of course, not surprising because for Eddie Roger is merely annoying, whereas Jessica threatens the basic tenets on which Eddie bases sexual identity. She appears to be what she is not, dupes her partner, and plays pattycake with Marvin Acme. Therefore she cannot be trusted. Her promiscuity and her deceptive sexual appearance make her a murder suspect.

Following these suspicions, he follows Jessica into Toon Town, believing she has covered her initial crime by killing the movie producer, Mr. Maroon. Instead of finding evidence against Jessica, he is chased out of Toon Town by a female (or femalelike) toon, who nearly chases him into a fatal accident, screaming: "A man! Kiss me!" The danger of being kissed by a strange "female" toon becomes analogous with the danger of succumbing to Jessica's seductive appearance and, possibly, her deadly schemes. When Jessica saves Eddie, however, he discovers that he was wrong about Jessica and eventually discovers that the villain is Judge Doom, who is involved in a real estate conspiracy to acquire Toon Town.

_____ *Figure 39* _____

Jessica Rabbit threatens the basic tenets on which Eddie bases sexual identity. She appears to be what she is not.

In a final confrontation in Marvin Acme's warehouse, we discover that Judge Doom is not only a toon in disguise but also the same toon who killed Eddie's brother. The telltale red of Doom's eyes, furthermore, is revealed to be blood when the eyes turn into menacing daggers. Like the dip shooting out of phallic hoses at the bound-up Roger and Jessica, the blood at the tips of Doom's eyes suggest the dangerous fluid that not only threatens to destroy all the toons but also is capable of killing Eddie's brother or Eddie himself. In the final struggle, however, Eddie destroys Doom with his own dip, saves Roger and Jessica, and uncovers the deed that saves Toon Town for the toons. The dangerous dip is then carried away by a miraculous train, and Eddie demonstrates his changed attitude toward Toons by kissing Roger.

Who Framed Roger Rabbit? is one of the earliest films to deal with the themes of the AIDS epidemic employing codes that have become somewhat conventional: the community at risk, facing extinction from some inexplicable evil; the breakdown in the normal social and personal defense systems;

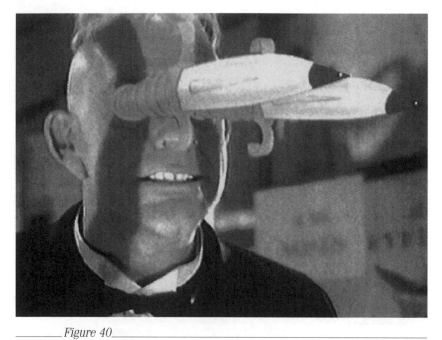

_____ *Figure 40*_____
The telltale red of Doom's eyes is revealed to be blood when the eyes turn into menacing daggers.

the association with sexual ambiguity; the mystery of origins, connected with the sexual history of the suspects; the destructive power of an uncanny twin, sibling, or self-as-mutant Other; the threatening liquid (in this case dip, but more often blood); and, as the "framing" of Roger suggests, the blaming of the victim.

Who Framed Roger Rabbit? thus can be read as a benign allegory about the AIDS epidemic. It represents AIDS as a disease threatening the gay community and asks for compassion rather than blame: Roger Rabbit is the victim, not the perpetrator. But if he has been framed, by whom? At the inscrutably evil and miraculously benevolent margins of this narrative, we find the unfathomable world of the toons. Judge Doom is a closeted toon, a perverse toon, a sick toon, a toon just as uncanny as the miraculous Toon Town train that removes the vats of dip. While being a narrative about blaming the victim, therefore, the film raises troubling questions about the arbitrariness of framing on which cinematic narrative depends. Technically, the film depends on the insertion of the invidious into the visual frame. Its justly acclaimed advances in the integration of animate humans and animated drawings create a unique control of the mise-en-scène. The makers of the film have framed Roger Rabbit such that he becomes central in a human environment rather than beyond its margins.

The humanizing of the (gay) victim has been a motif in most of the (relatively few) films more or less directly about AIDS, most notably *Philadelphia* and *Longtime Companion*, and less overtly (or more arguably) *Prelude to a Kiss*, *Dying Young*, *Lorenzo's Oil*, and even possibly *Memphis Belle*, a film, like *Longtime Companion*, that surveys a male community at risk, building its tension around the question of who will survive the statistical odds.

At the center of all of these films is the idea of a family or community. In *Philadelphia*, for example, director Jonathan Demme goes to great lengths to remind the audience that the victim is not only a gay man but also a son and brother. The concluding shots after Andrew Beckett's (Tom Hanks) funeral show a sequence of home movies that represent him not as a sexually active adult but as a prepubescent child playing with the parents and siblings who have now gathered with his friends in his loft. These friends and siblings in many cases have brought children of their own, any one of whom by implication could grow up to face the same disease and/or prejudice that Andrew did. Throughout the film, we have been reminded constantly of the family, of children entering a world of risk, fear, and discrimination. As Andrew's black lawyer, Joe Miller (Denzel Washington), comes to recognize this, he becomes more cognizant of his love for his own wife and child. The film, in other words, develops the bond between Andrew and Joe more overtly on the basis of their common experience in family units than as members of discriminated-against minority groups. At the height of his compassion for Andrew's imminent death, Joe goes home deeply moved by passionate concern for his own wife and child.

The final shots of the home movies thus allow the diseased adult, who has been buried offscreen, to reenter the frame as the loved and innocent child. This is Demme's act of reframing that motivates the film, in the same way that the reframing of Roger Rabbit motivates both the plot of the film's detective story and the extradiegetic technology that empowers it. That technology, however, has its limits within the story and outside it. Content within the formulaic ending characteristic of the classical style of Hollywood films,

_____ *Figure 41*_____
The concluding shots after Andrew Beckett's funeral in *Philadelphia* show home movies on a TV screen that represent him not as a sexually active adult but as a pre-pubescent child.

to which this film alludes, *Who Framed Roger Rabbit?* ties up all the loose ends and privileges the personal goals of the individuals over a confrontation with the more messy conditions that caused their problem, or the broader implications of their resolutions. The causes of Judge Doom's genetic aberration, like the consequences of the Toon Town train's collision with the destructive dip, remain outside the frame of the screen and of the plot. The plot to frame Roger Rabbit is undone by the plot that unframes him through a reframing of his behavior.

In a similar fashion, much of the discussion of AIDS in the 1980s has focused on ways to frame the debate, about which President Reagan was virtually silent. Only in 1987 did he first make any statement on the topic, in part motivated by the revelation that Rock Hudson—a movie star, a friend of Nancy Reagan's, and a lifelong Republican—had died of AIDS. The position Reagan took was to advocate universal testing, while ignoring the importance of education and research, two areas advocated by the medical community but disdained by political conservatives, especially those among the Religious Right.

Throughout the course of the Reagan presidency, the administration was slow and inadequate in its funding and policy responses to the problem. As the epidemic continued to broaden, federal funding was constantly cut back in Reagan's proposed budgets. Repeated requests for adequate funding from the assistant secretary for health, Dr. Edward Brandt, were routinely ignored by his superior, Secretary of Health and Human Services Margaret Heckler. In 1983, a House report documented severe underfunding of federal efforts to fight AIDS, and in 1984 a crucial Brandt funding memo lay on Heckler's desk for two months; she only responded to it after it was leaked to the press, at which time she rebuffed Brandt's request for additional funds for AIDS research.

Much of the resistance to funding came from Reaganism's attitude toward the AIDS epidemic, which resembled its attitude, discussed in Chapter 2, toward the crack epidemic. Like drug addiction, Reaganism viewed AIDS as the disease of the Other, from which President Reagan's America needed to be insulated. Randy Shilts, in *And the Band Played On*, his extensive study of America's response to the epidemic, details month by month the ways in the first half of the 1980s that political agendas, pandering to a combination of fear, homophobia, and moralism, missed numerous opportunities in the areas of research and education because of virtual opposition to government response. A vivid example comes in his discussion of the 1984 Republican convention:

> AIDS was a topic of much discussion at the Republican Convention, although all of it was off the convention floor. At a party barbecue held at the estate of a millionaire Republican businessman, a fundamentalist minister delivered an invocation that included a reference to the fact that God was using AIDS to mete punishment to the immoral. At a breakfast for Republican business executives a day later, the president of American Airlines opened his talk by telling guests that the word "gay" stood for "got AIDS yet?" . . .
>
> For all the behind-the-scenes talk, however, AIDS remained a largely unspoken subtext in the election. When the issue was considered at all, it was generally in the context of what each political party thought was wrong with the other. For the Democrats, AIDS was another example of the woes

that would be cast upon the world by aggressive reductions in domestic spending. For Republicans, the epidemic was a just desert, the result of permissiveness bred by the secular humanism of liberals, being visited upon people they largely did not care for.[2]

While the Democrats and Republicans framed their issues, the narrative of the epidemic admitted no clear cinematic resolution, no simple distribution of guilt and innocence. And thus it fell outside the America framed by President Reagan's discourse, a discourse in which the play and orientation of desire create no ambivalence.

The *way* Jessica is drawn—to look like a woman? to pursue men?—raises questions not only about her sexual orientation but also about her culpability. In *Who Framed Roger Rabbit?* both are represented, ultimately, as benign. Jessica's sexual history is more innocent than it appears and her attraction not fatal. In *Fatal Attraction*, the same issues are at stake, but in this case the femme fatale is Jessica's opposite. Whereas Jessica helps clear the lovable rabbit, in *Fatal Attraction* Alex Forrest (Glenn Close) cooks the pet rabbit belonging to Dan Gallagher's daughter.

This lapin motif suggests both the similarities and differences in these films, for in many ways Alex Forrest is Jessica Rabbit's evil Other. Both Jessica and Alex are successful in their careers, and both are marked by compulsive drives. Both evoke, moreover, responses of gender confusion. Despite her appearance, Jessica, as we noted, is not a woman, and Alex not only has a masculine name but also manifests the aggressive characteristics associated in many narratives of the dominant culture with masculinity. In *Roger Rabbit*, Jessica, who is drawn to appear feminine, turns out merely to have been misunderstood, whereas in *Fatal Attraction*, Alex, who assumes a masculine name and role, turns out to personify evil. This could be looked upon as a vilification of the successful career woman—and certainly those implications cannot be expunged[3]—but I also think it participates in the film's more pervasive injunction against gender confusion.

The basic plot of the film is rather simple. A successful Manhattan lawyer has a weekend fling with a publishing executive, while his wife and daughter are away. Although the woman promised that there would be no strings attached, she is incapable of abating, making constant demands for his time and attention. The problem becomes worse when she discovers that she is pregnant. When rebuffed by the lawyer, she becomes vengeful and destructive, trashing his car, sending threatening tapes to his home, killing his daughter's pet rabbit, briefly kidnapping the child, and eventually entering his home wielding a butcher knife, which necessitates his (and his wife's) killing her.

Certainly this is a cautionary tail about the dangers of extramarital relations, but that "message" is framed in the film by injunctions about the danger of sex in general, especially when combined with gender confusion. At the reception near the opening of the film, in which Dan (Michael Douglas) and Alex first meet, Bob, one of the executives in Dan's firm, is wearing a neck brace because of an injury sustained while "he was screwing his wife." The wife, we are told, had to be taken out in a stretcher. The injury is alluded to again at the business meeting in which Dan and Alex meet for the second time. From the outset, we see that sex can be dangerous, even when practiced by married couples. The film, in fact, assaults the idea that the "happily married" nuclear family can be immune from the sexual danger. It is not Toon Town that is threatened in this film but the land of heterosexual domesticity, of middle-class family values, that circumscribes it. "In the spirit if not the style of 1950's television families like the Nelsons, the Cleavers and the Andersons," Liahna Babener points out, "*Fatal Attraction* offers up a romantic reaffirmation of old-fashioned domesticity, maternal solicitude, fatherly governance and bourgeois materialism, conveniently situating the hazard to such laureled values in the person of a lethal woman whose monomaniacal villainy is rendered in melodramatic excess, which makes it easy to marginalize, defeat and dismiss."[4]

In true backlash fashion, characteristic of President Reagan's America, Doom here—the genetic aberrant who threatens to destroy its complacent happiness of this domesticated world—is represented as the independent career woman, but it is important to note that the initial attraction is mutual. The fatal attraction of the title refers equally to Alex's obsession with Dan and Dan's initial attraction to her. Like Judge Doom, Alex is the irrational constant in the formula, the latent killer who, once she becomes active, runs her unstoppable course to death—hers and, potentially, others'. We never know what draws Dan to Alex, but when he rejects her, Alex accuses Dan not of being a womanizer or philanderer but rather of being homosexual. In a tape she sends him, Alex call Dan "a cocksucking S.O.B." and says, "I bet you don't

Figure 42

The somewhat androgynous child in *Fatal Attraction* cross-dresses in order to play Miles Standish in the school play.

even like girls, do you? You're a flaming, fucking faggot." This theme is re-iterated in the tape when Alex says, "I bet you don't even like girls. Probably scare you."

This film shows a traditional nuclear family (with a somewhat androgynous child who cross-dresses in order to play Miles Standish in the school play) at risk from a sexual intruder whose blood becomes an instrument of terror, a point demonstrated most graphically by the fact that *Fatal Attraction* is the only film about a homicidal maniac that I know of in which virtually the *only* blood shed is that of the slasher herself. Her blood-smeared apartment, where she attempted suicide, portends her psychotic invasion of the Gallagher's suburban bathroom, where she threatens Dan's wife, Beth (Anne Archer), by using a butcher knife to gouge a slit in her *own* leg; the pool of blood that spreads at Alex's foot is further troped by the overflowing bathtub that starts seeping through the floor to the kitchen ceiling. Like the

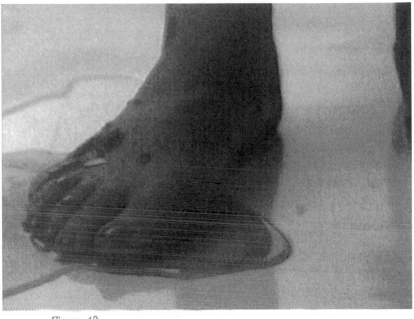

Figure 43

Having gouged a slit in her *own* leg, Alex creates a pool of blood around her own foot, spreading her blood in the Gallagher household, . . .

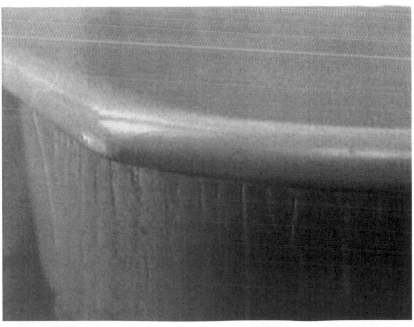

Figure 44

. . . this infusion of liquid is troped by the overflowing bathtub.

corrosive dip in the final confrontation of *Roger Rabbit*, a invasive liquid here seems to portend the destruction of the domestic couple. Even when Alex starts slashing at close range, however, she fails to cut Beth, and in the ensuing struggle with Dan she manages only to inflict an apparently superficial wound. Alex is eventually drowned in the tub and subsequently shot, so that her blood stains the invaded home's white tiles in the same way that it did the pillars of her own loft, and drips into the couple's bath just as it did into her own sink.

As in *Roger Rabbit*, the death of the true villain and the washing away of the dangerous fluids are greeted by kudos from the community and the law-enforcement system that had failed to defend it. *Fatal Attraction*'s commitment to family values, moreover, is first subtly emphasized by the fact that, despite the screaming slasher and the screaming wife, despite the violent struggle, brutal drowning, and subsequent shooting, the sleeping child does not wake up, which for some yuppie suburban couples would constitute a horror at least as great as having a visit from Norman Bates. *Fatal Attraction* ends, moreover, with the police inspector shaking Dan's hand on the front lawn, in a scene clearly suggesting that, having found murdered in the upstairs bathtub the woman whom Dan had already reported as a pest and menace, the officer was congratulating Dan for his civic-mindedness. This scene reveals clearly how one can differentiate Dan Gallagher from Rodney King.

And like the stories of Roger Rabbit or Rodney King, this film relies on the distribution of innocence and guilt. Just as the media has lodged upon a set of codes that identify hemophiliacs as "innocent" victims of AIDS, implying an alternative "guilty" set, *Roger Rabbit* and *Fatal Attraction* absolve the innocent by constructing a narrative that delimits guilt, although the narratives differ greatly in that Roger Rabbit attempts to absolve sexual indeterminacy and *Fatal Attraction* attempts to implicate it. Neither film, however, divorces (implicit) sexual orientation from fatal consequences and invidious liquids. Nor, perhaps, is such a goal possible so long as causes and effects remain not only inextricably bound to one another but also inextricably confused.

This is, of course, exactly what disease does: it contaminates the causes with the effects and vice versa. The realm of "risk" mediates the boundary between causality and randomness in which contagion operates. Thus to say that AIDS is not a gay male disease risks ignoring the historically specific consequences for the American gay male population, that is, risks ignoring peo-

Figure 45.

Fatal Attraction ends, in the style of 1950s sitcoms, with a close-up of the framed family photo.

ple at risk. By the same token, to say that AIDS is a gay male disease is to risk implicating people and practices causally in what was a random phenomenon. AIDS is transmitted by fluids, not by types of people, and therefore in parts of Africa the infected population is overwhelmingly heterosexual. Because there is no defense against the effects of the fluids, concern has focused on practices, which in turn have been absorbed within an array of cultural narratives that frame the risks. In *Fatal Attraction*, sexual ambiguity (represented as Dan's attraction to Alex) is absorbed by a narrative that asserts the fatal potential of acting on that attraction and the domestic security acquired by killing off the sexually attractive Other.

This fantasy resolution underscores cultural anxiety about the breakdown in protective mechanisms, such that the fallibility of the immune system becomes associated with any aberrations from the standard practices of the anecdotal American family to which Reaganism ascribed paradigmatic status. Thus the threatened defense systems extend beyond the impotent police and legal systems of *Fatal Attraction* and are more typified by Judge Doom, for whom the normal protection systems have mutated into their opposites.

Internal Affairs, for example, is about the proliferation of death spread by police corruption. The villain, Dennis Peck (Richard Gere), is a ubiquitous menace, whose activities have infused the myriad operations of the Los Angeles police force. He is involved with narcotics, graft, and business shakedowns; he even does contract killing. He also "helps" his fellow officers, by arranging for them to have lucrative moonlighting jobs providing security for underworld figures, and he plants evidence to help them escape misconduct charges connected, for example, with illegal shoots or police brutality. This network of favor and reward ensconces Peck at the center of an internal economy that allows him to draw on those who owe him favors in order to control the scheduling and allegiance of the police with whom he works. He becomes, in other words, a counterforce within the police hierarchy, one that allows an alternative source of power and income. Since such a counterforce, as it spreads, threatens to corrupt the entire system, and consequently the larger social system it is supposed to protect, the force has its own internal defense mechanism, the Internal Affairs Division (IAD). IAD aids the force in defending itself from corruption.

The central conflict in *Internal Affairs* is between Peck and an idealistic policeman, Raymond Avila (Andy Garcia), who joins IAD. He and his gay partner, Amy Wallace (Laurie Metcalf), discover a multifarious and infectious web of corruption that revolves around Peck. Initially they become suspicious when investigating Dan Stretch (William Baldwin), a policeman with numerous reprimands for excessive force, who has been charged with planting evidence. Stretch, an old friend of Avila's, is Peck's partner and is entangled in Peck's illegal activities. When Stretch verges on cracking under investigative pressure, his protector, Peck, turns on him, arranging for his murder. After Stretch is shot, Peck also assassinates the man with whom he had contracted the murder.

These events mark the point when Peck becomes an active killer, turning not only on the general community to which he is a symbol of protection but specifically, as well, on those who associate with him or rely on him for protection. He has the murderer's accomplice killed as well as a policeman who gives information to IAD. He contracts to kill the parents of an affluent man,

_____Figure 46_____

The final confrontation with Peck comes in Avila's bedroom, where the bleeding Peck threatens to become a rapist/murderer.

Arochas, and then kills Arochas and his wife, Tova. He shoots, perhaps fatally, Avila's partner, and he tries to kill Avila and his wife.

These killings, moreover, are pervasively linked to Peck's sexual activity: he is having an affair with the wife of the partner whom he has killed, and after the contract killing of the Arochas' parents, Peck has sex with Tova Arochas. When her husband comes in, Peck convinces him to kill his wife, after which Peck shoots him. Peck's way of countering Avila's investigation, moreover, is to lead Avila to believe that Peck is sexually involved with Avila's wife. Peck, furthermore, stresses on many occasions his and the women's preference for anal sex, in terms of AIDS a high-risk activity.

The internal affairs, in other words, are not just police matters but questions of sexual promiscuity. The clues that complete the investigation of Peck are those that link his sexual indiscretions to his criminal acts, and Avila's marriage is saved by the discovery that his wife's sexual history has not been tainted by association with Peck. Thus the final confrontation with Peck comes in Avila's bedroom, where the bleeding Peck threatens to become a rapist/murderer. His blood, like that of Alex Forrest, has invaded the privacy of the domestic site, where in this case the defender of public safety has become the biggest menace to it.

The professional and physical similarities between Andy Garcia and Richard Gere (and William Baldwin), emphasized by similar haircuts, mark the villain in this film, as in many others, by an uncanny doubling. In *Unlawful Entry*, the doubling takes the form of male bonding between Kurt Russell and Ray Liotta. We also see doubling in the psychotic seductive sisters in *Final Analysis*, the twin sisters played by Sean Young in *A Kiss before Dying*, or those played by Delia Sheppard in *Mirror Images*, and in the mirroring of Bridget Fonda by Jennifer Jason Leigh (who in the story had a dead twin) in *Single White Female*, of Jeanne Tripplehorn by Sharon Stone in *Basic Instinct*, or in Drew Barrymore's haunting by her own homicidal and nose-bleeding double in the *Doppelganger*. These films suggest, in other words, an alter ego or evil Other as representative of a system turning on itself.

In many of these, the doubling is troped by the transference involved in psychotherapy, just as the breakdown in the defense system is troped by the sexual compromising of therapist-patient relationship. In *Final Analysis*, Gere is a therapist having an affair with his patient's sister; in *Basic Instinct*, Tripplehorn is Michael Douglas's therapist and lover; in *Doppelganger*, the villain is Barrymore's deranged psychiatrist. In *Body of Evidence*, a psychiatrist becomes sexually involved with a patient who manipulates her lovers into committing murders.

In *Whispers in the Dark*, Ann Hecker (Annabella Sciorra) is a psychiatrist who compromises her professional ethics by becoming sexually involved with a female patient's lover. When that patient's apparent suicide is revealed to be a murder, a series of deaths ensue surrounding Hecker's friends and patients. The actual murderer, it turns out, is Hecker's therapist Leo (Alan Alda), who is irrationally in love with her. What typifies this murder mystery as an AIDS film is the linking of the characters' sexual history to the investigation. As in *Internal Affairs, Basic Instinct, Doppelganger, Final Analysis, Body of Evidence, Mirror Images*, and *A Kiss before Dying*, if we can learn enough about people's sexual history, we will know if they are the killers; until then, sex always courts death.

This courtship is the focus of *Sea of Love*, another film about the ways in which sexual desire compromises the defenses of a policeman. A series of men who put rhymed advertisements in a singles' column turn up murdered. They are all lying facedown in their beds, naked, with bullets through their head, and there are signs that a woman has recently left the apartment. A police team, headed by Frank Keller (Al Pacino), sets a trap for the murderer by running a rhymed ad, meeting the respondents in a bar, and getting fingerprints off their drinks. One woman, Helen (Ellen Barkin), however, refuses to touch the drink, and consequently when a relationship develops between her and Frank, they cannot know if she is a murderer. Thus in *Sea of Love*, that metaphoric sea merges torch song with deadly liquid, and the search for the murderer focuses on the sexual history of Helen. Frank becomes involved with her sexually but wonders, in so doing, if he is not risking his life. His doubts arise from his having failed to take the proper prophylactic precautions in testing her fingerprints to ascertain definitively her guilt or innocence. As it turns out, this is another instance of blaming the victim, although the clues do come from her sexual history: her former husband has been following her and killing her lovers. We mistakenly thought the killer was a woman, when it was really a man, one whose mode of executing naked men replicated the coupling in an act of anal sex." The presence of the killer, however, had contaminated the sea of love, linking, as the two implications of the song do, love and death.

In *Unlawful Entry*, similarly, the menace comes from the policeman who installs the house security system. Assaulted by a black burglar who nearly slashes her throat, Karen (Madeleine Stowe) and her husband, Michael (Kurt Russell), find themselves befriended by one of the investigating policemen, Pete Davis (Ray Liotta). As someone who moonlights in security systems, he arranges to have a state-of-the-art system installed in their home. He also arranges for Michael to go on a police patrol ride-along, during which time he captures and brutally beats the intruder who had initially threatened Karen and Michael. Pete's behavior strongly discomforts Michael, who further rebuffs Pete when he wants to handle security on a renovated concert theater that Michael is promoting. From this point on, Pete becomes increasingly unstable, invoking equally his knowledge of Michael's home security system and of the larger legal system to destroy Michael's life.

We have another instance of the defense systems designed to protect the upper middle class turning perverse. In the process, it drives the sociopathic

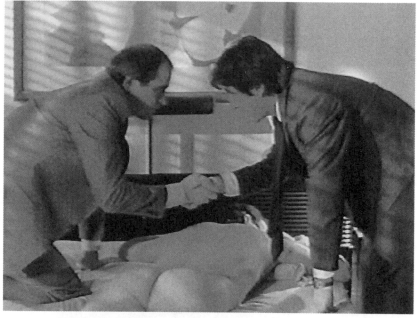

_____*Figure 47*_____
In *Sea of Love*, the police wear prophylactic gloves when examining murder victims.

qualities of the protector out of their latency, such that he not only terrorizes Karen and Michael but also kills his own partner and Karen's friend. Here, too, the breakdown is motivated by Pete's sexual attraction to Karen. In the narrative he has constructed about their relationship, she doesn't want her husband because he is not capable of protecting her; all of his assaults on Karen's life, including the near rape at the end, are thus performed in the interest of protecting her.

Issues of class surround this film, for several reasons. Karen and Michael are the quintessential yuppies who thrived in President Reagan's America. Karen is a schoolteacher in a private school, but the couple's main source of income is the money Michael makes arranging business deals. His income, therefore, is uneven, and at the outset of the film, they are near the edge of their credit limit. This, of course, does not prevent them from living in a luxurious home in a posh neighborhood. In every way they represent the world from which Pete is normally barred. His personal relationships are with other policemen and with women he considers "sleazy lowlife whores."

Manifesting the dark side of the Del Griffith–Neil Page relationship in *Planes, Trains, and Automobiles*, Pete inserts himself in Michael and Karen's life with the same tenacity with which Del latches on to Neil, albeit not with the same good humor. Motivated by anger as well as envy, Pete violates the sanctity of the home, thus connecting the house at financial risk with one threatened by physical and sexual dangers. Because the precariousness of their credit-driven lives make the couple particularly vulnerable to the unlawful entries in their life, the film unavoidably links the motifs of AIDS films to those of the house and daughter at risk. At the end of *Internal Affairs*, Peck sums up a similar anger in his dying words shouted at Avila and his wife: "You selfish yuppies!"

This phrase describes equally well the beleaguered couple in *Pacific Heights*. In that film, too, the entire law-enforcement system, instead of protecting the family from the invader, turns on the hero by wrongly incarcerating him and thus making his sexual partner susceptible to the menacing villain. Like *Unlawful Entry*, this film draws on the house-at-risk motif common to many films of President Reagan's America. As in *Beetlejuice*, a child less yuppie couple acquires and renovates a turn-of-the-century house, only to have it threatened by a vulgar and demented intruder, in this case Carter Hayes, played by Michael Keaton. Hayes combines the upper-class affluence and entrepreneurial interest in real estate as investment associated with *Beetlejuice*'s Dietzes and the irresponsible vandalism associated with Beetlejuice himself. In many ways *Pacific Heights* is the dark version of *Beetlejuice* in that it is informed by the matrix of speculation and renovation—once again that movement back to the future—in which the narratives of President Reagan's America are so heavily invested. The yuppie couple, Patty Parker (Melanie Griffith) and Drake Goodman (Matthew Modine), also have a beneficent black friend who attempts to help them in crisis, giving sage advice, loaning money, allowing Drake to stay at his apartment, but he, too, is helpless against the malevolence of Hayes. And in this version, there are no ghostly powers to save the home when danger threatens.

Hayes is a both a con man and a sociopath. Evading a deposit or rent, he cons his way into apartments and then uses the tenant-favorable eviction laws to maintain occupancy while he makes the building unlivable for other tenants and/or the owner. Making noises at all hours of the night, setting hoards of roaches loose in walls, and stripping the interiors of all their fixtures, he financially destroys his landlords, and when he eventually leaves, if he has provoked them into violence, he can also initiate civil litigation that may threaten all of their remaining assets, as is the case for Patty and Drake, who have overextended themselves to buy the San Francisco home.

Their investment in the house is permitted by their faith in the economic optimism of Reaganomics. After abandoning the prospect of a balanced budget through "the elimination of waste and mismanagement," Reagan argued that "growth" would eliminate the deficits. This assertion was, of course, fantastic; at no time in even the height of the Reagan boom years did the growth of the economy come close to equaling the growth of the debt that accompanied the boom. Replicating on a personal level the principles of Reaganomics, Patty and Drake should eventually have to confront the spiraling economic failure that should follow from the fact that their debt exceeds their capacity to meet it. This is what happened to many American farmers after they refinanced their farms in the 1970s and early 1980s. In the "save the farm" movies that *Field of Dreams* inadvertently parodies, this economic crisis is real and tragedy usually imminent. *Field of Dreams* averts tragedy, as we have noted, by evoking a supernatural patriarch. Lacking such a patriarchal figure (dead or alive), Patty and Drake should fail in their attempt to turn the renovated living space of an earlier America into currency.

And at one point they do. Patty and Drake have lost their other tenant, fallen irrevocably in arrears on their mortgage payment, and seen the renovated interior of Hayes's apartment completely destroyed. In addition, Drake has been shot by Hayes when he violates a court restraining order that barred Drake from his own premises and left Patty vulnerable to Hayes. The cause of their failure thus becomes Hayes's dishonesty and psychosis, rather than their own faulty economic judgment, and Hayes personifies the feared stranger who can move in and destroy a neighborhood. The film makes a point of indicating that he is not a surrogate black by showing as the preferable alternative to Hayes a black prospective tenant whose application accidentally gets lost. Nevertheless, Hayes draws on all the fears of a stranger in one's house: that he will be dirty and criminal; that he will bring in undesirables and wreck the property; that he will make the house a dangerous place in which to live.

The same fears are evoked at the beginning of *The Hand That Rocks the Cradle*, which cuts between the beautiful interiors of a spacious, renovated

Victorian home in a quiet residential neighborhood and a hulking black man (Ernie Hudson) slowly pedaling his way into that neighborhood. The cross-cutting between still, medium shots of the house's open, static interiors and the tracking close-ups that isolate parts—arm, leg, shoulder—of the black man on the bicycle have the effect of imposing him on the house, suggesting yet again the iconography of the house at risk. The real menace in the film comes from the innocent-looking, blonde live-in babysitter (Rebecca De Mornay), just as the real menace in Pacific Heights is the affluent Hayes, and the greater menace in *Unlawful Entry* is not the black burglar but the policeman who arrives to protect the home from him.

Although these films reject the specifics of black menace to the neighborhood, they evoke the narrative of black menace as the context in which white psychopaths are supposed to be surprising and shocking anomalies. But the context that jeopardizes the couples in *Unlawful Entry* and *Pacific Heights* is their economic situation, a fact that the films' attention to the psychopath obscures. The pathology of deficit spending is thus replaced by the pathology of the perverse stranger who replaces the rational narrative of the ledger sheet with the irrational narrative of mental disease. This is the sickness of the invasive Other, not necessarily about AIDS, but unavoidably tainted with the elements of its narratives.

In a facile equation that draws on and promotes the narrative, in the Reagan-Bush era, of the beleaguered nuclear family, as a group these films thematize not only the ways in which love itself is represented as a disease—a compulsive, destructive, and self-destructive obsession with an Other—but also the ways in which the disease of love represents disease itself. This move enables a reversal, wherein the obsession *with* the Other is the obsession *of* the Other, and the Otherness of disease—the invidious virus, the deformed Other within—can be exteriorized. That exteriorizing of the sick Other thus becomes a family-values narrative, and the family of President Reagan's America, represented as already assaulted from the outside by too many taxes and not enough police, by the absence of prayer in the schools, and by the wrong kind of people moving into the neighborhoods, now has to fend off as well the external invasion of its own Otherness, its evil double who originates, as the film titles suggest, from a *Basic Instinct* or a *Fatal Attraction* (or *Mirror Images*, or *Indecent Behavior*, or *Body Language*, or a *Body of Influence*, or a *Body of Evidence*, or *Body Chemistry 1, 2,* or *3,* or from an *Ultimate*

Desire, a *Fatal Temptation*, or just *The Temp*) that always threatens an *Unlawful Entry*, for diseases are always *Internal Affairs*.

One significant exception, Francis Ford Coppola's *Bram Stoker's Dracula*, refuses to construct a narrative externalizing AIDS as the product of evil intrusion but rather represents it as a form of subjectivity. The disease-of-love as the love-of-disease that informs *Bram Stoker's Dracula*'s narrative treats love as a technology of gender constructed by the cinematic gaze. In this context, the film examines the ways in which technology (i.e., cinema) can drive people past the limits of technology (i.e., medicine). In Coppola's narrative, AIDS is not caused by an invading virus but rather by an attitude that is the product of the cinematic consciousness that informs contemporary sensibilities. There is not space here to detail the numerous and varied techniques Coppola uses to reconfigure the working of the cinematic apparatus in that film. Indeed, a monograph could easily be devoted to a segmented study of the cinematic grammar Coppola employs in *Bram Stoker's Dracula*.

More briefly, I want to concentrate on the ways in which he divides the screen and disorients the cinematic gaze to underscore its arbitrary qualities, and the ways he connects the fragmented and arbitrary gaze with technology. If blood is a constant image in the film—at the greatest distance infusing walls, drenching rooms, at closer view dripping and seeping from small cuts and punctures, and at the microscopic level displaying its animated components—the shots in the film constantly bleed into one another. Sunsets create red smears on a bias across the wide screen; ocean waves suffuse or dissolve into human figures and vehicles in motion; faces and images saturate portions of a scene. The film reminds us constantly of the fluidity of image, a motif echoed by Dracula's (Gary Oldham) myriad forms and appearances.

Particularly cogent is the way that eyes emerge out of and recede into scenes and actions, suggesting the ubiquity of Dracula's gaze not only in relation to the other characters but also in relation to the audience. Dracula is, in other words, the audience's Other, watching what we watch and also watching us. In point-of-view shots that, at high speed, show violent sexual assaults, we construct Dracula's presence by assuming completely his gaze, in other words, by occupying the site of the gaze that has already penetrated our own. The technological virtuosity of these juxtapositions underscores the connection between the subjectivity of the viewer and the cinematic appara-

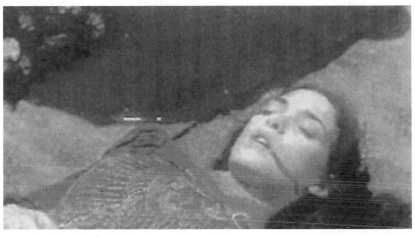

_____ *Figure 48*_____ _____ _____
Blood is a constant image in *Bram Stoker's Dracula*, covering floors . . .

_____ *Figure 49*_____
. . . and drenching rooms.

tus. The driving passion of Dracula, that of transcendent love, merges here with the technological mastery. It is, thus, purely and self-consciously cinematic, the sine qua non of technology.

In this light it is important to note that the film uses its techniques in order to present a pastiche of clichéd images and motifs from the history of Western cinema. Not just an encyclopedia of other vampire films, it also alludes to virtually every form of Hollywood genre, from the romantic "woman's picture" to the western, in which women are generally peripheral, from the period adventure story to the porn film; it even has touches of the scientist biopics and, perhaps more subtly, of film noir. Dracula first encounters Mina (Winona Ryder) when she is on her way to see "the cinematograph" that she terms "the wonder of the civilized world," and their first encounters occur in that viewing parlor, surrounded by the silent projections of the earliest form of moving pictures. These moving images allude to the world of romance in such a way as to suggest that the romance is with technology; it is a love of the power to construct and situate—however tenuously—the subjectivity of the Other. The film, in other words, gazes at the conventions of cinematic seduction while systematically undermining the seduction of the cinematic gaze. It does so, moreover, in a world experiencing a technological explosion, as represented in the film by a proliferation of "modern" machines, such as a typewriter or Dictaphone, in their rudimentary versions.

Thus Coppola presents the conflict between technology and technology's narrative power as an AIDS story, a story, in other words, in which the loss of blood is a benign experience, in contrast to the horrific decision to let someone else's blood into one's system. The decision is the act of love that acquires transcendence by virtue of its commitment to death, but it acquires meaning by virtue of its cinematic power. AIDS is not represented as an outsider who is assaulting the family but as a product of the cinematic consciousness that has contributed to the construction of contemporary subjectivity. It is, in other words, no more the fault of the victim than is allowing the power of cinematic representation to qualify someone for the presidency. This, too, could be a manifestation of a cultural death wish.

The point that I have been making throughout this book is that the power of the Reagan presidency was its ability to construct narratives that manifested the assumptions on which film viewing relied. In foregrounding and problematizing those assumptions, Coppola has not only connected the risks of AIDS to the pleasures of cinematic technology; he has also provided, however unintentionally, a profound critique of Reaganism by laying bare the dangers of accepting the transparent continuity of cinematic narrative. The disease is proliferated by the privileging of specific narratives as much as by the contact with bodily fluids. As long as those infected were considered "de-

_____ *Figure 50*_____

The final shot of *Bram Stoker's Dracula* frames the story by representing the domed ceiling as a camera lens containing idealized images of Dracula and Mina.

viants" or the recipients of divine punishment, the appropriations for research and education languished. As long as the infected were viewed as outsiders, invasive threats, contaminators, too much emphasis was placed on testing or quarantining. As long as the infected constructed themselves within the romantic narratives propagated by films, modifying practices and instilling responsible behavior remained difficult.

If sex is not safe or dangerous until it is situated in a narrative, the practice of "safe sex" requires the defeat of cinematic narrative, a point painfully underscored when Mina of her own volition accepts Dracula's blood into her system. Making the immortality of love, as situated in its cinematic history, the alternative to disease, she says to Dracula, "Take me away from all this death." In the concluding scene, as Mina lies with the beheaded corpse of her Dracula, awaiting the time when she will join him, we look up at the domed ceiling with the painting of the lovers in Renaissance style and see that the dome looks like a camera lens. The whole scene of love and death painted on that lenslike dome thus becomes the site of the god's view from which the mortality of the lovers is played out.

Conclusion

The Enduring Power of Reaganism and the Movies

Reaganism is with us still. Its incapacity to deal with AIDS, like its incapacity to deal with the economy, or race, or health, safety, and housing, in no way diminished the cogency of its narratives. Such is the power, at the close of this century, of film. For every "fact," or piece of "evidence," or call to "logic" that enters the discourse, thousands of times daily cinematic forms reinforce another kind of argumentation. In that form, citizens are spectators embedded in a series of protocols about order, frame, space, distance, and ellipsis, and the narratives that insulate that spectatorship thus remain unavoidably buttressed by the act of spectating.

Hence it does little good, for example, to tell a Newt Gingrich that "government is the problem" is the problem, or remind a Dick Armey that lower taxes did not end the deficit but multiplied the debt, or explain to a Clarence Thomas that affirmative action also assisted many competent people, or point out to a Phil Gramm that his political philosophy closely resembles anarchism, or tell a Bob Dole anything (to cite a few of the most prominent re-iterators of the narratives of President Reagan's America at the moment of this writing). They have latched, each of them in his way, on to fragments of the narrative that played well when it starred Ronald Reagan. The narratives of President Reagan's America continue to grip spectators and assure them that citizenship is another kind of consumer choice, effected through the ability to buy tickets or switch channels.

By 1992, the gap between the limited national economy and the limitless economy of cinematic representation became so large that George Bush's limited acting ability could not broach it, and change became the thematic of the presidential election, such that both (or all three) candidates presented themselves as the agents of change.

They were, however, agents without agency. For numerous reasons, one could argue, the conditions connecting campaign to agenda to performance simply did not exist. Although documenting and analyzing those conditions would be the topic of another book, I do want to make one point germane to this study: conventional wisdom maintains that American presidential election campaigns start too early and last too long. The problem that gives rise to that wisdom, however, has little to do, I think, with when the campaigns start but rather that they are unable to stop. As one more battle in a larger campaign for control of popular narratives, elections provide dramatic focus by highlighting the goals and motivations of individuals; they supply the narrative form, in other words, of Hollywood films. And whatever else Hollywood has or has not proved, it has proved that there has always been a strong audience for sequels.

Conditioned by a lifetime of television programming that repeats formulas on a weekly basis, in several separate versions, on several separate channels, the population under fifty displays extraordinary acceptance of sequels and tolerance for reruns. At the younger end of the spectrum, those who have lived a chunk of their lives with video games, VCRs, and cable access may feel even more comfortable with repetitions, sequels, and series. For members of such an audience—which is what the electorate is—what constitutes "change"? Changing channels only calls forth another form of repetition, a different formula, some other rerun.

In many ways, the American electorate seems stuck on a kind of Gilligan's Island, its members surrounded not by water but by countless clichéd versions of themselves, countless televised narratives reproduced exponentially that are hopelessly recognizable in reference to one another but refer less and less to anything the audience can recognize in their own lives. By the same token, watching the repetitions has become their lives. They want it to change, but the only means they know of is to change the channel, which is no change at all. Like the readers of Paul Fussell's *Class*, they are trapped within the representations of themselves.

This situation all too precisely glosses the plot of *Groundhog Day*. In that film Phil Conners (Bill Murray), a Pittsburgh weather forecaster, goes to Punxsutawney, Pennsylvania, with his producer, Rita (Andie MacDowell), and cameraman (Chris Elliott) to cover the February 2 emergence of the groundhog that will forecast the end of winter. Once there, however, he finds himself unable to leave. With the highways closed and the phone lines down because of an unexpected blizzard, he is trapped in Punxsutawney for the evening. On the following morning, however, he awakes again to February 2, with the same events occurring exactly as they had before. The problem for Phil is how to chart a course of action that will restore his agency, give his actions consequences. The film is about, in other words, Phil's fumbling attempts to forge a mandate for meaningful change.

The early February date is significant, therefore, in the way that it echoes the season of the New Hampshire primary, usually considered the unofficial start of the campaign season.[1] The repeated appearances at public gatherings, outdoor rallies, and fund-raising parties, with their rote activities punctuated by an occasional new gimmick, replicate all too accurately the bus-tour, jet-hopping, whistle-stop campaigns that characterize the election season. No doubt in many ways the towns and people must start to look alike, and one of the ordeals for any candidate in a long campaign is how to sound fresh for an audience that is experiencing the stump speech for the first time. *Groundhog Day* merely literalizes the redundancy of campaign narratives.

Like the narratives of Reaganism, of course, *Groundhog Day*'s play with the space-time continuum is also dependent on the power of cinema. And like Reagan (and his administration), Phil exploits his privileged position in the narrative for personal gain. Gauging carefully the habits of the community, Phil is able to seduce women, steal money, and place himself above the law. He is able to indulge, in other words, the traits most commonly associated with the worst politicians. In his attempts to seduce Rita, however, his practiced study, finely tuned adjustments, and carefully planned deceits run amok when they become perceived as performance. The infinite replay of everyday life in a world of the momentary rather than the remembered allows him infinite attempts at the same seduction. His attempts, however, suffer rather than improve with refinement. The problem is not in the way memory affects his audience but in the way it affects his performance. He is the victim of his own memory, one so full of cues and bits, studied responses and rehearsed acts that he becomes visible as performer and hence unacceptable.

Nor does honesty help. Confiding in and proving to Rita that he is reliving the same day engages her compassion but in no way allows him to escape his entrapment in the endless search for change. In light of the fact that no matter how he changes things, nothing changes, he tries a third tack, which is to change himself. He learns how to play the piano, finds out where problems exist in the town, and works out a schedule wherein he can solve every problem in one day—save a man from choking, change a flat tire for some older women, make charitable contributions, play the piano at the evening party. In terms of other films, he turns himself into the Superman of the 1978 film who, coming newly into his powers, dazzles Metropolis by doing everything from rounding up criminals to rescuing cats from trees. Phil is also apparently like Superman in that he has two identities, one as an ordinary person and the other as a superhuman. The superhuman quality of Phil's performance, however, is really his mastery over his medium. Trapped within a cinematic reality, he has learned how to employ its devices not only to his own ends but to those of the public good. If the conventions of Reaganism and Reaganomics had mortgaged the future, then the reclaiming of the future, *Groundhog Day* suggests, is not a return to some normative "truth" but a redeployment of cinematic illusion to new ends.

The other alternative to the conundrum of the space-time continuum at the center of cinema is supplied by Robert Zemeckis, who helped initiate the films of President Reagan's America with *Back to the Future*. As the bookend to that text, in the wake of the Reagan presidency, he takes us back to the past with *Forrest Gump*. The advertisements for that film argued that you will never look at the world the same way again once you have seen it through the eyes of Forrest Gump. Gump (Tom Hanks) is, in other words, Marty and Doc's time machine, the cinematic apparatus that can naturalize and make normative a revisionist history. The story of a white, southern moron—exact IQ 78—with a form of disability that requires leg braces, who starts elementary school in 1954 (the same period that is critical in *Back to the Future*), *Forrest Gump* returns at the end, in the 1980s (the other critical decade in *Back to the Future*), to the same school bus stop and bus driver, with Gump delivering his son to the bus in the same way that his mother delivered him. His mother has died; his black best friend has died (in Vietnam); his wife has died of AIDS (without contaminating him). The nation has gone through tumultuous times, while the moronic Gump has been uncannily successful and become independently wealthy; without the aid of significant reasoning power, moreover, he has become the source of much of the conventional wisdom in America's popular culture. If the message of *Groundhog Day* is that we can find a way to change, the message of *Forrest Gump* is that we can escape change; if we just trust America to witless white men and get rid of all the women and blacks, we can have a life exactly like the one we imagined in that definitive moment in the 1950s—the moment of Clark Griswald's home Christmas movies—while the French were still handling the Vietnam problem and the schools in the South were still segregated. We no longer need the ghost patriarch or the beneficent black as long as we place our faith in average white morons.

What is particularly arch about this back-to-the-past alternative is its attempts to erase blacks from American history. In 1952, the landmark publication of Ralph Ellison's *Invisible Man* called attention to the transparency of blacks in American culture. As I have argued extensively, Ellison was attempting to construct a symbolic rereading of American history, culture, and literary criticism that would call attention to the ways in which everything recognizably American had its visible form because of the unacknowledged presence and contribution of black Americans.[2] While the contributions of Americans were inextricable along racial lines, recognition in the dominant discourse remained separate and unequal. In terms of facilities, education, housing, and employment, the judicial and legislative branches of government would—with varying degrees of success—address the inequalities shortly after *Invisible Man*'s publication and in the decades that followed. Only in the last decade, however, with attention to the issue of multiculturalism, have many of the invisibilities suggested by *Invisible Man* focused public debate or motivated public action.

And *Forrest Gump* is the response. As much as Ellison and many, many others have tried to demonstrate the presence of blacks in American culture, *Gump* attempts systematically to erase that presence, to deny it ever existed. As a young child, for instance, the little moron Gump has a disability that requires that he wear leg braces, which in consequence make him walk with a peculiar, gyrating motion. This motion is noticed by a boarder at his mother's boardinghouse, a young Elvis, who decides to imitate the motion as part of his performance. A great deal, needless to say, has been written about Elvis Presley, and regardless of how one regards his music or what level of originality or derivativeness one ascribes to it, regardless of whether one prefers Elvis's version of "Hound Dog" or Big Mama Thornton's, there is little debate that Elvis was drawing on black American music for his style. The search for origins amid the miasma of adaptation, imitation, and parody in American popular music, as Andrew Ross has shown, is an impossible task, because of the rich and complex interweaving of the strains that make up American musical culture.[3] *Forrest Gump* simplifies the problem by straining out the strains. After we see the world through the eyes of Forrest Gump, we no longer have to worry about the black strains in American music.

Or in anything else. When the little moron Gump was first starting school, public transportation in his neck of the woods was routinely and uniformly segregated. Rosa Parks had not yet refused to move to the back of the bus, and Martin Luther King had not yet led the Montgomery, Alabama, bus boycott. On little moron Gump's bus, nevertheless, there is a problem with being seated because, as the film has it, normal white schoolchildren don't want to sit next to someone with leg braces. Once again, the social issues connected with the imposition of racial distinction in the public space are replaced with the much more idiosyncratic problem of one white boy. This is *not* to suggest that people with disabilities do not suffer problems about access or discrimination but rather to suggest that those problems are not being engaged in *Forrest Gump* but instead exploited as a way of denying the racial problem for which they substitute.

Even as an inappropriate replacement for race, the issue of Gump's disability is not engaged but escaped when Gump, one miraculous day, runs away from his problems and the braces that supported them, becoming one of the fastest runners in the world. His speed allows this moron to attend the University of Alabama on a football scholarship, although there is no doubt that he would not have qualified on academic grounds. And so we watch Gump first enter the University of Alabama at exactly the same time that blacks did. In the computerized composites, for which the film is well known, we see Gump starting school while Governor George Wallace, in defiance of federal court orders, bars access to a black student. What thus should be a historically important confrontation between the forces of segregation and those of equal access becomes trivialized as a somewhat bewildering event in which all of our attention is drawn to the inappropriate figure in the scene, a bewildered white moron who is our "hero" for witnessing the heroism of the black students. We are asked, in other words, to see the desegregation of American universities in terms of its impact on a white moron instead of its impact on the thousands of blacks who struggled and suffered for this hard-earned and not always pleasant "privilege."

This scene is all the more troubling because Gump's unquestioned right to be a student at Alabama is based solely on his athletic ability, whereas the black students are there based on their academic qualifications. Much has been said about the merits and drawbacks of athletic scholarships. Many have argued that they have afforded minority students from disadvantaged backgrounds educational opportunities that would otherwise have been unavailable to them; others have held that athletic scholarships exploited their talents without ever repaying them with a genuine education. But there is little disagreement that the scholarships have brought many underprepared students and many minority students onto college campuses. And there is also little disagreement that the integration of athletic programs has contributed to easing the difficult integration process at formerly all-white schools. Just as the qualified black students were marginalized by the insertion of the figure of the oblivious white moron into the site of their struggle, the black athletes have been rendered invisible by their Gump replacement, who becomes the latest in a string of great white hopes who will establish white supremacy in the public athletic arena.

Finally, the meeting with George Wallace becomes another bit of Gump memorabilia whereby he can reminisce or ponder the prominent people he met who were subsequently shot. They include John Kennedy, Robert Kennedy, and George Wallace, but as Tom Byers points out, not Martin Luther King:

> The exclusion of Dr. King's murder in a history of the assassinations of the period is simply astonishing. It doesn't even make sense in terms of the way Forrest is drawn, since he is portrayed both as prone to discuss assassinations and as highly sympathetic toward and disposed to identify with Southern Blacks. This is the film's most striking erasure of a single event, and I think it can only be understood symptomatically, as produced by the wish to attach victim status to white men and the concomitant need to cover over any systematic exploitation of others by them.[4]

The scene of Gump's college years substitutes not only Wallace for King but also the inflexibility of segregationists for the discipline of those participating in nonviolent sit-ins. The civil rights cry "we shall not be moved" is here represented by the intransigence of George Wallace, and barred college doors, not lunch counter sit-ins, illustrate the civil rights movement in the eyes and mind of Gump.

When in the service, Gump does become the best friend of a black soldier, Bubba (Mykelti Williamson), whose dream of becoming a shrimp fisherman Gump fulfills after Bubba's death. He in fact replaces Bubba in his entrepreneurial opportunity and also in the black church choir, so that the black man's loss becomes the white moron's gain. Gump also brings along with him the white militaristic lieutenant whom he managed to save in Vietnam. Having lost both of his legs in the war, the lieutenant (Gary Sinise) takes the place of Ron Kovics and all the other veterans against the war, substituting Ahab-like tirades against the elements for any form of political action or social protest.

Gump's uncritical view of the war is balanced in the film by white peace protesters and black militants. Both of these groups are represented as irrational, violent, and hypocritical, especially in comparison with the naive logic, easygoing demeanor, and sincere emotions of Gump. Although the film never says that the Vietnam War was right, it clearly suggests that those who opposed it were wrong, a point vividly made when Jennie (Robin Wright), Gump's only childhood and adolescent friend, now turned flower child, is struck by her abusive peacenik boyfriend at a peace rally in Washington. If the boyfriend is a mockery of the antiwar movement, the black militants at the rally are pure caricatures, mindlessly shouting vacuous clichés, such as to discount or discredit any of the issues of racism or inequity that provoked black radicalism in the 1960s.

Thus the blacks who fought and who died in Vietnam in disproportionate numbers are not the victims of injustice but rather the agents that pave the way for the psychological redemption and economic prosperity of the white moron and his commanding officer. In Gump's version of American history, black contributions disappear; even the black security guard who discovered the Watergate break-in is replaced by the moronic Gump, whose mindless behavior is always validated, particularly in comparison with overly introspective and hopelessly confused Jennie, the love of Gump's life. Throughout the film she is searching for meaning as she dons the fashion and the rhetoric of successive periods in American history from the 1950s to the early

1980s, when she finally marries her longtime moron friend and then dies of AIDS.

In coming to grips with the loss of his love, Gump finally finds contentment in replacing his own mother as he sees his son off to school at the same location from which she originally saw him off. The narrative that made Gump affluent did so at the expense of all the blacks and women. With their removal, he also gains control of the time machine, as he is able to entrust his son to the *same* school bus driver with whom his mother had entrusted him, thirty years earlier. With a naïveté, optimism, and trust in the anecdotal power of the American small town, rivaled perhaps only by Ronald Reagan himself, Gump returns to the fork in the space-time continuum with proof that America works, in other words, that it distributes its rewards cinematically.

The hell of being trapped forever in a small town on February 2 becomes the nirvana of being able to relive forever the first day of school, with all its innocence and hope. The school that little Gump will attend in all probability has given up trying to teach the lessons of history, lessons that proved after all to be over his father's head. Instead they will probably substitute some video representation—perhaps a series prepared by Newt Gingrich— that will have all the well-learned credibility of a movie.

Filmography

Listed below are all the movies mentioned in the text, with date of release, director, and writer. Those discussed under the rubric of "President Reagan's America" have been arranged chronologically, by year. Earlier films are listed below, alphabetically.

Films of President Reagan's America and the Aftermath

1983

National Lampoon's Vacation. Harold Ramis, d; John Hughes, w.
Trading Places. Jon Landis, d; Timothy Harris, Herschel Weingrod, w.

1984

Sixteen Candles. John Hughes, d & w.

1985

Back to the Future. Robert Zemeckis, d; Zemeckis, Bob Dale, w.
The Breakfast Club. John Hughes, d & w.
National Lampoon's European Vacation. Amy Heckerling, d; John Hughes, Robert Klane, w.
Weird Science. John Hughes, d & w.

1986

9 ½ Weeks. Adrian Lyne, d; Patricia Knop, Zalman King, Sarah Kernochan, w.
Ferris Bueller's Day Off. John Hughes, d & w.
The Fly. David Cronenberg, d; Cronenberg, Charles Edward Pogue, w.
Pretty in Pink. Howard Deutch, d; John Hughes, w.

1987

Barfly. Barbet Schroeder, d; Charles Bukowski, w.
Black Widow. Rob Rafelson, d; Ronald Bass, w.
Broadcast News. James L. Brooks, d & w.
Fatal Attraction. Adrian Lyne, d; James Dearden, w.
House of Games. David Mamet, d & w.
No Way Out. Roger Donaldson, d; Robert Garland, w.
Planes, Trains, and Automobiles. John Hughes, d & w.
Siesta. Mary Lambert, d; Patricia Louisiana Knop, w.
Some Kind of Wonderful. Howard Deutch, d; John Hughes, w.
The Untouchables. Brian de Palma, d; David Mamet, w.
Wall Street. Oliver Stone, d; Stone, Stanley Weiser, w.

1988

Beetlejuice. Tim Burton, d; Michael McDowell, Warren Skaaren, w.
Clean and Sober. Glenn Gordon Caron, d; Tod Carroll, w.
Gorillas in the Mist. Michael Apted, d; Anna Hamilton Phelan, w.
Mississippi Burning. Alan Parker, d; Chris Gerolmo, w.
Mr. Mom. Stan Dragoti, d; John Hughes, w.
Who Framed Roger Rabbit?. Robert Zemeckis, d; Jeffrey Price, Peter S. Seaman, w.
Working Girl. Mike Nichols, d; Kevin Wade, w.

1989

All Dogs Go to Heaven. Don Bluth, d; David N. Weiss, w.
Back to the Future II. Robert Zemeckis, d; Zemeckis, Bob Gale, w.
Batman. Tim Burton, d; Sam Hamm, Warren Skaaren, w.
Bill and Ted's Excellent Adventure. Stephen Herek, d; Chris Matheson, Ed Solomon, w.
Chances Are. Emile Ardolino, d; Perry Howze, Randy Howze, w.
Field of Dreams. Phil Alden Robinson, d & w.
The Little Mermaid. John Musker, Ron Clements, d & w.
National Lampoon's Christmas Vacation. Jeremiah S. Chechik, d; John Hughes, w.
Sea of Love. Harold Becker, d; Richard Price, w.
Uncle Buck. John Hughes, d & w.

1990

Back to the Future III. Robert Zemeckis, d; Bob Gale, w.
Body Chemistry. Kristine Peterson, d; Jackson Barr, w.
Darkman. Sam Raimi, d; Raimi, Chuck Pfarrer, Ivan Raimi, Daniel Goldin, Joshua
    Goldin, w.
Edward Scissorhands. Tim Burton, d; Caroline Thompson, w.
Flatliners. Joel Schumacher, d; Peter Filardi, w.
Ghost. Jerry Zucker, d; Bruce Joel Rubin, w.
Ghost Dad. Sidney Poitier, d; Chris Reese, Brent Maddocks, S. S. Wilson, w.
Home Alone. Chris Columbus, d; John Hughes, w.
Internal Affairs. Mike Figgis, d; Henry Bean, w.
Jacob's Ladder. Adrian Lyne, d; Bruce Joel Rubin, w.
Longtime Companion. Norman René, d; Craig Lucas, w.
Memphis Belle. Michael Caton-Jones, d; Monte Merrick, w.
Pacific Heights. John Schlesinger, d; Daniel Pyne, w.
Pretty Woman. Garry Marshall, d; J. F. Lawton, w.

1991

Bill and Ted's Bogus Journey. Pete Hewitt, d; Ed Solomon, Chris Matheson, w.
Body Chemistry 2: Voice of a Stranger. Adam Simon, d; Jackson Barr, Christopher
    Wooden, w.
Curly Sue. John Hughes, d & w.
Drop Dead Fred. Ate De Jong, d; Carlos Davis, Anthony Fingleton, w.
Dying Young. Joel Schumacher, d; Richard Friedenberg, w.
Fried Green Tomatoes. Jon Avnet, d; Fannie Flagg, Carol Sobieski, w.
A Kiss before Dying. James Dearden, d; Mike Southon, w.
Late for Dinner. W. D. Richter, d; Mark Andrus, w.
Man in the Moon. Robert Mulligan, d; Jenny Wingfield, w.
Mirror Images. Alexander Gregory Hippolyte, d; Georges Des Esseintes, w.
My Girl. Howard Zieff, d; Lawrence Elehwany, w.
Paradise. Mary Agnes Donoghue, d & w.
Rambling Rose. Martha Coolidge, d; Calder Willingham, w.
Ultimate Desires. Lloyd A. Simandl, d; Ted Hubert, w.

1992

Basic Instinct. Paul Verhoeven, d; Joe Esztehas, w.
Body Language. Arthur Allan Seidelman, d; Dan Gurshin, Brian Ross, w.
Bram Stoker's Dracula. Francis Ford Coppola, d; James V. Hart, w.
Doppelganger: The Evil Within. Avi Nesher, d & w.
Final Analysis. Phil Joanou, d; Wesley Strick, w.
The Hand That Rocks the Cradle. Curtis Hanson, d; Amanda Silver, w.
Home Alone II: Lost in New York. Chris Columbus, d; John Hughes, w.
Lorenzo's Oil. George Miller, d; Miller, Nick Enright, w.

Prelude to a Kiss. Norman René, d; Craig Lucas, w.
Single White Female. Barbet Schroeder, d; Don Roos, w.
Unlawful Entry. Jonathan Kaplan, d; Lewis Colick, w.
Whispers in the Dark. Christopher Crowe, d & w.

1993

Body of Evidence. Uli Edel, d; Brad Mirman, w.
Body of Influence. Alexander Gregory Hippolyte, d; David Schreiber, w.
Dennis the Menace. Nick Castle, d; John Hughes, w.
Groundhog Day. Harold Ramis, d; Ramis, Danny Rubin, w.
Indecent Behavior. Lawrence Landoff, d; Rosiland Robinson, w.
Philadelphia. Jonathan Demme, d; Ron Nyswaner, w.
The Temp. Tom Holland, d; Kevin Falls, w.

1994

Body Chemistry 3: Point of Seduction. Jim Wynorski, d; Jackson Barr, w.
Forrest Gump. Robert Zemeckis, d; Eric Roth, w.

Earlier Films

If I Were King. 1938. Frank Lloyd, d; Preston Sturges, w.
It's a Wonderful Life. 1946. Frank Capra, d; Capra, Frank Goodrich, Albert Hackett, w.
The King and I. 1956. Walter Lang, d; Ernest Lehman, w.
King's Row. 1941. Sam Wood, d; Casey Robinson, w.
Little Miss Marker. 1934. Alexander Hall, d; William R. Lipman, Sam Hellman, Gladys Lehman, w.
Mr. Deeds Goes to Town. 1936. Frank Capra, d; Robert Riskin, w.
Mr. Smith Goes to Washington. 1939. Frank Capra, d; Sidney Buchman, w.
My Fair Lady. 1964. George Cukor, d; Alan Jay Lerner, w.
My Man Godfrey. 1936. Gregory La Cava, d; La Cava, Morrie Ryskind, Eric Hatch, w.
The Prince and the Pauper. 1937. William Keighley, d; Laird Doyle, w.
Rear Window. 1954. Alfred Hitchcock, d; John Michael Hayes, w;
Sabotage. 1936. Alfred Hitchcock, d; Charles Bennett, Ian Hay, Helen Simpson, E.V.H. Emmett, w.
Saboteur. 1942. Alfred Hitchcock, d; Peter Viertel, Joan Harrison, Dorothy Parker, w.
Star Wars. 1977. George Lucas, d & w.
The Sting. 1973. George Roy Hill, d; David S. Ward, w.
Superman. 1978. Richard Donner, d; Mario Puzo, David Newman, Robert Benton, Leslie Newman, w.
Vertigo. 1958. Alfred Hitchcock, d; Alec Coppel, Samuel Taylor, w.
The Wizard of Oz. 1939. Victor Fleming, d; Noel Langley, Florence Ryerson, Edgar Allan Woolf, w.

Notes

Introduction

1. Irvin Ehrenpreis, "The Meaning of Gulliver's Last Voyage," in *Swift: A Collection of Critical Essays*, ed. Ernest Tuveson (Englewood Cliffs, N.J.: Prentice-Hall, 1964), 125.
2. Paul Fussell, *Class* (New York: Ballantine, 1983).
3. Ibid., 29, 84-85.
4. Ibid., 64.
5. Ibid., 60.
6. Susan Jeffords, *Hard Bodies: Hollywood Masculinity in the Reagan Era* (New Brunswick, N.J.: Rutgers University Press, 1994).
7. John Kenneth Galbraith, *The Culture of Contentment* (Boston: Houghton Mifflin, 1992); Barbara Ehrenreich, *The Worst Years of Our Lives: Irreverent Notes on a Decade of Greed* (New York: HarperCollins, 1990); Donald L. Barlett and James B. Steele, *America: What Went Wrong* (Kansas City: Andrews and McMeel, 1992). See also Kevin Phillips, *The Politics of Rich and Poor: Wealth and the American Electorate in the Reagan Aftermath* (New York: Random House, 1990).
8. Jean Baudrillard, *America*, trans. Chris Turner (New York: Verso, 1989), 107.
9. Ibid., 108.
10. Raymond Williams, *Television: Technology and Cultural Form* (Hanover, N.H.: Wesleyan University Press, 1992).
11. Baudrillard, *America*, 109.
12. Ibid.
13. Fussell, *Class*, 25.
14. Ibid., 24.

One   Back to the Futures Market

1. Lou Cannon, *President Reagan: The Role of a Lifetime* (New York: Simon and Schuster, 1991); Garry Wills, *Reagan's America: Innocents at Home* (New York: Doubleday, 1987).
2. Wills, *Reagan's America*, 372-373.
3. Quoted in Michael Schaller, *Reckoning with Reagan: America and Its President in the 1980s* (New York: Oxford University Press, 1992), 53.
4. Ibid., 54-55.
5. Wills, *Reagan's America*, 4.
6. Haynes Johnson, *Sleepwalking through History: America in the Reagan Years* (New York: Norton, 1991), 32.
7. Cannon, *President Reagan*, 229-230.
8. Ibid., 173.
9. Ibid., 177.
10. Rob Schieffer and Gary Paul Gates, *The Acting President* (New York: E. P. Dutton, 1989), 169.
11. Quoted in "Campaign '84: The Inside Story," *Newsweek*, "Election Extra" edition, November/December 1984, 36.
12. Interview with Rhett Dawson by Lou Cannon, in Cannon, *President Reagan*, 54.
13. Cannon, *President Reagan*, 54.
14. Quoted in Mark Green and Gail MacColl. *There He Goes Again: Ronald Reagan's Reign of Error* (New York: Pantheon, 1983), 39.
15. Ibid., 124.
16. Wills, *Reagan's America*, 169.
17. Quoted in Schieffer and Gates, *Acting President*, 168.
18. Wills, *Reagan's America*, 173.
19. Cannon, *President Reagan*, 56.
20. John Sears, in *Leadership in the Reagan Presidency Part II: Eleven Intimate Perspectives*, ed. Kenneth Thompson (Lanham, Md.: University Press of America, 1993), 71.
21. Cannon, *President Reagan*, 837.
22. Ibid., 41.
23. Ibid., 57.
24. Michael Rogin, *Ronald Reagan, the Movie: And Other Episodes in Political Demonology* (Berkeley and Los Angeles: University of California Press, 1987).
25. Schieffer and Gates, *Acting President*, 168.
26. See David Bordwell, Janet Staiger, and Kristin Thompson, *The Classical Style of Hollywood Cinema: Film Style and Mode of Production to 1960* (New York: Columbia University Press, 1985).
27. Baudrillard, *America*, 109.
28. Ehrenreich, *Worst Years*, 3.
29. See, for example, Larry N. Gerston, Cynthia Fraleigh, and Robert Schwab, *The Deregulated Society* (Pacific Grove, Calif.: Brooks/Cole, 1988).
30. Schaller, *Reckoning with Reagan*, 47.
31. Johnson, *Sleepwalking through History*, 256.

32. Ibid., 276-277.
33. Quoted in ibid., 279.
34. Schaller, *Reckoning with Reagan*, 117.
35. Schieffer and Gates, *Acting President*, 308.
36. Cannon, *President Reagan*, 801.
37. Donald L. Barlett and James B. Steele, *America: Who Really Pays the Taxes?* (New York: Touchstone, 1994).
38. Barlett and Steele, *America: What Went Wrong*, 4.
39. Ibid., xi.
40. Gerston, Fraleigh, and Schwab, *Deregulated Society*, 185.
41. Johnson, *Sleepwalking through History*, 229.
42. Barlett and Steele, *Deregulated Society*, 18.
43. Schieffer and Gates, *Acting President*, 220.
44. Galbraith, *Culture of Contentment*, 55-56.
45. Jimmie L. Reeves and Richard Campbell, *Cracked Coverage: Television News, the Anti-Cocaine Crusade, and the Reagan Presidency* (Durham, N.C.: Duke University Press, 1994), 114.
46. Ibid., 125.
47. Ibid., 131.
48. Johnson, *Sleepwalking through History*, 240-241.
49. Quoted in Jane Mayer and Doyle McManus, *Landslide: The Unmaking of the President, 1984-1988* (Boston: Houghton Mifflin, 1988), 36.
50. William Empson, *Some Versions of Pastoral* (London: Chatto and Windus, 1950).
51. Thomas Byrne Edsall and Mary D. Edsall, *Chain Reaction: The Impact of Race, Rights, and Taxes on American Politics* (New York: Norton, 1991), 196.
52. Ibid., 187.
53. It should be noted that Terrel Bell, Reagan's first secretary of education, did *not* reflect the administration's position. He recounts his battles with the administration in *The Thirteenth Man: A Reagan Cabinet Memoir* (New York: Free Press, 1988). His successor, William Bennett, codifies the position that Reagan first articulated in response to Bell's devastating report on the poor state of American education, which was to call for vouchers and school prayer.
54. See Jonathan Kozol, *Illiterate America* (Garden City, N.Y.: Anchor/Doubleday, 1985).
55. Jerry Adler et al., "The Year of the Yuppie," *Newsweek*, December 31, 1984, 14-24.
56. Ibid., 16.
57. Ibid., 17.
58. Ibid.
59. Ibid., 18.

Two Flatlining on the Field of Dreams

1. This idea of language as a "pharmakon," or drug that is both toxin and cure, is developed by Jacques Derrida in "Plato's Pharmacy," in *Dissemination*, trans. Barbara Johnson (Chicago: University of Chicago Press, 1981), 61-171.

2. Schieffer and Gates, *Acting President*, 181.

3. James David Barber, as quoted in Ronnie Dugger, *On Reagan: The Man and His Presidency* (New York: McGraw-Hill, 1983), 462.

4. Ibid.

5. Schieffer and Gates, *Acting President*, 181.

6. Larry Speakes and Robert Pack, *Speaking Out: The Reagan Presidency from Inside the White House* (New York: Avon, 1989).

7. Schaller, *Reckoning with Reagan*, 52.

8. Daniel C. Hallin, "Network News: We Keep America on Top of the World," in *Watching Television*, ed. Todd Gitlin (New York: Pantheon, 1986), 9-41.

9. This inversion can be seen in the disparity between Reagan's rhetoric and actions regarding immigrants; see Schaller, *Reckoning with Reagan*, 96-98.

10. Stephen Holden, "Today's Hits Yearn for Old Times," *New York Times Arts and Leisure Section*, August 13, 1989, 25.

11. It is worth noting, although I cannot develop the argument here, the kinship this film has with Steven Spielberg's *Hook*, especially given the latter film's emphasis on baseball and its attempt to establish the patriarch, as opposed to the mother, as in the Barrie original.

12. Viveca Gretton, "You Could Look It Up: Notes Towards a Reading of Baseball, History, and Ideology in the Dominant Cinema," *CineAction!* 21-22 (Summer/Fall 1990): 73-74.

13. Bill Maurer points out that the film "attempts to signify the supposedly 'archetypal' male quest for a return-to-(God-)the-Father." "Striking Out Gender: Getting to First Base with Bill Brown," *Public Culture* 4 (1992): 145. Gretton discusses the way in which baseball functions as the "primary ideological and metaphorical referent" for "reinstating the position of the Father" as "part of a larger and more pervasive strategy of reactionary political obfuscation within mainstream American film," "You Could Look It Up," 70-71. See also Bill Brown, "The Meaning of Baseball in 1992 (with Notes on the Post-American)," *Public Culture* 4 (1991): 43-69; and Vivian Sobchack, "Baseball in the Post-American Cinema, or Life in the Minor Leagues," *East-West Film Journal* 7 (1993): 1-23.

14. Cannon, *President Reagan*, 41.

15. Wills, *Reagan's America*, 94.

16. Cannon, *President Reagan*, 121, 122.

17. Ibid., 23.

18. Such films include *The River, Places in the Heart*, and *Country*.

19. Schieffer and Gates, *Acting President*, 231.

20. Cannon, *President Reagan*, 131.

21. Mayer and McManus, *Landslide*, 359.

22. Ibid., 131.

23. Cannon, *President Reagan*, 128-129.

24. Ibid., 130.

25. Cited in Dugger, *On Reagan*, 514. Dugger makes extensive use of the transcripts of these shows to demonstrate the continuity in Reagan's political philosophy.

26. Reeves and Campbell, *Cracked Coverage*, 90.

27. Wills, *Reagan's America*, 371.
28. Reeves and Campbell, *Cracked Coverage*, 91.
29. Galbraith, *Culture of Containment*, 20.
30. Johnson, *Sleepwalking through History*, 131.
31. Tom Morganthau, with Rick Thomas, Eleanor Clift, and Thomas M. DeFrank, "Second Term Tax Plans," *Newsweek*, November 19, 1984, 48.
32. Cannon, *President Reagan*, 261.
33. See Robert Corber, *In the Name of National Security: Hitchcock, Homophobia, and the Political Construction of Gender in Postwar America* (Durham, N.C.: Duke University Press, 1993).
34. Marsha Kinder writes that the restoring of the family in this film, "threatened by financial, emotional, and moral ruin . . . blamed primarily on the weakness of the father," depends on "the interchangeability of father and son within the patriarchal order that empowers them both." "Back to the Future in the Eighties with Fathers and Sons, Supermen and PeeWees, Gorillas and Toons," *Film Quarterly* 42 (Summer 1989): 5.
35. Susan Jeffords argues convincingly that Doc is a surrogate for Reagan. *Hard Bodies*, 78.
36. Susan Jeffords points out that control over the past, as represented in this film, "was to be one of the key insights of the Reagan ideologues: they could sell their version for the present if they could invent a version of the past that validated it." *Hard Bodies*, 73.
37. Reeves and Campbell, *Cracked Coverage*, 89.
38. Ibid., 83. Also see Wills, *Reagan's America*.

Three   The *Pretty Woman, The Little Mermaid,* and the *Working Girl* Become "Part of That World"

1. Susan Faludi, *Backlash: The Undeclared War against American Women* (New York: Anchor/Doubleday, 1991), xviii.
2. Kinder, "Back to the Future in the Eighties," 4.
3. Divine, perhaps the most successful drag queen in film history, was originally set to play the part of Ursula.
4. Merlin Stone, *When God Was a Woman* (New York: Dial, 1976), 18. See also Riane Eisler, *The Chalice and the Blade: Our History, Our Future* (San Francisco: Harper & Row, 1987), and Catherine Keller, *From a Broken Web: Separation, Sexism, and Self* (Boston: Beacon Press, 1986), chap. 2, 47-92.
5. Gloria Feman Orenstein, *The Reflowering of the Goddess* (Oxford: Pergamon Press, 1990), 129.
6. James Livingston, "What Does a Mermaid Want," *Cineaste* 16 (1990): 20.
7. Ibid., 20.
8. Faludi, *Backlash*, 232.
9. Harvey Roy Greenberg, "Pretty Woman's Co-opted Feminism," *Journal of Popular Film and Television* 19 (Winter 1986): 12.
10. Orenstein, *Reflowering*, 131.

11. Annette Kolodny, *The Lay of the Land: Metaphor as Experience and History in American Life and Letters* (Chapel Hill: University of North Carolina Press, 1984).
12. Schaller, *Reckoning with Reagan*, 101.
13. Robert Dallek, *The Politics of Symbolism* (Cambridge: Harvard University Press, 1984), 85.
14. Cannon, *President Reagan*, 531.
15. Ibid., 532.
16. Ellen Willis, "Putting Women Back in the Abortion Debate," in *From Abortion to Reproductive Freedom: Transforming a Movement*, ed. Marlene Gerber Fried (Boston: South End Press, 1990).
17. June Howard, *Form and History in American Literary Naturalism* (Chapel Hill: University of North Carolina Press, 1985).

Four   "I'm Not Really Bad. I'm Just Drawn That Way"

1. Since we never learn the actual name of the character, I am going to refer to her by the name of the actress whose screen persona unifies the multiple identities.
2. Teresa de Lauretis argues that the "heavy hints of lesbianism" are intended to "'blow the viewer's mind.' . . . If Alex had been allowed to be . . . the subject of her female desire for Catherine [Russell]—she would not have wanted *to be like* Catherine but *to have her*, or have *her* instead of *Paul*; and she, most likely, *might* have had her—and then, good-bye poker games and target practice with the boys, good-bye service to the Law protecting rich men from women, good-bye loyalty to their moral order. . . . Will someone ever remake *film noir* this way?" "Guerrilla in the Midst: Women's Cinema in the Eighties," *Screen* 31 (Spring 1990): 22.
3. Johnson, *Sleepwalking through History*, 180.
4. Ibid., 169.
5. Ibid., 145.
6. As Elayne Rapping points out, "Many people can relate to Jane's character, claim to know women like her; but no one would want her. Far better, the film subtly suggests, to be Aaron or Tom and really 'have it all.' Under the guise of showing a complex, interesting, true-to-life 'New Woman,' *Broadcast News* subtly undermines feminist demands for wholeness, for work as well as joy, and it paints career women so distastefully that few would want to pursue that course." "Liberation in Chains: 'The Woman Question' in Hollywood," *Cineaste* 15 (1989): 7.
7. See Bell's *Thirteenth Man*.
8. Diane Sippi, "Aping Africa: The Mist of Immaculate Miscegenation," *CineAction!* 20 (Fall 1989): 26.
9. This contextualizing of Fossey in a Darwinian hierarchy should not obscure the fact that the film also participates in a colonialist view of Africa and Africans, a point made convincingly by Sippi. "Fossey's quest for language and acceptance," Sippi points out, "[is] not among real Africans, imagined in the film as savages, but among real *apes*, imagined as noble Africans" (ibid., 24). See also Kinder, "Back to the Future in the Eighties," 9-11.
10. Sundiata K. Cha-Jua, "Mississippi Burning: The Burning of Black Self-Activity," *Radical History Review* 45 (1989): 131.

Five Home and Homelessness Alone in John Hughes's America, or Dennis the Menace II Society

1. In *The Breakfast Club* these traits are divided up among the five high school students on Saturday detention, with the point of the narrative being that each of these "misfits" has elements of the other.
2. Vicky Lebeau, "Daddy's Cinema: Femininity and Mass Spectatorship," *Screen* 33 (Autumn 1992): 256.
3. Hughes puts the child in charge where the parent has failed. This is the appeal, for example, of Ferris Bueller. In *Pretty in Pink*, Andie takes charge of her household, caring for her father, who has been unable to hold a steady job or take control of his life ever since they were both abandoned by Andie's mother three years earlier.
4. Bill Carter, "Him Alone," *New York Times Magazine*, August 4, 1991, 33.
5. Ronald J. Ostrow, "Panel Charges Pierce Steered Funds to Friends," *Los Angeles Times*, November 2, 1990, as cited in Cannon, *President Reagan.*
6. Cannon, *President Reagan*, 796.
7. Peter Marcuse, "Homelessness and Housing Policy," in *Homelessness in America*, ed. Carol Caton (New York: Oxford University Press, 1990), 148.
8. Ibid., 152.
9. Mary Ellen Hombs, *American Homelessness: A Reference Handbook* (Santa Barbara, Calif.: ABC-CLIO, 1990), 7.
10. Ibid., 9-10.
11. Roberta Youmans, "The Shortage of Low-Income Housing: The Role of the Federal Government," in *Homelessness: A Prevention-Oriented Approach*, ed. Rene I. Jahiel (Baltimore: Johns Hopkins University Press, 1992), 265.
12. Marcuse, "Homelessness and Housing Policy," 152.
13. *Homeless Families: Failed Policies and Young Victims*, (Washington, D.C.: Children's Defense Fund, 1992), 13.
14. Ibid., 15.
15. Cannon, *President Reagan*, 24.
16. Edsall and Edsall, *Chain Reaction*, 206.
17. Ibid., 216.
18. Andrew Ross, "Ballots, Bullets, or Batman: Can Cultural Studies Do the Right Thing?" *Screen* 31 (Spring 1990): 26-44.

Six Seas of Love and Murderous Doubles

1. See Corber, *National Security*; Elaine Tyler May, *Homeward Bound: American Families in the Cold War Era* (New York: Basic Books, 1988); and Alan Nadel, *Containment Culture: American Narratives, Postmodernism, and the Atomic Age* (Durham, N.C.: Duke University Press, 1995).
2. Randy Shilts, *And the Band Played On: Politics, People, and the AIDS Epidemic* (New York: Penguin, 1988), 474.
3. This is a recurrent theme, for example, in the collection of eight essays devoted to the film in the *Journal of Popular Culture* 26 (Summer 1992): 1-89. In her intro-

duction, Liahna Babener, the guest editor of the collection, underscores the consensus among the essays that the film "offers up . . . a shrilly anti-feminist and profoundly anti-female declaration" (2).

4. Liahna Babener, "Patriarchal Politics in *Fatal Attraction*," *Journal of Popular Culture* 26 (Summer 1992): 25-26.

5. Nickolas Pappas has demonstrated a strong homoerotic motif in the film that works, particularly, to draw parallels between Frank and the murderer. "A *Sea of Love* Among Men," *Film Criticism* 14 (Spring 1990): 14-26.

Conclusion

1. Of course, the hunger to make presidential campaign news coverage perennial has driven the media into reporting, and thus making significant, formerly insignificant events such as the Iowa Republican straw poll in which the "delegates" had to pay in order to vote. With each new "premature" media event, the unofficial start becomes murkier.

2. Alan Nadel, *Invisible Criticism: Ralph Ellison and the American Canon* (Iowa City: University of Iowa Press, 1988).

3. Andrew Ross, *No Respect: Intellectuals and Popular Culture* (London: Routledge, 1989).

4. Thomas Byers, "History Re-Membered: *Forrest Gump*, Postfeminist Masculinity, and the Burial of the Counterculture," *Modern Fiction Studies* 42 (Summer 1996): 428. This essay presents a fine detailed reading of the film as the reconstruction of American masculinity by the consolidation of conservative values achieved through vigilant historical revisionism.

Index

Page references to illustrations are in italics.

abortion, 111–112

Ackroyd, Dan, 29

Acquired Immune Deficiency Syndrome (AIDS), 176, 177, 182; defining populations at risk, 188–189; and films, 9–10, 175–201; as form of subjectivity, 198, 200; and high-risk behavior, 191; politicians' responses to, 182–184, 202; semiotic codes about, 179–180

Adams, Arlin, 162

addiction, 121; sexual, 118

adolescence, 10, 33; and time travel fantasies, 76–85; and wealth, 153

Advent calendar, 150, *151*

affirmative action, 40

Agriculture, Department of, 119

AIDS, *see* Acquired Immune Deficiency Syndrome

Aid to Families with Dependent Children (AFDC) grants, 163–164

alcoholism, 118, 130

Alda, Alan, 192

Alexander, Grover Cleveland, 19; Reagan in role of, *20*

All Dogs Go to Heaven, 50

Allen, Woody, 11

Altman, Robert, 11

Ameche, Don, 29, 32

America: What Went Wrong (Barlett and Steele), 4, 26

America: Who Really Pays the Taxes (Barlett and Steele), 26

American Christian Cause, 96

American Civil Liberties Union (ACLU), 171

amnesia, 52, 62, 63–64, 65, 74

anal sex, 191, 193

Anderson, Martin, 15

And the Band Played On (Shilts), 183–184

About the Author

Alan Nadel, professor of literature at Rensselaer Polytechnic Institute, is the author of *Invisible Criticism: Ralph Ellison and the American Canon* (University of Iowa Press, 1988) and *Containment Culture: American Narratives, Postmodernism, and the Atomic Age* (Duke University Press New Americanist Series, 1995) and the editor of *May All Your Fences Have Gates: Essays on the Drama of August Wilson.* His essay on Alice Walker's *Meridian* won the 1988 award for the best essay in *Modern Fiction Studies,* and his essay on *The Ten Commandments* as Cold War epic won the 1993 award for the best essay to appear in *PMLA.* His poetry has appeared in a number of journals, including *Georgia Review, New England Review, Paris Review, Partisan Review,* and *Shenandoah.* Currently he is editing a collection of essays on the infantilizing of American academics and is working on a book of essays on aspects of the relationship between visual representation and cultural narrative in late-twentieth-century America. Its working title is "Rodney King Live."